WITHDRAWN
UTSA LIBRARIES

SIR
Walter Ralegh

SIR
Walter Ralegh

A STUDY IN
Elizabethan Skepticism

BY
Ernest A. Strathmann

OCTAGON BOOKS

A DIVISION OF FARRAR, STRAUS AND GIROUX

New York   1973

Copyright 1951 by Columbia University Press

Reprinted 1973
by special arrangement with Columbia University Press

OCTAGON BOOKS
A DIVISION OF FARRAR, STRAUS & GIROUX, INC.
19 Union Square West
New York, N. Y. 10003

Library of Congress Cataloging in Publication Data

Strathmann, Earnest Albert, 1906-
    Sir Walter Ralegh; a study in Elizabethan skepticism.

        Reprint of the ed. published by Columbia University Press, New York.

        1. Raleigh, Sir Walter, 1552?-1618.   2. Skepticism.
DA86.R2S86   1973   211.7'092'4   73-8897
ISBN 0-374-97640-6

**Manufactured by Braun-Brumfield, Inc.
Ann Arbor, Michigan**

Printed in the United States of America

TO
Cynthia

Preface

ONE OF THE PLEASURES of completing this study is the opportunity to express my thanks for the liberal support which I have enjoyed from the beginning of my work. For fellowships and grants which made the study possible I am indebted to the Trustees of the Folger Shakespeare Library, to the Trustees of the Henry E. Huntington Library, and to the John Simon Guggenheim Memorial Foundation. The plan of my book, to explore the thought of Sir Walter Ralegh as an exemplar of Elizabethan skepticism, was the outgrowth of a year devoted to more general reading in Elizabethan thought during the tenure of a Folger Shakespeare Library Fellowship. Work on the project, interrupted by increased academic duties during the War, was furthered by a grant-in-aid from the Henry E. Huntington Library in the summer of 1944, and in 1947 the book was virtually completed in its present form under a Fellowship of the John Simon Guggenheim Memorial Foundation. Funds allotted to me by the Research Committee of the Claremont Graduate School have provided typing assistance. I wish to thank also President E. Wilson Lyon of Pomona College for his continued personal interest in my study and the Trustees of the College for their uniformly generous policy in granting sabbatical leaves of absence.

In the work itself I am no less indebted to friends and fellow workers who have shared with me their knowledge and experience. Dr. Louis B. Wright has advised and helped me throughout, both in research and publication; my thanks to him as a scholar and an old friend extend far beyond the narrow limits of this study. In the early stages of my work I was privileged to enjoy the wise and friendly counsel of Dr. Joseph Q. Adams, late Director of the Folger Shakespeare Library; and Dr. James G.

McManaway, of the Folger Library staff, gave me the benefit of his wide knowledge of bibliography and Elizabethan printing. Dr. Frederick Sorensen allowed me to use his unpublished Ralegh bibliography, which greatly facilitated the checking of reference materials. I have noted in the text the helpful contributions of fellow workers, but my thanks are due also for many suggestions not necessarily reflected in any one particular passage. The pleasant associations of the Huntington Library facilitate just this easy and stimulating exchange of knowledge, as readers there well know. Staff members of the libraries in which I have worked, notably Miss Mary Isabel Fry at the Huntington and Dr. Giles E. Dawson at the Folger, have been constantly helpful in all reference problems.

I have acknowledged the indispensable financial assistance received toward the publication of this volume, but I wish to thank personally those who helped me with friendly interest: Professor William A. Nitze, Chairman of the Pacific Coast Committee for the Humanities, and Professor Hugh G. Dick, its Secretary, who made my problem their own; Dr. Henry Allen Moe, Secretary General of the John Simon Guggenheim Memorial Foundation; and Dean Harold W. Bradley and other members of the Committee on Publications of the Claremont Graduate School. In the course of publication I have profited by the advice and suggestions given me by the staff of the Columbia University Press.

For permission to reprint or to adapt those parts of my study already published I owe thanks to the editors of *The Huntington Library Quarterly*, *Modern Language Quarterly*, *Modern Language Notes*, and *American Quarterly*; and to the Trustees of the Folger Shakespeare Library, publisher of *Joseph Quincy Adams Memorial Studies*. I have indicated in the footnotes any extended passages which follow closely a published article.

Of the works on Ralegh which I have used I have found especially helpful the biographies by John Oldys and Edward Edwards, despite errors in fact and a tendency to excuse all faults in their hero. Oldys has "prevented" me in a number of details

Preface   ix

concerning Ralegh's posthumous reputation, which I review in Chapter VIII. With obvious exceptions (as in passages involved in textual interpretation and a few proper names) I have modernized both the spelling and punctuation of quotations from early printed books and of their titles. References to Ralegh's *History of the World* are to the first edition (1614): in the Preface, by signature; in the text, by book, chapter, section, and page—a form which I believe can be adapted to any of the numerous editions of the work.

E. A. S.

Claremont, California
March, 1950

Contents

1 Problems and Evidence — 3
2 The Record — 17
3 Elizabethan Meanings of "Atheism" — 61
4 Of God and the Soul — 98
5 Of the Architecture of Fortune — 148
6 Of Miracles; and of Men before Adam — 172
7 Of Human Knowledge — 219
8 The Judicious Historian — 254
Index — 277

SIR
Walter Ralegh

Chapter 1

Problems and Evidence

For common bruit is so infamous an historian as wise men neither report after it nor give credit to anything they receive from it

History, I, vii, 10, pt. 10, p. 123

THE FORTUNES of Sir Walter Ralegh underwent many changes in the fifteen years from the defeat of the Spanish Armada to his imprisonment in the Tower in 1603. During these critical years he climbed still higher the winding stair to great place, found the standing thereon slippery—and slipped, partly because of his marriage and partly for reasons which are now obscure.[1] After his disgrace and his exclusion from court in 1592, he recovered his footing at a somewhat lower and more precarious level which he maintained until his conviction on a charge of treason thrust him down to struggle, but not to rise again. In the last decade of the sixteenth century he achieved two military victories, one at Cadiz in collaboration with the Earl of Essex and one at Fayal in unfortunate opposition to his great rival and, at that time, commander; independently he made the voyage to Guiana which increased his fame in Europe, yet was the prelude to a tragedy played out more than twenty years later.

---

[1] As commonly told, the story is that Ralegh seduced Elizabeth Throckmorton, married her, and incurred the wrath of the Queen, who sent the couple to the Tower. But the earliest authentic reference to the seduction is in an edition of Camden's *Annals* (1625) published after the death of both Camden and Ralegh. See Fred Sorensen, "Sir Walter Ralegh's Marriage," *Studies in Philology*, XXXIII (April, 1936), 182–202. I note that Anthony Bacon implies more than one cause for Ralegh's loss of favor; in a letter to Anthony Standen written some time after February, 1593, Bacon remarks: "Sir Walter Ralegh having been almost a year in disgrace *for several occasions*, as I think you have heard, is yet hovering between fear and hope, notwithstanding his great share out of the rich carrack." *Memoirs of the Reign of Queen Elizabeth*, ed. Thomas Birch, 2 vols. (London, 1754), I, 93, cited by Arthur Cayley, *Life of Ralegh*, 2 vols. (London, 1805), I, 129; italics mine.

4   Problems and Evidence

While great actions were in progress abroad and the weaved-up follies of rivalry were unraveled at home, Ralegh carried himself with a pride and arrogance that won him the hatred of the people, displayed an extravagant vanity in dress that was conspicuous even at Elizabeth's court, and uttered his opinions boldly, with complete disregard of the misinterpretation that can befall even the most carefully worded statements.

During these days of prominence and power, when he was, in his own phrase, "permitted to draw water as near the well-head as another," [2] Ralegh's religious beliefs were first publicly questioned. Like other great men of his day, he was poet as well as politician, scholar as well as soldier. From his early association with George Gascoigne, whose motto *Tam Marti quam Mercurio* he later appropriated, to the literary activities of his imprisonment in the Tower, Ralegh sometimes dabbled and sometimes delved in the intellectual pursuits of his time: versifying, music, mathematics, navigation, geography, history, political theory, philosophy, theology. He brought to his studies a mind almost always independent and sometimes original, and his inquiring disposition led him to pick brains where he found them. At one time or another the preacher-geographer Hakluyt, the mathematician Harriot, and the poet Spenser were found in his retinue.

Given the rivalries of great men, the complicated religio-political struggles of the age, the uneven advances of knowledge in a period of transition, and the close interrelations of many activities which today are segregated in the compartments of specialization, it was almost inevitable that Ralegh's academic pursuits should be challenged as "atheistic" and he and his associates called "atheists." The charges faded in men's minds,

---

[2] *The History of the World* (London, 1614), Pref., sig. E4r. Hereafter all references to the *History* will be to book, chapter, and section (and part, when that subdivision is indicated), followed by the page reference to the first edition (1614). The book and chapter references make it possible to find quotations in other editions than the first, and for the first edition (paged 1 to 651 for Bks. I–II, and 1 to 776 for Bks. III–V) will indicate in which half of the volume the page reference falls. References to the preface are by signature in the first edition.

Problems and Evidence

though they never dropped completely from memory, as personal misfortune and political change transformed Ralegh from a hated monopolist to an admired symbol of English patriotism for men like Hampden, Cromwell, and Milton. For more than two centuries, while *The History of the World* was read as a guide to life and a model of prose, and not as an antiquarian curiosity with some purple passages, Ralegh the historian and patriot overshadowed Ralegh the scheming courtier and alleged atheist. During the past half century, a renewed interest in the intellectual activities of the last years of Elizabeth and the first years of James has manifested itself in novel theories—in some quarters held as facts—concerning the beliefs and the personal and literary relations of Elizabethan courtiers and writers, among them Ralegh, Marlowe, and Shakespeare. The trend of these studies has been to reestablish Ralegh as the freethinker of his Elizabethan reputation, even to present him as markedly in advance of his time. He has been made the center of a group of poets, scholars, and courtiers, known by a phrase from *Love's Labour's Lost* as the "School of Night," whose esoteric beliefs and pretensions to learning met the ridicule of Shakespeare himself and other partisans of Essex.[3]

The primary purpose of my study is to reexamine in their Elizabethan setting the charges of atheism which Sir Walter Ralegh's contemporaries made against him and to survey anew his religious and philosophical beliefs. At the same time, the variety of topics which such a study entails may lead to some clarification of Elizabethan ideas on the relations of faith, reason, and knowledge, subject always to the avowed limitation of the subtitle of my book: a study in, not of, Elizabethan skepticism. Yet the very reasons that prompt a new study of the thought of Ralegh justify attributing to the results some representative value. Ralegh was a prominent courtier, concerning whom, in the years of his power, we have more extensive biographical information than for most of his contemporaries; he was charged with

[3] For bibliographical references on this theory, see below, chap. viii.

holding unorthodox beliefs; and he has left behind a substantial body of writings which record—in the first person—his opinions on many questions and which were influential in the century following his death. Of no other Elizabethan writer do all three statements hold true. There were men of higher position at court than Ralegh, although Burghley himself sometimes sought his aid; charges of atheism were so common as to present a problem in semantics; and for sheer bulk of writing the chroniclers or theologians may surpass him. It is the union in one person of the three qualifications which I have listed that prompts a restudy of Ralegh's active and contemplative life, for its own sake and for the light it throws on the intellectual life of the time. Not that the study of one man is the study of his age; in focusing the investigation upon Ralegh I am attempting to make concrete an important problem of Elizabethan life and literature: the reconciling of ancient faith and authority with new learning. The problem is recurrent, and the Elizabethans are by no means original in their attempted solutions. Ralegh's answers are given with a fullness of context that makes it possible to distinguish with some assurance his fundamental beliefs and to attempt an explanation of the seeming paradox between them and his reputation.

The province of this study is described by the term "skepticism" in preference to "atheism," with its varied Elizabethan meanings, or "rationalism," which has more positive denotations than are warranted by the state of philosophy in the late sixteenth and early seventeenth centuries. I have not hesitated to use freely, especially in those chapters which illustrate and explain Elizabethan usages, "atheism" and its derivatives. Some Elizabethan meanings of the term fall within the modern definition of "skepticism," and Ralegh studies in recent years have placed so much emphasis upon the unorthodox aspects of his thought that a review of his alleged religious skepticism is indispensable to a discussion of his philosophical skepticism. But "skepticism" need not presuppose religious disbelief, even though that has become the dominant element in its meaning; nor does it presuppose a systematic philosophy of doubt. "Skepticism" is a term in which, for once, philosophical and popular definitions come together. By it I understand a tendency to question authority and to submit prescribed beliefs to the test of experience or experiment. The term has merit in describing attitudes in a time when old beliefs may be held sincerely by men who are gathering the tools to shape new patterns of thought. Such men are not necessarily uncompromising rebels or iconoclasts, nor need one expect a tough consistency in their thought. A skeptical attitude may comprise shifting combinations of belief and disbelief, of conformity and rebellion. "Skepticism" is further distinguished by its principal meanings: systematic philosophical doubt, like that of Pyrrho or the Middle Academy; doubt about the capability of human reason or the possibility of knowledge; religious doubt; and doubt about the validity of received customs and morality. Although these distinctions can be applied quite usefully to the study of Ralegh's thought and will be explained further [4] in the light of his own writings, the broad definition of skepticism as willingness to doubt and to question will suffice as an introductory guide to our survey.

It is a comparatively simple task to define the objectives of this investigation in a series of questions which, implied or expressed, determine the order of my discussion. What records do we have of Ralegh's reputation with his contemporaries and how are we to interpret their hostile comments? What do their terms, especially the frequently used "atheism," mean? How do these meanings apply to Ralegh's opinions on God, the soul, the Bible, ethics, and science? Out of this survey and other relevant material, what can we conclude about Ralegh's ideas on the powers and limitations of the intellect? How well do his opinions accord with the theories about him advanced in studies of the "School of Night"? Although it is thus easy to frame the questions, the evidence for the answers is beset in turn by problems

[4] In chap. vii.

of interpretation which must be analyzed before we can proceed. Chief of these problems are the Elizabethan range of Ralegh's interests, the reliability of his testimonies about himself, and the varying authority of his works as representative of his opinions.

The diversity of Ralegh's employments, being external, was early marked and admired; the opinion of one seventeenth-century biographer, John Shirley, is illustrative of many: "Authors are perplexed under what topic to place him, whether of statesman, seaman, soldier, chemist, or chronologer; for in all these he did excel. He could make everything he read or heard his own, and his own he could easily improve to the greatest advantage." [5] An account of any one aspect of Ralegh's life incurs the danger of foisting upon him a specialization which he himself did not profess. He took pride, it is true, in his knowledge of military, naval, and political strategy, and under Elizabeth his counsel was attended with respect. But his strength lay in a humanistic breadth of learning and in his Renaissance endeavors to combine the contemplative and the active life rather than in a precise knowledge of one limited field or even in a record of solid accomplishment. It has been remarked that Ralegh's many

---

[5] *The Life of the Valiant and Learned Sir Walter Ralegh*, 8vo. ed. (London, 1677), p. 242. For an account of the authorship and editions of this book see T. N. Brushfield, *A Bibliography of Sir Walter Ralegh*, 2d ed. (Exeter, England, 1908), No. 3. This variety in the talents and occupations of Ralegh attracted the historian Edward Gibbon, who during a period of almost a year contemplated writing a biography of the Elizabethan. Gibbon's enthusiasm for the subject grew, and then waned as he considered the deficiencies in the evidence bearing on some of the most interesting events in Ralegh's life, especially in his private life. As a remedy for this defect, Gibbon considered enlarging upon the "circumjacent history of the times, and perhaps in some digressions artfully introduced, like the fortunes of the Peripatetic philosophy in the portrait of Lord Bacon." After further consideration he abandoned the biography of Ralegh: "The events of his life are interesting; but his character is ambiguous, his actions are obscure, his writings are English, and his fame is confined to the narrow limits of our language and our island. I must embrace a safer and more extensive theme." *The Memoirs of the Life of Edward Gibbon*, ed. G. B. Hill (London, 1900), pp. 144–46.

Problems and Evidence 9

designs failed of completion, at least under his direction: the settlement of Virginia, the Guiana venture, his hope to be of the Privy Council, *The History of the World*. Yet he could "toil terribly": one can detect in the phrase the surprise which Sir Robert Cecil felt when he saw the Ralegh whom he knew as a courtier and politician working among the men of Devon to straighten out the pillaging of the "great carrack."[6] Ralegh cannot be pigeonholed, in action or thought; one cannot study the scholar unmindful of the soldier, the philosopher unmindful of the courtier. Although the materials for a study of his skepticism are found predominantly in a few of his works, including the voluminous *History*, one must be heedful of his protean quality and must also observe his changes as well as his single role of author.

The character of the man presents a greater difficulty in judging his words than does his many-sided life. Is he trustworthy? The long and dangerous course of what he called in the preface to the *History* a "tempestuous life," from youthful soldiering to disaster on the Orinoco, with his son killed and his best friend a suicide; the trickeries, evasions, and shifting loyalties of court politics; the dislike by many of his contemporaries: all compel a recognition that his tower was not ivory nor was his residence there voluntary. What he said and what was said about him alike require an awareness of the context and circumstances of the remarks. "What booteth it to swear the fox?" asked Essex at his trial, when Ralegh was called to testify.[7] Although not so

---

[6] Edward Edwards, *Life of Sir Walter Ralegh*, 2 vols. (London, 1868), I, 154.

[7] David Jardine, *Criminal Trials*, 2 vols. (London, 1832–35), I, 329. During Ralegh's last imprisonment in the fall of 1618, his keeper, Sir Thomas Wilson, referred to him as "arch-hypocrite" and "arch-impostor," and told him that "he had so lost his reputation for truth that no one believed a word he said." Wilson's indignation has its comic side, for he wrote that he had not promised Ralegh any favor in the King's name, "but has merely used the hope of mercy as a bait, being the only one that could draw him to confess anything." Sir Robert Naunton, who later was to write a not unsympathetic sketch of Ralegh in *Fragmenta Regalia*, likewise referred to the prisoner as "the hypocrite." See *Cal. State Papers Dom.*, *1611–18*, pp. 570–73, 583.

severe as Essex in their judgments, less partisan critics have had their reservations about Ralegh's integrity, to the annoyance of his many admiring biographers. The adverse judgments by David Hume [8] have been matter for controversy; Lord Acton said that he venerated "that villainous adventurer for his views on universal history"; [9] an authority on Elizabethan maritime history has labeled Ralegh "the greatest costume actor in any age." [10] Nor is it simply a matter of balancing favorable and unfavorable opinion; a sympathetic editor of his poems writes: "It is difficult to believe in Sir Walter Ralegh. There is and always has been something legendary, something fantastic and not quite credible about him." [11] Ralegh on the scaffold, with a humility appropriate to the occasion, confessed himself "a great sinner of a long time, and in many kinds, [my] whole course was a course of vanity." This is conventional enough, but he came closer to the problem faced by one who would understand his works when he called himself "a sea-faring man, a soldier, and a courtier, the least of these were able to overthrow a good mind, and a good man." [12] Ralegh was neither the blackguard hated by the Essex faction nor the unselfish hero of his seventeenth-century admirers. In terms of fiction, which his life so often suggests, his actions may sometimes belong to romance, even to melodrama, but his character has the lifelike contradictions and inconsistencies which a skilled novelist does not hesitate to give to his creatures. This complexity of character, natural enough in any man of wide experience and unusual talents but greatly heightened in Ralegh, enjoins upon the student of his thought a careful regard for his

[8] *The History of England*, 2 vols. (Philadelphia, 1840), II, 171, 666–67 (note 2M).
[9] In a letter dated May 21, 1869, quoted by Charles H. Firth, "Sir Walter Raleigh's *History of the World*," *Proceedings of the British Academy*, VIII (1918), 20.
[10] J. A. Williamson, introduction to G. B. Parks, *Richard Hakluyt and the English Voyages* (New York, 1928), p. xv.
[11] Agnes M. C. Latham, ed., *The Poems of Sir Walter Ralegh* (London, 1929), Introd., p. 1.
[12] *The Works of Sir Walter Ralegh*, 8 vols. (Oxford, 1829), VIII, 779.

Problems and Evidence

motives in any part of his writings marked by subjectivity or self-interest. Fortunately, when we turn to his writings and to reports of what he said, we find a wealth of materials which by their quantity and diversity make it possible to get at Ralegh's opinions. By setting one passage against another, by following a theme through different contexts, by noting any signs of compulsion which may attend his remarks, we may attempt with some assurance to define his position on a number of critical problems. Other distinctions suggest themselves. Ralegh's impulsiveness and his carelessness of popular favor during most of his life made for some degree of frankness to offset the insincerity of court flattery and politic caution. (Even here we are not without guides, when, for example, we can counter the adulation of a living Queen, who had favors to grant, with the praise of Elizabeth dead.) The differences or similarities between documents prepared for an occasion and private messages, or between the formal expositions in *The History of the World* and the personal asides; the correspondences between speeches which were given a sinister interpretation and similar statements in print which went unchallenged: such differentiations are helpful in understanding his words. But a study of the works of Ralegh is attended by other complications, proceeding in part from their author and in part from the age in which they were written: the uncertainty of the canon, the frequent borrowings in his writings, and the difficulty of tracing changes in his opinions.

Three of Ralegh's major works were published in his lifetime: his account of the last fight of the *Revenge; The Discovery of Guiana*; and *The History of the World*. There was no authorized edition of his poems, a few of which got into print, and most of the miscellaneous writings in prose included in the last volume of the collected *Works* (1829) were first published after his death. His posthumous fame as a hero and sage made the printing of his "Remains" a desirable venture in the seventeenth century, and numerous volumes bearing his name, with contents in varying combinations, came from the press, just as his "ghost" was invoked to enhance the appeal of political tracts.[13] But, as Anthony à Wood noted,[14] some of the long list of writings credited to Ralegh may have been the works of others credited to him "for sale sake"; and modern scholars have removed several items from the canon. Further, some of the discourses published posthumously appear, upon close study, to be notes taken on reading rather than independent essays occasioned by his reading.

Even a work properly attributed to Ralegh may have its own problems of originality, since Elizabethan fondness for piracy on the seas of thought is now a familiar story. The question is not one to be decided on the degree of originality but on the use made of the borrowed material. The distinction which I am making is between essays which are in effect translations (like *Causes of the Magnificency and Opulency of Cities* and *The Skeptic*) [15] and essays which incorporate the borrowings in a new synthesis. *The Cabinet-Council* and the *Maxims of State*, close as they are to their originals, are somewhat more independent in plan than the tracts which I have cited as translations. But the greatest authority as a guide to Ralegh's thought is found in the *History of the World*, which has the distinct advantages of publication in his lifetime, a highly personal preface, and an

[13] Brushfield, *Bibliography*, pp. 77–83, gives an account of the editions of Ralegh's collected works, and (pp. 161–62) lists some of the books which carry "Ralegh's Ghost" in their titles. A study of the Ralegh canon which would incorporate the findings of modern scholars is badly needed. A new edition of the letters was reported in progress several years ago. I have indicated at the appropriate places in my discussion any doubts about the authenticity of writings which are pertinent to this study.

[14] *Athenae Oxonienses*, II (London, 1815), 240, 243.

[15] The *Causes* consists of extracts translated from Giovanni Botero, *Tre libri delle cause della grandezza e magnificenza delle città* (1589); see A. Buff, "Über drei Ralegh'sche Schriften," *Englische Studien*, II (1879), 392–416. I have noted a few close correspondences between the tract assigned to Ralegh and the English translation of Botero's work by Robert Peterson (London, 1606), which Buff cites (p. 398, n. 1). *The Skeptic* is a summary translation of three of the skeptical tropes of Sextus Empiricus; see G. T. Buckley, *Atheism in the English Renaissance* (Chicago, 1932), pp. 146–49. For further discussion of the place of *The Skeptic* in Ralegh's work, see below, chaps. iv and vii.

Problems and Evidence

encyclopedic range of comment. Admittedly the *History* too has its problems of originality, even of authorship; but it has the hallmark of its compiler's approval. Passages were taken verbatim from other works; assistants gathered some of the materials, helped with translation, gave advice, and quite possibly wrote portions of the work.[16] None the less, we have in the *History*, however disordered and unwieldy, some kind of design with Ralegh as overseer. When he adopts another's opinion or even another's words in such a work, he makes them, in something like the sense of John Shirley's words quoted above, his own.[17] Elizabethan ideas on the legitimacy of such borrowing were decidedly less strict than our own. In the seventeenth century it is not unusual to find favorable references to the *History* as "compiled" by Ralegh, and one separately printed extract is described on the title page as "gathered out of Polybius and other authors by that famous historian Sir Walter Raleigh."[18] A borrowing worked into its proper place in a volume of more than fourteen hundred folio pages has a somewhat different

---

[16] Well known, for example, is Ben Jonson's claim to part of the work: "That Sir W. Ralegh esteemed more of fame than conscience. The best wits of England were employed for making of his *History*. Ben himself had written a piece to him of the Punic war which he altered and set in his book." See "Ben Jonson's Conversations with Drummond," in *Works*, ed. C. H. Herford and Percy Simpson (Oxford, 1925–), I, 138. Professor C. J. Sisson, in *Modern Language Review*, XLI (1946), 74, notes without further comment, "an unpublished Chancery record in which Ben Jonson is involved, which has bearings upon his share in Raleigh's *History of the World*." Ralegh's acknowledgment of assistance (Pref., sig. E4^r) is limited to the help he received in translating Hebrew. Some of his biographers have been unduly sensitive to statements that Ralegh had help; the nature of his project and the conditions under which he worked were such that some kind of assistance was indispensable.

[17] Hardin Craig, *The Enchanted Glass* (New York, 1936), pp. 254–55, emphasizes the importance of this kind of borrowing as reflecting the author's thought and temperament. He goes so far as to say of some passages in Ben Jonson that they are, "paradoxically speaking, absolutely original though borrowed outright."

[18] *A Notable and Memorable Story of the Cruel War between the Carthaginians and Their Own Mercenaries* (London, 1647). See Brushfield, *Bibliography*, No. 239. Some of the seventeenth-century meanings of "compiled" allow for direct borrowing.

status than a few sheets of a translation published posthumously. Aside from its inestimable value as a magnum opus published in the author's lifetime, the plan of the *History* encouraged in Ralegh that constant inclination to digression and personal comment which he excuses with somber humor on the ground that "the life of man is nothing else but digression." [19] To illustrate at random, he has his say, in few words or many, on the wars in France, the insolence of Sir John Perrot, the improper diet of pregnant women, the seven ages of man, the vanity of human wishes, the location of the terrestrial paradise, death, immortality, the origin of law, and the defense of England. No topic is too great or too trivial for Ralegh's notice if the context or his own inclination leads him to it. This fondness for comment in the first person makes the *History*, of all his works, the most dependable guide to his opinions on many questions relative to a study of his skepticism.

Problems of authenticity and originality are far more open to solution than the third difficulty of interpretation which I mentioned: tracing the development of Ralegh's thought. With him as with other Elizabethans a study of change or growth in chronological terms is attended by uncertainties. *A Report of the Truth of the Fight about the Isles of Azores* (1591) and *The Discovery of Guiana* (1596) are dated precisely by the events narrated, but they have only a secondary importance for this study. *The History of the World* (1614) was written in the Tower when Ralegh was well past fifty years of age. As for the miscellaneous writings in prose, when a precise date is lacking it is generally assumed that the work was written after 1603; but in most cases the assumption has only plausibility to support it. It is possible, as we shall see, to discern the influence of long imprisonment on Ralegh's temperament; but it is not possible, or any evidence now available, to trace with confidence a development in Ralegh's thought from youthful radicalism to mature conservatism. The contrast which M. Beau suggests between the "intellectual intransigeance of his youth" and the

[19] Pref., sig. E3ᵛ.

Problems and Evidence 15

time when he is willing to concede the value of a faith is misleading: the period of "youth" in M. Beau's distinction would have to fall in the 1590's, when Ralegh, about forty years old, described himself with Elizabethan lugubriousness as "in the winter of my life." [20] Aside from the awkwardness of extending Ralegh's youth to the time of life when he was a hard-bitten veteran of wars and court intrigues, the contrast between the statements credited to him at Cerne Abbas in 1594 and corresponding expressions in the *History* is not so marked as it is often represented to be. In effect, our dependable evidence on Ralegh's opinions, from himself and from others, comes in his middle years; in any consideration of changes in Ralegh's philosophy or religion, we must reckon with our scanty information about his youth and also be wary of the inviting contrast between the court favorite and the Tower prisoner.

Like Ralegh's own works, another important source of information about him—the comments of his friends and enemies—must be used with an eye to the context. Obvious as it is, the precaution is not always observed faithfully. For example, most of his biographers and critics are well aware that the Jesuit Robert Parsons had little reason to speak well of Ralegh; yet his reference to Ralegh's "school of atheism" [21] has frequently assumed the status of historical evidence, despite a dutiful caveat or two, and is one of the props of evidence in theories about a "School of Night." By a similar reading of other evidence Ralegh has been credited with a spirit of tolerance worthy of a nineteenth-century liberal but quite at variance with his actions and with opinions expressed in his letters. Often the reading of the evidence becomes a matter of definition: if sixteenth-century epithets like "atheist" do not always have twentieth-century meanings, neither are they always general terms of abuse.

John Shirley, writing but two generations after Ralegh's death,

[20] J. Beau, "La Religion de Sir Walter Ralegh," *Revue Anglo-Américaine*, XI (1934), 410–22; p. 417. Ralegh's phrase is from the dedication of his *Voyage to Guiana* (1596).
[21] A detailed account of the background of Parsons' statement is given in chap. ii.

tried to assess the changes for better or worse which time imposes upon our recollections of the dead. The speculation is of a kind which Ralegh himself found congenial in verse and prose.

Indeed his shadows cannot now well be left exact, seeing they must be taken so long after his death, when time hath defaced his best features and shed oblivion on the most beautiful of his actions. . . . Distance of time doth sometimes, like some mediums, make the straightest actions seem crooked, and sometimes gives them the advantage of landscapes, which appear taking and agreeable afar off, though when nearly searched and pried into by a curious and intelligent eye, they seem rude, harsh, and unpleasant. We must therefore despair of a just and exact account of him, unless we could by some magic power (as the author of a pamphlet has done to terrify and make Gondomar speak the truth) raise him from the dead and converse a while with his ghost.[22]

Time has continued to blur our picture of Ralegh, and its ravages have been repaired only in part by our access to a greater fund of primary information, such as letters and state papers, than the early biographer knew. Some of Ralegh's straightest actions have been made crooked, and acts which were "rude, harsh, and unpleasant" have been softened by time. Shirley's comment, made in terms of general biography, is no less applicable to a study of Ralegh's thought; if in biography we may expect at best a good likeness rather than a finished portrait, so an attempt to define his beliefs may not attain more than that approximation of the truth with which Ralegh the historian often had to rest content. To come close to a "just and exact account" of his religious and philosophical opinions, we must compensate for the falsifying perspective of time by restoring as best we can the Elizabethan proportions of Ralegh's thought. Subject to the restrictions of the evidence here analyzed, that is the purpose of my book.

[22] *Life of Ralegh* (1677), pp. 6–7. The pamphlet to which Shirley refers is by Thomas Scott, *Sir Walter Ralegh's Ghost* (Utrecht, 1626).

Chapter 2

The Record

I never travailed after men's opinions when I might have made the best use of them

History, Preface, sig. E4ʳ

WHEN Ralegh came into prominence at the Court of Elizabeth early in the 1580's, he had been through a grim schooling in warfare in France and Ireland and he had served a brief apprenticeship at sea. If detailed knowledge of this youthful life of action is lamentably sketchy, even more fragmentary is the record of Ralegh's early opinions and beliefs. Henry Oxinden's note on the information of Simon Aldrich in 1641, that Ralegh was an atheist in his younger days, is of too late a date to have independent value. The informant, Aldrich, received his degree from Cambridge in 1597, at a time when Ralegh's religious beliefs were much in question.[1] It is most probably to this period that Aldrich, looking backward, applies his phrase "younger days," rather than to the time almost twenty years earlier when Ralegh was emerging from obscurity.

With the publication, in 1592, of a widely circulated book in which Ralegh is charged with atheism, clues and suggestions are superseded by more material evidence: first in Catholic replies to the severe edict of 1591, then in the charges and recriminations centering largely about Christopher Marlowe in 1593, and most directly in a formal investigation of unorthodox opinions allegedly held by Ralegh and some of his followers. These records, closely related in time, are at the very center of any discussion of Ralegh's reputation as a freethinker. After 1594, during his lifetime and in his posthumous fame, opinions about Ralegh's "atheism" are numerous and varied, but not all have independent value. Clues to Ralegh's youthful opinions and, more significantly, the open

---

[1] Mark Eccles, "Marlowe in Kentish Tradition," *Notes and Queries*, CLXIX (1935), 20 ff.; refs. pp. 41, 58.

and bitter attacks by his contemporaries, especially in 1592–1594, are the subject of this chapter.

I

The soldier of eighteen had been a student at Oxford, and the captain of twenty-eight had resided in the Middle Temple. He had made the acquaintance of George Gascoigne, the versatile and accomplished soldier-poet whose early fame was dimmed by the brilliance of his successors, and had written commendatory verses for Gascoigne's *The Steel Glass* (1576). For what it is worth, the adventurous Gascoigne was in his day charged with atheism—and with all the other misdeeds his disappointed creditors thought remotely plausible.[2] More significant for our purpose is the indication that Ralegh was at an early date interested in literature and friendly with men of letters.

Of his intellectual development at this time we can only guess —and briefly, since there has been guessing enough about Sir Walter. Tradition as recorded by Wood credits Ralegh with the exercise of a sharp mind in his student days.[3] Mr. George T. Buckley[4] has made some shrewd observations about the possible effect upon Ralegh of his residence in France when that country, torn apart by religious controversies and charges and countercharges of unbelief, was the scene of philosophical speculation somewhat more bold than England knew. Ben Jonson, in telling how he was the victim of an irreverent prank by the son of Sir Walter, credits Lady Ralegh with the observation that "his father young was so inclined":

S. W. Ralegh sent him governor with his son anno 1613 to France. This youth being knavishly inclined, among other pastimes (as the setting of the favor of damosels on a codpiece) caused him to be

---

[2] C. T. Prouty, *George Gascoigne* (New York, 1942), p. 61. Further evidence of the acquaintance may be found in Gascoigne's publication of *A Discourse of a Discovery for a New Passage to Cataia* (1576), by Sir Humphrey Gilbert, Ralegh's half brother.

[3] Anthony à Wood, *Athenae Oxonienses*, II (1815), 235.

[4] *Atheism in the English Renaissance* (Chicago, 1932), pp. 151–52.

The Record

drunken and dead drunk, so that he knew not where he was, thereafter laid him on a car which he made to be drawn by pioneers through the streets, at every corner showing his governor stretched out and telling them that was a more lively image of the crucifix than any they had, at which sport young Ralegh's mother delighted much (saying his father young was so inclined) though the father abhorred it.[5]

Young Walter's knavish trick smacks more of extreme Protestant prejudice than of unbelief; Elizabethan sailors saw no occasion to treat reverently the images in the Spanish churches which they plundered. Finally, in this brief survey of hints and suggestions, Ralegh is mentioned as one of the auditors of ungodly remarks in 1580 or 1581. Among the many charges brought by Charles Arundel (no impartial witness) against the Earl of Oxford is "Blasphemy vs. scripture and Christ in presence of a number as my Lord Winsor, Mr. Russell, and Ralegh. God dealt well with those that deserved evil and vice versa; after this life we should be as if we had never been. . . ."[6] But Ralegh's association with Oxford, whom Arundel had accused of plotting to murder both Sir Philip Sidney and Ralegh himself, was not one of trusting friendship. In 1583, acting on the request of no less a personage than Lord Burghley, Ralegh interceded with the Queen on behalf of Oxford, Burghley's son-in-law. Reporting on his indifferent success, Ralegh wrote to Burghley: "I am content, for your sake, to lay the serpent before the fire, as much as in me lieth, that, having recovered strength, myself may be most in danger of his poison and sting."[7] Ralegh sensed

---

[5] "Ben Jonson's Conversations with Drummond," in *Works*, ed. C. H. Herford and Percy Simpson (Oxford, 1925–), I, 140–41. A Different version of the story is given in the notes to Wood's *Athenae Oxonienses*, II (1815), 612. See also John Aubrey, *Brief Lives*, ed. Andrew Clark, 2 vols. (Oxford, 1898), II, 15; Izaak Walton's statement there printed is obviously wrong in its dates.

[6] *State Papers Dom., Eliz.*, 151:46. I am indebted to Professor Helen E. Sandison for transcripts (not verbatim) of this item and of other parts of Arundel's charges against Oxford in *State Papers Dom., Eliz.*, 151:45 and 46. See also *Cal. State Papers, Dom., 1581–90*, pp. 39, 40 (items 151:49 and 57).

[7] Edward Edwards, *The Life of Sir Walter Ralegh*, 2 vols. (London, 1868), I, 58–60.

the danger in Oxford's friendship, and all that we can conclude from Arundel's accusations is the bare fact that Ralegh, on the word of a man who was himself in serious trouble, heard some unorthodox opinions voiced by Oxford.

Although the known record of the years before Ralegh became a court favorite produces nothing conclusive about his beliefs, the story of the 1580's is another matter. These are the years of Ralegh's ambitious designs for colonization, projects which in a series of dedications to him are connected with the glory of God and the relief of the savages' miserable estate. However strange the intermingling of conquest and piety may seem to us, it would be anachronistic to assume that the Elizabethans were hypocritical in combining as a lure for adventurers the material profits of gold mines, agriculture, and commerce, with the spiritual profits of saving the heathen from idolatry or the religion of Rome.[8] Missionary zeal was uninhibited by the study of comparative religion or by the hesitation of tolerance. Ralegh, of course, is only one of many leaders who were exhorted by Richard Hakluyt, and by others with Hakluyt's prodding, to plant colonies and save souls; but in the 1580's Ralegh is the dominant figure in plans to settle Englishmen in the New World. The important point for this study is that the preacher Hakluyt sees nothing untoward in addressing a religious plea to Sir Walter or in encouraging others to do likewise.

The glory of God is asserted as a motive for colonization by Martin Basanier in dedicating to Ralegh his edition of Laudonnière's *L'Histoire notable de la Floride* (1586). Basanier praises Ralegh for his interest in navigation, all the more admirable a study because of the aid it draws from mathematics, and for his lavish expenditure in the cause of planting colonies. Also in 1586 Hakluyt asks Ralegh to let him know "if there be anything else that you would have mentioned in the epistle dedicatory" to his new edition of Peter Martyr's *De Orbe Novo*. Whether or not the patron replied to the request we do not know,

[8] See L. B. Wright, *Religion and Empire* (Chapel Hill, N.C., 1943).

but when the book was published in Paris the next year (1587) it carried a sufficiently fulsome Latin dedication. Divine Providence, wrote Hakluyt, has reserved for Sir Walter the completion of Sebastian Cabot's work. Ralegh has enlisted the help of the preeminent mathematician Thomas Harriot to assist in the development of navigation. Those who spread rumors of the barrenness of Virginia are like the bad spies who brought Moses false reports of the promised land.

That God will be with you, you have no reason to doubt, for his glory, the salvation of countless souls, and the increase of the Kingdom of Christ is at stake. Up then, go on as you have begun, leave to posterity an imperishable monument of your name and fame, such as age will never obliterate. For to posterity no greater glory can be handed down than to conquer the barbarian, to recall the savage and the pagan to civility, to draw the ignorant within the orbit of reason, and to fill with reverence for divinity the godless and the ungodly.[9]

In the same year (1587) Hakluyt dedicated to Ralegh an English translation of Laudonnière's *History of Florida*, which had already been dedicated to him in the French edition. Hakluyt's propaganda here is stronger than ever, and the latter part of the dedication reads like an exhortation to Ralegh, who may well have had qualms about the heavy drains of the Virginia ventures upon his purse. But the religious note is again struck hard. Hakluyt concedes that the "fewest numbers" of those attempting discovery have as their end "the glory of God and the saving of the souls of the poor and blinded infidels."

Yet because diverse honest and well-disposed persons are entered already into this your business, and that I know you mean hereafter to send some such good churchmen thither, as may truly say with the Apostle to the savages (2 Cor. 12:14) We seek not yours but you: I conceive great comfort of the success of this your action, hoping that

---

[9] *The Original Writings and Correspondence of the Two Richard Hakluyts*, ed. E. G. R. Taylor, "Publications of the Hakluyt Society," 2d. ser., LXXVI and LXXVII (1935), 368. The last phrase is more emphatic in the Latin original (p. 361): ". . . atheos & a Deo alienos divini numinis reverentia imbuere."

the Lord, whose power is wont to be perfected in weakness, will bless the feeble foundations of your building.[10]

In harmony with this theme (although not in chronological order here) are some of the principal arguments in the treatise "Of the Voyage for Guiana," written "by or for" Sir Walter Ralegh [11] as a supplement, unpublished in his lifetime, to *The Discovery of Guiana*. The Guiana enterprise is honorable because "by this means infinite numbers of souls may be brought from their idolatry, bloody sacrifices, ignorance, and incivility to the worshipping of the true God aright to civil conversation," and their bodies saved from the cruelty of the Spaniards. The conversion of the natives to the true religion will "stop the mouths of the Romish Catholics, who vaunt of their great adventures for the propagation of the gospel." In an argument the broad tolerance of which is somewhat weakened by self-interest in its application, the author denies the right of Christians "under pretence of Christianity only, and of forcing men to receive the gospel" to conquer a free people. "We ourselves hold it unreasonable . . . that an excommunicate person (whom Christ denounceth to be as an heathen) or a Mahumetist coming into our country for traffic, or an alien atheist (if any were among us) not seducing our people, should be assaulted in goods or person, by any private man, or other whosoever, under whose jurisdiction he is not placed." Nevertheless the Guianans are expected to acknowledge their vassalage to Elizabeth, and the first condition of that vassalage is "to renounce their idolatry, and to worship the only true God, unto which unless they will yield it may be doubted whether we being Christians may join with them in

[10] *Original Writings*, p. 376.
[11] Sloane MS 1133, fol. 45, printed in *The Discovery of Guiana*, ed. R. H. Schomburgk, "Publications of the Hakluyt Society," III (1848), 135–53. Schomburgk argues for Ralegh's authorship, largely on stylistic grounds. V. T. Harlow in his edition of *The Discovery of Guiana* (London, 1928), p. 138, describes the treatise as written "by or for" Ralegh. See also Edwards, *Life*, I, 198; T. N. Brushfield, *A Bibliography of Sir Walter Ralegh* (Exeter, England, 1908), No. 118.

arms against the Spaniards or not." The point is argued with Biblical citations pro and con. For the modern reader there is unintentional irony in the juxtaposition of such benefits to the natives as "3. That we will instruct them in liberal arts of civility behooveful for them that they may be comparable to any Christian people. 4. And lastly that we will teach them the use of weapons, how to pitch their battles. . . ." [12] The missionary purposes of colonization set forth in the treatise "Of the Voyage for Guiana" are neglected in *The Discovery of Guiana,* wherein Ralegh is concerned chiefly with the vindication of himself and his enterprise on materialistic grounds; but the idea is alluded to in the concluding pages of his account of the last fight of the *Revenge.*

Just outside the orbit of Hakluyt's pioneering zeal, the antiquary John Hooker dedicated to Ralegh *The Irish History* printed in the second volume of Holinshed's *Chronicles* (1587). Translating the work of Giraldus Cambrensis, Hooker extended the narrative to the date of publication, and in so doing gave prominence to Ralegh's exploits in Ireland. Despite the discussion of Virginia again, it is not necessary to assume that Hakluyt secured this dedication for Ralegh [13] (as he certainly did others) as part of a propaganda campaign; Hooker was a historian of Devon, a genealogist well acquainted with the Ralegh family

---

[12] For the quoted passages see *The Discovery of Guiana,* ed. Schomburgk, pp. 135, 142, 146, 148–49. Cf. *History of the World* (1614), V, ii, 2, pt. 4, p. 386: ". . . that civility and religion shall be propagated into barbarous and heathen countries."

[13] Eleanor Rosenberg, "Giacopo Castelvetro: Italian Publisher in Elizabethan London and His Patrons," *Huntington Library Quarterly,* VI (1943), 119–48, argues plausibly that the intended patron of *The Irish History* was Sir Henry Sidney, who died five months before the date of Hooker's dedicatory epistle. She considers Hooker's remarks on Virginia a digression "which speaks with the very voice of Hakluyt" (p. 129). Less plausible, for the reasons given above, is the assumption that Hakluyt secured the dedication for Ralegh. The section on Ralegh in Miss Rosenberg's article is concerned chiefly with Castlevetro's dedication to him of a poem by Julius Caesar Stella, *Columbeidos* (1585). Correcting John Hooker's assumption that the dedication is evidence of Ralegh's fame abroad, she places the work in the context of the dedications secured by Hakluyt to promote the Virginia colony.

history, and according to Oldys,[14] a kinsman of Ralegh. The dedication, which fills almost five closely printed folio pages, contains some interesting anticipations of Ralegh's later work. The praise of history culminates in an oft-quoted description attributed to Cicero which, years later, found pictorial illustration in the frontispiece of Ralegh's *History of the World:* ". . . the witness of time, the light of truth, the life of memory, and the mistress of life." The ancient family of Ralegh, fallen on modest days, has been raised up again; God has blessed Walter, the youngest son of many, even as he did Joseph, one of the youngest sons of Jacob. The explanation of God's special favor is found in Cicero: ". . . that you should be beneficial and profitable to all men . . . for we are not born to ourselves alone, but the prince, the country, the parents, friends, wives, children, and family, every of them do claim an interest in us, and to every of them we must be beneficial." Ralegh's Virginia venture is praised as redounding to "the advancement of the name of God, the honor of the prince, and the benefit of the commonwealth. For what can be more pleasant to God, than to gain and reduce in all Christian-like manner, a lost people to the knowledge of the gospel, and a true Christian religion?" Hooker commends Ralegh for the public-spirited use of his wealth: "You have been rather a servant than a commander to your own fortune." Nevertheless, the writer exercises the privilege of age to admonish the powerful courtier of the thanks he owes to God for his advancement and to caution him that true nobility lies not in birth but in virtue.

Conventionalities of language and thought in these dedications [15] and the propagandist intent of some of them sharply restrict their value as evidence of Ralegh's beliefs in the 1580's.

---

[14] *The Life of Sir Walter Ralegh,* in *The Works of Sir Walter Ralegh,* 8 vols. (Oxford, 1829), I, 7: all references to the *Life* by William Oldys (1st ed. 1736) are to the 1829 edition. Hooker's flattering genealogy did not go unchallenged; cf. Edwards, *Life,* I, 3–5.

[15] The list is incomplete; only those dedications which bear on Ralegh's reputation are cited in this study.

The Record

On the other hand, it is not mandatory that an author digress into matters of religion, as the reading of any random selection of dedicatory epistles will show; such references are commonly limited to a pious wish, in the last sentence, for the patron's welfare. The evidence of the dedications is negative; if Ralegh had been already "scandalized with atheism" [16] in this decade, the scandal failed to impress the preacher Hakluyt and the antiquary Hooker, both sufficiently engaged in worldly matters to know a hawk from a handsaw. If we record as evidence of Ralegh's religious opinions the words of his personal enemies and religious opponents, let us record also that a patriotic minister of the gospel saw no incongruity in urging religious motives upon the patron of attempts to found an English colony in the New World.

II

Ralegh's many biographers, as far back as William Oldys,[17] have noted and variously interpreted the charge by Robert Parsons that Ralegh sponsored a "school of atheism":

> Of Sir Walter Ralegh's school of atheism by the way, and of the conjurer that is M[aster] thereof, and of the diligence used to get young gentlemen to this school, wherein both Moses and our Savior, the Old and New Testament are jested at, and the scholars taught among other things to spell God backward.[18]

Thus the statement appears in *An Advertisement*, a condensation in English of Parsons' lengthy and detailed *Responsio*, written in Latin under the pseudonym "Andreas Philopater." In the Latin version, Parsons had enlarged upon what might happen, if, as everyone expected, Ralegh were made a member of the Privy Council. That was a reasonable prospect, accord-

---

[16] John Aubrey's phrase; see his *Brief Lives*, ed. Clark, II, 188.
[17] Ralegh, *Works* (1829), I, 166–74. Section II follows in the main my article entitled "Ralegh and the Catholic Polemists," *Huntington Library Quarterly*, VIII (1945), 337–58.
[18] *An Advertisement Written to a Secretary of My L. Treasurers of England, by an English Intelligencer as He Passed through Germany towards Italy* (1592), p. 18.

ing to Parsons, since Ralegh had been raised merely by the Queen's favor from a common soldier to a powerful leader. If Ralegh were a Councilor, then we might have at some time or other from that Magian and Epicure who is Ralegh's instructor an edict, published in the Queen's name, which would quite plainly reject all divinity and the immortality of the soul and would stigmatize as disturbers of the realm those who objected in any way to the sweet reasonableness of libertinism:

> Et certè si Gualteri quoque Raulaei schola frequens de Atheismo paulo longius processerit, (quam modo ita notam et publicam suis in aedibus habere dicitur, Astronomo quodam necromantico praeceptore; ut juventutis nobilioris non exiguae turmae, tam Moysis legem veterem, quam novam Christi Domini, ingeniosis quibusdam facetiis ac dicteriis eludere, ac in circulis suis irridere didicerint) si haec inquam schola radices ac robur caeperit, et ipse Raulaeus in senatum delectus fuerit, quo reipub. quoque negotiis praesideat (quod omnes non sine summa ratione expectant, cum primas apud Reginam post Dudlaeum et Hattonum teneat, et ex gregario propè Hiberniae milite virum principem ac potentem Reginae sola gratia nullis praecedentibus meritis effectum videant) quid (inquam) erit expectandum aliud, nisi ut aliquando etiam edictum aliquod a Màgo illo atque Epicuro Raulaei praeceptore conscriptum Reginae nomine evulgatum cernamus, quo planè omnis Diuinitas, omnis animae immortalitas, et alterius vitae expectatio dilucidè, clarè, breviter et citra ambages denegetur, et laesae majestatis accusentur, tanquam reipub. perturbatores, qui contra istiusmodi doctrinam tam placidam ac in carnis vitiis volutantibus suavem, scrupulos cuiquam aut molestias moveant.[19]

These accusations by Parsons, in both English and Latin versions, have been frequently cited or quoted by biographers of Marlowe as well as of Ralegh. Less emphasized is the relative position of the statement about Ralegh in a work which, in Latin, fills approximately three hundred pages in most editions and

---

[19] *Elizabethae, Angliae Reginae Haeresim Calvinianam Propugnantis, Saevissimum in Catholicos sui Regni edictum . . . cum Responsione . . . per D. Andream Philopatrum* (Augsburg, 1592), sec. 43, p. 36. Hereafter references to this work will be to this edition by the abbreviated title, *Responsio*.

which consists largely of attacks upon high officials of the Elizabethan government; or the fact that Parsons' book is only one —although the best one—of many replies to the anti-Catholic edict of 1591, some of which also indict Ralegh, by name or by inference.

The immediate occasion of these controversial works was the strongly worded proclamation by the Queen, dated October 18, 1591, and entitled "A declaration of great troubles pretended against the realm by a number of seminary priests and Jesuits, sent, and very secretly dispersed in the same, to work great treasons under a false pretence of religion, with a provision very necessary for remedy thereof." [20] The proclamation charges the King of Spain with making undeclared war upon England and with maintaining one of his creatures as pope; attacks the seminaries on the Continent as institutions for instruction of fugitives, rebels, and traitors in "school points of sedition" (a phrase with which Parsons makes merry); affirms that in England men are punished for treason, not persecuted for religion; states that Parsons and Allen have assured the Spanish King of the help of a Catholic "Fifth Column" when he invades England; and for all these reasons orders a severe search throughout the country for disguised and hidden priests and a new check upon recusants. The proclamation further provides for local commissions to conduct inquiries, and attached to the proclamation is a sheet entitled "Articles annexed to the Commission for a further instruction to the Commissioners how to proceed in the execution thereof."

The response from the Catholic press on the Continent was immediate and vociferous. Three books appeared bearing dates in March, 1592: *Exemplar Literarum, Missarum, E Germania, Ad D. Guilielmum Cecilium Consiliarium Regium,*[21] by Joseph

---

[20] Printed in broadside (three sheets, *Short-Title Catalogue*, No. 8207), with the "Articles Annexed" (*STC* 8209) on a fourth sheet; and also in quarto (*STC* 8208). According to the writers who answered it, the proclamation was published November 20 or 29, 1591.

[21] The original has a misprint: "Conisliarium."

Creswell, using the pseudonym "John Pernius"; *A Declaration of the True Causes of the Great Troubles, Presupposed to be Intended against the Realm of England,* most probably by Richard Verstegen; and *Apologia Pro Rege Catholico Philippo II,* by Thomas Stapleton. No doubt a fourth reply, Parsons' *Responsio,* also appeared early in 1592, for the prefatory letter of the English abridgment, dated August, 1592, states that *Philopater* (the popular title for Parsons' book in the sixteenth century) has been "sent hither to be printed *again.*" The abridgment itself, *An Advertisement Written to a Secretary of My L. Treasurers of England,* appeared in 1592 as a translation on which Sir Francis Englefield, Henry Walpole, and Joseph Creswell seem to have collaborated in some haste. By the end of 1593, the *Responsio* by Parsons, who had been attacked by name in Elizabeth's proclamation, went through eight editions: five (and possibly six) in Latin and one each in English (the abridged *Advertisement*), French, and German. Frequent references to it during the next twenty years attest to its continuing circulation and popularity; and in 1612 it was again reprinted.[22] The wide distribution of the book, I believe, contributed not a little to rumors of Ralegh's "atheism." It is noteworthy that other significant references in the years 1592–1594 to Ralegh's beliefs are in manuscript sources; Parsons' book carried far and wide in print its report of Ralegh's "school of atheism."

These replies to Elizabeth's edict, differing in length, in the mode of attack, and in severity of language, are much alike in content. As a group, the answers to the proclamation stress the lowly origins of the Councilors (especially of Cecil), describe the painful deaths of Leicester and Walsingham as just retribution for their hounding the Catholics, and treat scornfully the religious

---

[22] For further bibliographical data on the books listed in this paragraph see "Ralegh and the Catholic Polemists," *Huntington Library Quarterly,* VIII (1945), 339–43, 356–58; *Unpublished Documents Relating to the English Martyrs,* ed. J. H. Pollen ("Publications of the Catholic Record Society," V; 1908), pp. 259–67, and *passim;* and J. B. Code, *Queen Elizabeth and the English Catholic Historians* (Louvain, 1935), pp. 1–102.

motives alleged in the proclamation. The Turks, say the Catholic writers, allow greater liberty of conscience than the English. Elizabeth is upbraided for her dealings with the Turk, the common enemy of Christendom. She, not Philip, has been the aggressor in international affairs—witness the shameful piracies of her seamen; and the boasted peace of England is a sham peace, marred by internal strife and religious persecution. For men are being done to death for their religion, whatever the government may say about punishing only for treason. The proclamation slanders the seminarists, who are men of good birth and great learning and who show the justice of their cause by their willingness to die for it. Further, say the writers, the persecution defeats its end by strengthening the faith of true Catholics. Not all these arguments, of course, are in all the answers; but many of the charges are common to two or more of the books written against Elizabeth's proclamation.

Nor do all the books attack Ralegh by name. Creswell, in the *Exemplar Literarum*, questions the religious motives of the government; Verstegen, who makes one noncommittal reference to Ralegh by name, is critical of the Virginia venture and prints an epitaph on Leicester which has been credited to Ralegh; Stapleton attacks both Leicester and Ralegh for the suffering which their military ventures have brought to England.

Of the replies to the edict of 1591 Parsons' *Responsio* is the most comprehensive and at the same time the most detailed. Translating the proclamation into Latin, passage by passage, he answers at length each item in Elizabeth's bill of particulars and treats with the same thoroughness the "Articles Annexed." A comparison of the Latin and English versions of the passage on Ralegh quoted above illustrates the superiority of Parsons' Latin original. The suggestion of a proclamation ordering conformity to an Epicurean belief is an ironic burlesque of the proclamation actually issued, the writing of which Parsons and his fellows credited to Burghley. At one stroke Parsons discredits Ralegh and implies that an order requiring conformity to the established faith is as capricious and ill-founded as an order which would require adherence to libertine doctrines.

Despite the superiority of the *Responsio*, the English version is useful for the present study not only because it is an abridged translation but also because of the method of summary used in *An Advertisement*. The translator does not adhere strictly to the order of his original; although he follows it in general, he exercises freedom in the selection and occasionally in the transposing of details. He may summarize a paragraph of abuse in a choice epithet of his own selection: thus the term "atheist" is used more freely in the English version than in the Latin, but its use is always justified by the language of the original text.[23]

The attack upon Cecil in *An Advertisement*, after the writer has disposed of Sir Nicholas Bacon, Leicester, and Hatton, offers a fair measure of the charges against Ralegh. Since Burghley is the principal adversary, no possibility of abuse, however trivial, is overlooked. The writer, says the translator, "maketh pastime at large against my L. Treasurer, and his broken rhetoric," which also merits the epithets "ridiculous and raving." Burghley is charged with plotting to marry his grandson to Arabella Stuart, who was considered a possible successor to Elizabeth. Burghley is a "malignant and wrangling worm"; even his wisdom in civil government is overrated; and there might still be hope for moderation "if her Majesty would follow her own princely disposition and leave the bloody humor of this old ambitious serpent." But more nearly parallel to Parsons' attack on Ralegh is his abuse of Burghley's religion. The seminary priests died for the faith of their fathers, not for crimes of life and manners, "whatsoever the slanderous tongue of Cecil the old atheist affirmeth to the contrary." Contrasting the good order and sobriety of the seminaries with the riotous living in the English univer-

---

[23] The difference is relative, for the epithet "atheist" is used vigorously in the *Responsio* too: e.g., sec. 197, p. 135; sec. 52, p. 43. *An Advertisement* is written entirely in indirect discourse to maintain the fiction that the book is a report by one of Burghley's "intelligencers." The reader is not allowed to forget that he is reading an abstract of another work.

sities, Parsons is reported as saying that "Cecil, Leicester, and such other like, rather cancellors of all virtues than chancellors of universities, have overthrown all, broken down the walls and hedges of all discipline, exiled all sound and solid learning, extinguished all modesty, shamefastness, and religion, have laid open the way to dissolution, ruffianry, and atheism." And the passage is concluded "with a place or two of S. Gregory Nazianzene against Julian the Apostata, very bitterly applied against my L. Treasurer." Cecil calls men to prayer, "whereas it is well known, by testimony of such as live with him, and others, and see their lives, and have served them in their chambers, that neither he, nor Leicester, nor some others that have been heads of threatening these bugs do ever lightly use that exercise of prayer, but live as mere atheists, and laughing at other men's simplicity in that behalf." [24]

In short, according to Parsons, Cecil is no less an atheist than Ralegh: Cecil laid open the way to atheism in the universities, and Ralegh conducted a school of atheism; Cecil laughed at the simplicity of men who pray, and Ralegh fostered disrespect for the Scriptures. It would be unreasonable to accept one charge as a fact and the other as a libelous fiction. What we have in these passages are examples of Parsons' skill in the niceties of sixteenth-century controversy, a skill which alarmed the English Catholics who had to bear the consequences of the Jesuits' polemics. In time, as the breach between the lay Catholics and the Jesuits widened, criticism of Parsons' methods became open and vigorous, especially in the division occasioned by the Archpriest controversy at the end of Elizabeth's reign.[25] The numerous books and pamphlets which that controversy called forth and the continuation of the struggle during the following decade are marked by protests against the language used by Parsons. The translator

[24] For the quoted passages see *An Advertisement*, pp. 33, 38, 43–46, 59–61, 64, 67.

[25] For an account of this conflict, with an annotated bibliography, see Thomas G. Law, *A Historical Sketch of the Conflicts between Jesuits and Seculars in the Reign of Queen Elizabeth* (London, 1889).

of the *Responsio* had said that the book was sharply and odiously written, but that the writer "doth not in deed use open railing terms"; [26] the description, relative at best, is certainly not echoed by the secular priests. William Watson complains that Parsons calls upon all men to accept such a sovereign as he will appoint them, "otherwise to be noted for atheists, fools, rebels, malicious politics." [27] "W. C." in his *Reply to a Libel* (1603) is even more specific:

> [*Philopater*, that is the *Responsio*] is full of most bitter railing, and arrogant exasperations, as every man that hath read it can tell; besides foolish scoffings against great persons, which no man of wisdom and charity would have used in these times, unless he had meant to whet a double edged sword to cut Catholics' throats.[28]

In criticism of Parsons' *Manifestation* (1602), "W. C." writes:

> Also he draweth in atheists, heretics, apostates, seditious, contentious, tumultuous, disastrous, and dissolute, to be inveighers against him; as though he were the only innocent, and pillar of truth, against whom all such people did inveigh; . . . A proud, arrogant, and contemptuous speech.[29]

To the modern reader of controversial literature of the sixteenth and seventeenth centuries, the abusive style used by Par-

---

[26] *An Advertisement*, p. 7.

[27] *A Decacordon of Ten Quodlibetical Questions* (1602), p. 317. Watson criticizes the language of the *Responsio*; see pp. 71, 265–66, 270–71, 284. Accepting the common belief that Parsons wrote *Leicester's Commonwealth*, Watson says (p. 266) that he might have left "such scoggerie" to Tarleton, Nashe, or some Puritan Marprelate. Watson, whom T. G. Law (*Jesuits and Seculars*, pp. lxxix, xc) calls "an erratic, vainglorious, and not altogether veracious priest," is himself guilty of "such scoggerie." He was executed Dec. 9, 1603, for his part in the "Bye" or "Priests'" plot at the time when Ralegh was convicted of complicity in the "Main" treason against James. See *Dict. Nat. Biog.*, s.v. William Watson.

[28] Fol. 73ᵛ.

[29] *Reply to a Libel*, fol. 91ʳ; cf. fol. 73ʳ. In an appendix of eleven pages, entitled "A Table of the passionate and uncharitable words and sentences, used by Fa: Parsons in his Libel of *Manifestation*," W. C. gives chapter and page references for Parsons' terms of abuse, among them (*Manifestation*, pp. 87–89), "impiety," "Lucianism," and "infidelity."

The Record

sons seems to be neither better nor worse, in manners, than that of his contemporaries. What troubled his adversaries, though they had difficulty putting a finger on it, was his individual skill in the manipulation of such conceits as controversy keeps in pay. T. G. Law, who believes that Parsons' "habitual recklessness" in blackening the character of an opponent makes his denunciations suspect, pays tribute to this skill. "He was a master," writes Law, "in the suppression of the true and the suggestion of the false." [30]

Other replies to Elizabeth's proclamation also impugn the religious motives of the English government and at the same time extend the attack to other fields. Although they certainly help to explain the Jesuit writers' hostility to Ralegh, they are not directly concerned with his personal religious beliefs and therefore may be dismissed with brief comment. Father Creswell, writing as "Joannes Pernius," treats sardonically the religious pretensions of his adversaries, "ab omni Religione alieni"; points righteously to the wretched deaths of Leicester and Walsingham; and comments upon the wealth which the Spanish wars have brought to some courtiers.[31] Richard Verstegen's only mention of Ralegh by name is designed to discredit Burghley rather than Ralegh; it is a reference to "Ralegh's dream," in which Henry VIII appeared to marvel at the rise of the Cecil family from rural obscurity.[32] But Verstegen does get in a palpable hit in his remarks on the heavy loss of life in foreign war, "besides all the brave men and mariners consumed in sundry voyages or piracies by sea, sent forth to seek new habitations in Virginia, and by one such means or other made away. . . . And if any man should think, that all these troops have been but sent forth in May games he may call to memory that their coming home again declared it not." [33] Although Ralegh had been involved in more than one

---

[30] *Jesuits and Seculars*, pp. lv–lvi, xcii; cf. pp. cii, cxi, and *passim*.
[31] *Exemplar Literarum*, pp. 120 (cf. 73, 75), 175, 122.
[32] *A Declaration of the True Causes*, p. 63.
[33] *Ibid.*, pp. 56–57. One other remotely possible connection between *A Declaration of the True Causes* and Ralegh's activities is the inclusion (pp. 53–54) of a

of the military expeditions criticized by Verstegen, the reference to the disastrous attempts at colonizing Virginia points directly to him.

Whereas Verstegen is content with general references to losses in the wars and in Virginia, Thomas Stapleton makes charges specifically against Cecil, Leicester, and Ralegh as beneficiaries of the corrupt administration of justice in England. Leicester and Ralegh, not the commonwealth, have benefited by thirty-three years of Elizabethan "peace" in which thousands of Englishmen have been led to ignominious deaths. Another particular in Stapleton's bill of indictment is that pirates are made knights. He attacks not only Elizabeth's officers of state like Cecil but also "suavissimos Adonides suos," among whom Ralegh is named in the marginal note. Stapleton is especially vigorous in condemning Elizabeth's friendly relations with "Epicurean" and "Ethnic" princes and in calling her religious policy atheistic. The defense of King Philip II is positive as well as negative, and much of the *Apologia* is given over to a recital of his honorable dealings in contrast with Elizabeth's perfidy.[34]

It is not difficult to understand the feelings which motivated the vigorous attacks by Parsons, Creswell, Verstegen, and Stapleton on the Elizabethan religious policy and the men who formulated it. But why did Ralegh, who was not a member of the Privy Council, come in for even a small share of incidental abuse? The Catholic writers did not trust to chance to collect the facts and rumors with which they documented their answers to the proclamation of 1591. A paper which Lord Keeper Puckering

---

biting epitaph which has been attributed to Ralegh, but only in a seventeenth-century manuscript. See E. A. Strathmann, "An Epitaph Attributed to Ralegh," *Modern Language Notes*, LX (1945), 111–14.

[34] For the references to Ralegh see *Apologia pro Philippo*, sigs. B3^r, B7^v, L4. On the atheism of Elizabeth's religious policies see sigs. K8^v–L1^r, A8, P3^r, R2^r. The charge of knighting pirates (B8^r) is made also by one John Prestall, who said that the Queen "made such knights as other countries spoke much shame of; meaning Sir Walter Raleigh and Sir Fras. Drake" (*Cal. State Papers, Dom.*, *1591–94*, p. 19).

endorsed, "Instructions by way of questions from traitors beyond the sea, touching the state here," suggests that inquiries be made concerning the state of religious, political, and court affairs, specifically, "inquiries to be made and information to be given of any sickness that shall happen to the Queen; of the religion and dispositions of those in favor with her, and of those chief in Council, and their opinions about religion and the succession of the crown; also of any variations among the courtiers, or mutiny in any part of the realm." [35] Just this kind of information and misinformation appears in the books criticizing the religious policy of the government. To what extent Ralegh figured in the reports to the Continent it is difficult to say without access to manuscript records. But the *Calendar of State Papers* contains hints that he was a person whose movements were of interest to the Catholic refugees. His departure for sea is reported ("probably from abroad, in faint orange juice or milk writing") in the postscript to a letter [36] which contains information of the kind requested in Lord Keeper Puckering's document. Even more puzzling is the mention of Ralegh's name in instructions of February, 1592, from Thomas Phelippes to William Sterrell (alias *Saintmain*) about what appears to be a mission in spying.[37] But these references, unsupported by additional information, are no more than signs of an interest on the Continent in the activities of Sir Walter Ralegh.

More certain ground for Catholic antagonism is found in Ralegh's connection with the Puritans early in 1591. The writers against the proclamation blamed Puritan influence in high places for the stern measures against the Catholics; and outwardly at least Ralegh may have seemed to be under that influence. On March 11, 1591, a person of strong Puritan leanings wrote to Anthony Bacon an anonymous letter commenting on the imprisonment of "a profitable preacher" John Udall: "I can see

---

[35] *Cal. State Papers, Dom.*, *1591–94*, pp. 161–62; conjecturally dated 1591. The original is three pages long.
[36] *Ibid.*, p. 207. [37] *Ibid.*, p. 183.

nothing else but a way preparing to bring in popery; for atheism is in already, and in short time will overflow the land. . . . Sir Walter Ralegh was made an instrument of the prolonging hitherto of Udall's life."[38] Thomas Phelippes, writing a few days later (March 22), is even more explicit: ". . . the Puritans are the weaker by far, but they hope well of the Earl of Essex, who makes Ralegh join him as an instrument from them to the Queen, upon any particular occasion of relieving them."[39] If such activity as this, whether at Essex's request or on his own initiative, resulted in the popular association of Ralegh's name with the Puritan cause,[40] the Catholics would have one more reason for including him in their abuse of Elizabeth's government.

Although the events follow the attacks upon him, Ralegh's actions under this very proclamation may have some value as indicating his attitude, politically at least, toward the Jesuits. On April 14, 1594, he wrote to Sir Robert Cecil of the taking of a Jesuit priest, John Cornelius, alias Mohun—or, according to Ralegh, John Mooney.

This night, the 13th of April, we have taken a notable Jesuit in the Lady Storton's house,—wife to old Sir John Arundel,—with his copes and bulls. There hath been kept in this house, as I have formerly informed you, above thirty recusants.

Sir George Trenchard, Sir Ralph Horsey, and myself are now riding to take his examination, which, by the next, you shall receive at

[38] *Memoirs of the Reign of Queen Elizabeth*, ed. Thomas Birch (2 vols., 1754), I, 61–62. In the light of Ralegh's later reputation, it is amusing to find the spread of "atheism" lamented in the same letter which acknowledges his helping a Puritan.

[39] *Cal. State Papers, Dom.*, *1591–94*, p. 21. For further details about Ralegh's intervention in Udall's case see Edwards, *Life*, I, 132–34. Ralegh's opposition to repressive measures against the Brownists is of too late a date (April, 1593) to figure in the Catholic criticism of him in 1592. See Edwards, *Life*, I, 271–72, and W. K. Jordan, *The Development of Religious Toleration in England* (London, 1932), pp. 214–18.

[40] Ralegh inserted in *The History of the World* (Bk. V, chap. v, sec. 2) a marginal note bitterly resenting the charge by "Eudaemon John Andrew, a Cretan" that he was a Puritan. See Oldys, in Ralegh, *Works*, I, 438.

large. Sir George and Sir Ralph have used great diligence in the finding of this notable knave.

Being in haste, I do for the present humbly take my leave. From Sherborne, this 14th of April [1594].

Yours, ever to do you service
W. Ralegh

[Postscript.] He calls himself John Mooney, but he is an Irishman and a notable stout villain; and I think can say much.[41]

The official examination of the captive was taken a week later before Sir Ralph Horsey, John Williams, and Sir George Trenchard.[42] Trenchard had been host at the dinner party where the Reverend Ralph Ironside and Ralegh had debated the nature of the soul; and rumors originating in popular versions of that conversation had resulted in an investigation by a commission of which Horsey and Williams were members.[43] Ralegh's part in the taking of Cornelius appears to have been unofficial: as Lord Lieutenant of Cornwall, Ralegh was required to report, along with other Lord Lieutenants, on arms and armor taken from recusants;[44] but in the Devonshire incident which he reported to Sir Robert Cecil he does not seem to have been acting in an official capacity.

The mention of Father Cornelius in the letter to Cecil only by the priest's family name—"Mooney" or Mohun—has obscured

---

[41] Edwards, *Life*, II, 91.

[42] April 21, 1594; *Cal. State Papers, Dom.*, *1591–94*, pp. 488–89; a report to Puckering was made June 16, 1594 (*ibid.*, p. 521). There are references to Cornelius in other examinations (*ibid.*, pp. 504, 511). He was hanged and quartered July 4, 1594. For the Catholic version of his story, see Richard Challoner, *Memoirs of the Missionary Priests*, ed. J. H. Pollen (London, 1924), pp. 198–202; and Henry Foley, "The Life of Father Cornelius," *Records of the English Province of the Society of Jesus*, III (1878), 435–74.

[43] See below, pp. 47, 49.

[44] *Acts of the Privy Council, 1592–93*, p. 13. I do not share Oldys' certainty (*Works*, I, 438) that Ralegh wrote "A Dialogue between a Jesuit and a Recusant," and I have omitted it from consideration. The dialogue, written some time after 1609, is attributed to Ralegh in an abridgment of *The History of the World* (1700, 1702) to which his grandson, Philip Ralegh, lent his name. See Brushfield, *Bibliography*, Nos. 229, 272.

the connection between Ralegh's part in the capture of the priest and a story of his tolerance in debating religious questions with a Jesuit. The fact that Ralegh's "notable stout villain" John Mooney is also the Jesuit of the conversations at midnight described by Henry Foley [45] has escaped a number of Ralegh's biographers [46]—not without favorable consequences to Ralegh's reputation. Indeed, one writer, who has accepted Foley's story of the persuasive powers of Father Cornelius as evidence of Ralegh's tolerance, has concluded that Ralegh was "one of the few Elizabethans who, while convinced Protestants, would not have persecuted Catholics." [47] Yet Ralegh applauded the capture of this same priest!

The inconsistency between the two stories appears greater than it is. Allowance must be made for the enthusiasm of Foley's narrative, based largely on the story told by Dorothy Arundel, who was a zealous disciple of the martyred priest. Not only in the story of Father Cornelius but also in other early narratives of the priests who died bravely for their faith one finds an eagerness to acclaim the martyrs' power to win converts. Foley's story of Ralegh's conversation with Cornelius has been widely told; less frequently cited is that part of the same narrative which tells how Ralegh prevented the priest from finishing an address to the crowd which had gathered to witness his execution.[48] It is quite probable that Ralegh discussed questions of religion with Father Cornelius, and even regretted, upon closer acquaintance, that the good man could

---

[45] *Records of the Society of Jesus*, III, 462. Foley writes of Ralegh: "He was so pleased with the Father's conviction and reasoning and with his modest and courteous manner, that he offered to do all he could in London for his liberation, and this although the Father had gently reproved him for his mode of life and conversation. Mrs. Trenchard also promised her aid for the Father's liberation. . . ." Foley tells also (III, 461) of a debate between the priest and Protestant divines, witnessed by Trenchard, Horsey, Ralegh, and others.

[46] A. L. Rowse, *Tudor Cornwall* (London, 1941), p. 366, connects the two stories by a reference, without comment, to the *Salisbury MSS*, in which Ralegh's letter to Cecil is published.

[47] Edward Thompson, *Sir Walter Ralegh* (London, 1935), p. 75.

[48] *Records of the Society of Jesus*, III, 471.

not go free.[49] But it is not at all probable, especially in the light of Ralegh's letter to Cecil, that his readiness to argue with a captive priest is a sign of willingness to extend toleration to Catholics. Whatever indirect part Ralegh may have had in checking upon English refugees on the Continent, whatever his reputation as a Puritan partisan may have been, and however active he may have been in opposing Jesuit activity in England, two of his roles would have been sufficient to make him a target of the Catholic writers. He was a powerful favorite of the Queen, and therefore could be presumed to influence her policies; and he was an outspoken advocate of strong measures against Spain, among which he advised attacking Spanish power at its source in the New World. The Jesuits, unlike the English Catholics at home, looked to Spain for temporal power in the conversion of England. The remarks of Verstegen and Stapleton quoted above are ample indications of the bearing of Ralegh's colonizing ventures upon Jesuit hostility toward him. One aspect of the attacks in 1592, therefore, marks the beginning of Ralegh's long career as a symbol of anti-Spanish feeling in England.

This reexamination of the full context of Ralegh's "School of Atheism" almost negates the value of Parsons' description as historical evidence—"almost" because even a general libel may contain specific truths. If Parsons' satirical reference is to be used as evidence of Ralegh's religious beliefs, its use is subject to the following considerations: (1) that the publication of Parsons' *Responsio* in eight editions and four languages within two years contributed greatly to the spread of Ralegh's reputation as an "atheist"; (2) that, even though the most popular, the *Responsio* is only one of a series of replies, of which several, in answering Elizabeth's proclamation against the Jesuits and seminary priests, attacked Ralegh by name or by implication; (3) that these replies, devoted principally to the indictment of Burghley, of Protestant

---

[49] Compare Ralegh's generous treatment of a captured Spanish navigator, Pedro Sarmiento (*The Original Writings and Correspondence of the Two Richard Hakluyts*, ed. E. G. R. Taylor, pp. 47-48, 354-55).

leaders in the Privy Council, and of Elizabeth, make very free use of the epithet "atheist"; (4) that Ralegh is merely a target of opportunity, not the main objective of the attack; and (5) that in one important aspect the attacks mark an early stage of Ralegh's long usefulness as a symbol of anti-Spanish policy and feeling. The chief point is that we should read Parsons' statement not as independent historical evidence but as a footnote in a bitter and long-enduring quarrel between the Jesuits and those who controlled the religious policy of England.

III

The libels from abroad were accompanied by suspicions at home. Among the references in 1593–1594 to Ralegh's "atheism" are several which place him in the company of other suspected individuals, of whom Marlowe is the most notable. The association of Ralegh and Marlowe has long been a tempting subject for conjecture and assertion, and conclusions have ranged from Sir Sidney Lee's sweeping generalization on their supposed intimacy to Dr. Samuel A. Tannenbaum's theory that Ralegh arranged for the assassination of the young dramatist.[50] Despite the thousands of words written about this pair, when we turn to the record we find only one bit of evidence that Marlowe was ever in conversation with Ralegh. An item in the "Remembrances of words and matter" against the spy Richard Cholmeley is:

That he saith and verily believeth that one Marlowe is able to show more sound reasons for atheism than any divine in England is able to give to prove divinity, and that Marlowe told him that he hath read the atheist lecture to Sir Walter Raleigh and others.[51]

[50] According to Lee, in *Great Englishmen of the Sixteenth Century* (2d ed., London, 1925), p. 143, Marlowe was Ralegh's "frequent companion. They debated together the evidences of Christianity, and reached the perilous conclusion that they were founded on sand." A similar statement occurs in the *Dict. Nat. Biog.* article on Ralegh, of which Lee is coauthor. Dr. Tannenbaum's theory is expounded in *The Assassination of Christopher Marlowe* (New York, 1928).

[51] Harleian MS 6848, fol. 190, in C. F. Tucker Brooke, *The Life of Marlowe* (New York, 1930), p. 65. According to Richard Baines (Harleian MS 6848, fol. 185, in Brooke, *op. cit.*, p. 99) "Ric. Cholmley hath confessed that he was persuaded by Marlowe's reasons to become an atheist."

The Record   41

The context of this testimony against Cholmeley is a story in which Marlowe, not Ralegh, is the person of central interest.[52] Beginning with the apprehension of the dramatist Thomas Kyd on suspicion of writing libels against aliens resident in London, the governmental authorities found among his papers evidences of heresy: a manuscript on Arian doctrine, now known to be extracts of heretical statements from a work designed to refute them, *The Fall of the Late Arian* (1549) by John Proctor.[53] Kyd said that the manuscript belonged to Marlowe, who was brought before the Lords of the Council and required to attend them daily until released. A few days later Marlowe was killed, just as one Richard Baines was supplementing Kyd's accusations with a detailed account of Marlowe's blasphemies.[54] Among them, according to Baines, was Marlowe's scoff that "Moses was but a juggler and that one Heriots being Sir W. Ralegh's man can do more than he." [55] In a second version of the Baines note, a copy sent to the Queen, the identification of Harriot as Ralegh's man is omitted. Baines further asserted that Marlowe had "quoted a number of contrarieties out of the Scripture which he hath given to some great men who in convenient time shall be named," [56]

[52] For documented accounts of the events here summarized see Frederick S. Boas, *Marlowe and His Circle* (Oxford, 1929), and *Christopher Marlowe* (Oxford, 1940); C. F. Tucker Brooke, *op. cit.*, with documentary appendixes; John Bakeless, *The Tragicall History of Christopher Marlowe*, 2 vols. (Cambridge, Mass., 1942). F. C. Danchin, "Études critiques sur Christophe Marlowe," *Revue-Germanique*, IX (1913), 566–87, and X (1914), 52–68, prints in full the principal documents bearing on the "atheism" of both Marlowe and Ralegh.

[53] W. D. Briggs, "On a Document Concerning Christopher Marlowe," *Studies in Philology*, XX (1923), 153–59. The heretic whose errors John Proctor undertook to refute has been identified by G. T. Buckley, "Who Was 'The Late Arrian'?" *Modern Language Notes*, XLIX (1934), 500–503.

[54] In the chronology of extant manuscripts Baines' note precedes Kyd's letters to Lord Keeper Puckering, the source of our information about his charges against Marlowe. But Kyd was arrested on May 12 and Marlowe on May 20, 1593; it is evident that Kyd, who was put to torture, had implicated Marlowe in his testimony. Marlowe was killed May 30.

[55] Harleian MS 6848, fols. 185–86, in Brooke, *op. cit.*, pp. 98–100. Danchin, *op. cit.*, IX, 570–73, prints in full both this and the second version of Baines' accusations (Harleian MS 6853, fols. 307–308).

[56] *Ibid.* According to Danchin the paragraph in which this occurs is marked through with a transverse line in the second version.

and it is sometimes assumed that Ralegh was one of these men.

But only the statement attributed to Cholmeley definitely associates Marlowe with Ralegh. All other evidence on the friendship is inferential: even the strongest, that they had in common several friends and acquaintances, is no proof of intimacy.[57] That Ralegh wrote an answer to Marlowe's "The Passionate Shepherd to his Love" does not show personal acquaintance. Such "clues" as that both Marlowe (in the Baines note) and Ralegh use the words "contrarieties" are meaningless: the word is commonplace in Elizabethan times, and Ralegh, who devotes to the agreement of the Testaments several pages in *The History of the World*, applies the word in *The Skeptic* to human testimonies, not to the divine revelations of the Scriptures.[58] In brief, the circles in which Marlowe and Ralegh moved seem to intersect, but they are not concentric. In those circles the person whose friendship bears most directly on Ralegh's religious reputation is not Marlowe, but Harriot; and Harriot's intimacy with Ralegh is attested not by twentieth-century inference but by sixteenth-century fact.

[57] Paul H. Kocher, *Christopher Marlowe: a Study of His Thought, Learning, and Character* (Chapel Hill, N.C., 1946), pp. 7–18, emphasizes the fallacy of this argument. For a summary of the "rather slender evidence" on the relations of Marlowe and Ralegh, see Bakeless, *op. cit.*, I, 127–28. Bakeless, however, accepts as confirming Cholmeley's statement the "fact" that "the general tenor of Ralegh's and Marlowe's theological questioning is about the same," although they differ in the mode of their investigations and in their conclusions.

[58] The parallelism is considered significant by Miss M. C. Bradbrook, *The School of Night* (Cambridge, England, 1936), pp. 17–18, and is cited after her by Boas, *Christopher Marlowe*, p. 256, and by Bakeless (*op. cit.*, I, 128), who calls the word "odd and unusual." But the word is adequately illustrated in the *New English Dictionary*, and of many additional examples one may be cited for its applicability to the usage in the Baines note: a speaker in a dialogue on the Trinity says, "It seemeth to me that there is a contrariety in this matter" (Peter Viret, *A Christian Instruction*, 1573, p. 146). The word appears frequently in Philip Mornay's *A Work Concerning the Trueness of the Christian Religion* (1587)—four times on p. 238. Arthur Broke, *The Agreement of Sundry Places of Scripture* (1563) attempts to reconcile more than a hundred pairs of seemingly conflicting passages from the Scriptures and rebukes those who seek out such discords to bolster their irreligious arguments. For Ralegh's views on the harmony of the Scriptures, see below, chap. iv.

The Record

Thomas Harriot, who was identified in the Baines note as Sir Walter Ralegh's man, is the most likely candidate for the post of "conjurer" in what Parsons called Ralegh's school of atheism.[59] In 1594, witnesses at Cerne Abbas, in answering questions designed to check upon rumors of unorthodox beliefs and practices among members of Ralegh's retinue, credited reports that Harriot "had brought the godhead in question, and the whole course of the Scriptures," that he had been "convented before the Lords of the Council for denying the resurrection of the body," and that in general he was suspected of atheism.[60] According to one account of Ralegh's trial in 1603, the judge who passed sentence warned Ralegh not to let "Heriott, nor any such Doctor, persuade you there is no eternity in Heaven, lest you find an eternity of hell-torments."[61] This seemingly dangerous companion, a distinguished mathematician and scientist, entered Ralegh's service as a tutor in mathematics and went with the unsuccessful colony of 1585 to Virginia. Upon his return he tried to offset the un-

---

[59] John Dee, however, apparently believed that he was the person slandered; see E. A. Strathmann, "John Dee as Ralegh's 'Conjurer,'" *Huntington Library Quarterly*, X (1947), 365–72. It is commonly conjectured (e.g., Boas, *Christopher Marlowe*, p. 114) that Thomas Nashe had Harriot in mind when he wrote in *Pierce Penniless* (1592): "I hear say there be mathematicians abroad that will prove men before Adam" (*Works*, ed. R. B. McKerrow, 5 vols. [London, 1904–10], I, 172).

Outside of the biographical dictionaries the only life of Harriot is that by Henry Stevens, *Thomas Hariot and His Associates* (London, 1900). There is no complete survey in print of the extensive manuscripts and notes which Harriot left, and many of our judgments on particular questions involving him are provisional until more information about the manuscripts is available. Jean Robertson, "Some Additional Poems by George Chapman," *The Library*, 4th ser., XXII (1941–42), 168–76, makes a good case for identifying the subject of two early portraits as Harriot.

[60] Harleian MS 6849, fols. 183–190, in Danchin, *op. cit.*, IX, 578–87. See below, footnote 70. No record of Harriot's appearance before the Council has been found. A single word in an ambiguous context, following a note of information against Cholmeley, may refer to Harriot: "Yong taken and made an instrument / to take the rest / hariet / borage dangerous" (Danchin, *op. cit.*, IX, 577).

[61] David Jardine, *Criminal Trials* (London, 1832), I, 450–51; quoted by Danchin, *op. cit.*, X, 67.

favorable reports of the disappointed colonists by writing *A Brief and True Report of the New Found Land of Virginia* (1588), a competent and readable survey of the economic resources of the new country. Some time after 1593, when he is still described as of Sir Walter Ralegh's household, Harriot left the service—but not the company—of Ralegh for that of Henry Percy, Ninth Earl of Northumberland.[62]

Because of the Earl's known interest in occult studies the new association was as suspect as the old, and, quite aside from public opinion, was to bring Harriot into unexpected political difficulties. In the dangerous excitement following the Gunpowder Plot, Northumberland was held to answer questions about a kinsman, and Harriot was taken into custody for a time, apparently because he was suspected of casting the King's horoscope for his employer. The incident produced two brief descriptive passages to enliven our picture of Harriot: the official who searched his study at Sion found there "books of all sorts of learning, and many: of all sorts and professions of religion," but nothing to the purpose of the government; and Harriot, protesting his innocence to the Council, said of himself that he was "contented with a private life for the love of learning, wherein his labors have been painful and great."[63] Northumberland was sent to the Tower, where he was to remain until 1621, the year of Harriot's death. The doubts of Harriot's orthodoxy expressed at Cerne Abbas in 1594 lingered on, and in his painful death from cancer of the lip some divines, according to Aubrey, saw evidence of God's judgment. Aubrey's

---

[62] On July 30, 1603, when Ralegh was recovering from a futile (and possibly histrionic) attempt at suicide, he asked permission to see "Mr. Heriott"; and Harriot's name is on the approved list of visitors to Ralegh in the Tower. See *Cal. State Papers, Dom.*, *1603–10*, p. 25; Historical MSS Comm., *Cal. of MSS at Hatfield House*, XVII (1938), 443–44. Ralegh and Northumberland, friends since 1586, were brought together again when Northumberland was sent to the Tower after the Gunpowder Plot. Both men enjoyed the company not only of Harriot but of other scholars.

[63] Hist. MSS Comm., *Cal. of MSS at Hatfield House*, XVII (1938), 507, 529–30, 554; cf. *Cal. State Papers, Dom.*, *1603–10*, p. 263. I do not know when Harriot was released. Dudley Carleton, held in a similar manner for questioning, was detained eleven days (*Cal. of MSS at Hatfield House*, XVII, 567).

notes, with their meaning somewhat distorted in Wood's better-known phrasing, state further that Harriot was a deist who nullified the Scriptures and infected Ralegh and Northumberland with his beliefs.[64]

As with Ralegh, the indictment of Harriot's beliefs is counterbalanced by attestations of orthodoxy. In *A Brief and True Report of Virginia* Harriot had shown interest in the natives' religion and a due concern for their heathen state. The Indians, he reported, believed in one god who was supreme over all other gods and in the immortality of the soul; but they were inclined to the opinion that the colonists, so obviously favored by God in their knowledge of crafts, enjoyed a religion superior to their own. Harriot therefore "made declaration of the contents of the Bible; that therein was set forth the true and only God, and his mighty works, that therein was contained the true doctrine of salvation through Christ, with many particularities of miracles and chief points of religion, as I was able then to utter, and thought fit for the time." [65] Harriot's book became widely known through its incorporation in Hakluyt's *Principal Navigations;* the remarks on the religious beliefs of the natives are reprinted in *Purchas His Pilgrimage;* [66] and the passage is cited in a seventeenth-century dispute about the origins of the American Indians.[67] The praise of Harriot by clergymen is, of course, for his skill in such studies as mathematics and astronomy; for the first he is commended by Hakluyt in the dedications of *De Orbe Novo* (1587) and of the second volume of *The Principal Navigations* (1599); and for the second he is invoked as an oracle by Richard Corbet, later Bishop of Norwich, who wrote of "deep Harriot's mine, In which there is no dross, but all refine." [68]

---

[64] *Brief Lives* (1898), I, 284–87; Anthony à Wood, *Athenae Oxonienses*, II (1815), 300. For further details see below, chap. iv.
[65] Sigs. E2^v–F2^v; quotation E4^r.   [66] 1614 ed., bk. VIII, chap. vi, p. 762 ff.
[67] Edward Stillingfleet, *Origines sacrae*, 8th ed. (London, 1709), pp. 74–75.
[68] "A Letter Sent from Dr. Corbet to Sir Thomas Ailesbury, December the 9th, 1618. On the Occasion of a Blazing Star," in *The Poems of Richard Corbet*, ed. Octavius Gilchrist (London, 1807), pp. 88–93; quoted by Aubrey and Wood.

More direct and more personal testimony is found in a letter written by William Lower, who, alluding to the death of his only son, tells Harriot that "amongst other things I have learnt of you to settle and submit my desires to the will of God." Harriot himself five years before his death wrote to his physician a kind of confession of faith: "My recovery will be your triumph, but through the Almighty who is the Author of all good things. . . . I believe in God Almighty; I believe that medicine was ordained by him; I trust the physician as his minister." As if in refutation of doubts cast upon his orthodoxy, two close friends who composed his Latin epitaph described him as "In Mathematics, Natural Philosophy, Theology/A most studious investigator of truth/A most pious worshipper of the Triune God." [69]

This selection of opinions pro and con on Harriot's soundness in religion is part of Ralegh's story because of the long association of the two men in a variety of enterprises. Certain matters here briefly presented, such as Marlowe's reference to Harriot's skill in magic and Aubrey's note on his "Deism," are important in an evaluation of Ralegh's own writings and will receive further attention. But to continue the account of Ralegh's reputation among his contemporaries it is necessary to proceed now to the investigation at Cerne Abbas.

Although the record of that inquiry has been known for half a century,[70] there is still a wide diversity of opinion about its

[69] The letters and the translation of the epitaph are in Stevens, *op. cit.*, pp. 124, 148, 142, 145. In the original, the phrases quoted from the epitaph read as follows: ". . . mathematicis, philosophicis, theologicis, veritatis indagator studiosissimus, Dei Triniunius cultor piissimus." See Wood, *Athenae Oxonienses*, II (1815), 301. The inconsistency of the epitaph and Wood's statement that Harriot was a deist has been noted by the author of the article on Harriot in *Biographia Britannica* (London, 1747–1766), IV, 2539–43.

[70] Excerpts were published by J. M. Stone, "Atheism under Elizabeth and James I," *The Month*, LXXXI (1894), 174–87; and by Frederick S. Boas, "New Light on Sir Walter Raleigh," *Literature*, No. 147 (Aug. 11, 1900), pp. 96–98, and No. 148 (Aug. 18, 1900), pp. 113–14. The document (Harleian MS 6849, fols. 183–90) is printed in full by Danchin in *Revue-Germanique*, IX (1913), 578–87, and by G. B. Harrison in his edition of *Willobie His Avisa* (London, 1926), App. III. I have worked principally with Harrison's text,

meaning. The story, in brief, begins with a supper party at the home of Sir George Trenchard, Deputy Lieutenant of Dorset, one summer evening in 1593. The guests were Sir Ralph Horsey, also Deputy Lieutenant of Dorset; Sir Walter Ralegh; Sir Walter's brother Carew; Mr. John Fitzjames; Ralph Ironside, Minister of Winterborne; Ironside's friend, Mr. Whittle, Vicar of Forthington; and apparently others anonymously lumped together in an "etc." "Some loose speeches of Mr. Carew Ralegh's being gently reproved by Sir Ralph Horsey," Carew inquired of the preacher Ironside what danger he might incur by such speeches. He scoffed at the reply, that "the wages of sin is death," since death is the common lot of sinner and saint; but Ironside answered further, "That death which is properly the wages of sin, is death eternal, both of the body and of the soul also." "Soul," asked Carew Ralegh, "what is that?" And Ironside remarked that knowledge of how the soul was to be saved was preferable to close inquiry into its essence.

Although Carew may have been deliberately baiting his companion, his remarks, as we shall see, could easily be interpreted as falling within the broad compass of "atheism." At this point, Ironside "keeping silence," Sir Walter broke in upon the dialogue, and asked that Ironside, for their instruction, "would answer to the question that before by his brother was proposed." "I have been," said Sir Walter, "a scholar some time in Oxford, I have answered under a bachelor of art, and had talk with diverse; [71] yet hitherunto in this point (to wit what the reasonable soul of man is) have I not by any been resolved." Thereupon followed a discourse upon the nature of the soul which left Sir Walter unsatisfied, nor did he like better Ironside's circular remarks on the nature of God. "Marry," quoth Sir Walter, "these

---

checked by Danchin's version and a microfilm of the manuscript. A few verbal differences will be noted at the appropriate places; since I am modernizing the text, I shall not note discrepancies in spelling or punctuation.

[71] Harrison reads "diu*i*nes," but the symbol used in the MS clearly stands for *er*, not *in*. It appears in such words as "howsoe*uer*," "conv*er*tiblie," and "unc*er*taine"; and the word "devines" is written out a few lines down the page.

two be like, for neither could I learn hitherto what God is." Further explanations were likewise unsatisfactory, and Sir Walter wished that grace might be said, "for that, quoth he, is better than this disputation."

This account of the supper party at Sir George Trenchard's comes from the testimony concerning the conversation that has the greatest value as evidence: the sworn statement, written by himself, which Ironside gave to the commissioners who on March 21, 1594, met to take examinations on various rumors of ungodly speech and conduct in Dorset. The depositions made at Cerne Abbas are not all of equal value. Concerning Sir Walter himself, most witnesses have only hearsay testimony to offer. The common formula, with variations, is: "To the first interrogatory he can say nothing of his own knowledge; but he hath heard . . ." Other matters than the party at Trenchard's are touched upon— Parson Nicholas Jefferys (Jeffries) recollected the high-handed confiscation of his horse by the Ralegh brothers and the disrespectful words of Carew—but the principal subject is the colloquy of Ironside and the Raleghs. Country gossip had distorted the facts, and one church officer who testified from hearsay had the idea that Sir Walter had questioned the immortality of the soul and the deity and omnipotence of God. John Davis, Curate of Motcombe, answered one question:

. . . he hath heard that Sir Walter Ralegh hath argued with one Mr. Ironside at Sir George Trenchard's touching the being, or immortality of the soul, or such like; but the certainty thereof he cannot say further, saving asking the same of Mr. Ironside upon the report aforesaid, he hath answered that *the matter was not as the voice of the country reported thereof,* or to the like effect.[72]

This distinction between the sworn, written testimony of Ironside and the hearsay evidence of those who had heard the story at second or third hand is the first and most important point to observe in reading the account of the investigation at Cerne Abbas.

---

[72] My italics. The deposition of one secondary witness, Parson Nicholas "Jefferys," corresponds reasonably well with that of Ironside.

The men who conducted the inquiry exercised their authority by "virtue of a commission to us and others directed from some of her Majesty's High Commissioners in Causes Ecclesiastical." The investigating committee consisted of Thomas Howard, Viscount Howard of Bindon,[73] Sir Ralph Horsey, Chancellor Francis James, John Williams, and Francis Hawley. Horsey had been present at the supper party, and his reproof of Carew Ralegh's "loose speeches" had led to the brief colloquy on the soul and God. Further, three weeks after this investigation Ralegh joined Trenchard and Horsey in taking the examination of the captured Jesuit, Father Cornelius. Ironside acted on the advice of counsel in offering only his sworn statement of what he knew at first hand; "but for that he hath heard, and knoweth no author [i.e., authority] to justify the same, he is persuaded by counsel that he is in danger to be punished, and therefore refuseth to say any thing upon uncertain report unless he could bring in his author in particular." Ironside's report, therefore, made in a sworn statement and submitted in writing to a group of experienced men among whom was one that had heard the whole debate with the Raleghs, has considerable value in attaching an earlier date to Sir Walter's opinions than we can affix with confidence to most of his writings.

A second point to be observed in using the evidence offered at Cerne Abbas is the function of the investigating committee. The list of queries, "interrogatories to be ministered unto such as are to be examined," indicates plainly a search for information concerning specific rumors.[74] Although Sir Walter is the principal

[73] Several years later, in a letter which has been variously dated, Ralegh refers bitterly to legal difficulties involving Viscount Howard of Bindon. See Edwards, *Life*, I, 470–72, II, 250; *Cal. State Papers, Dom.*, 1595–97, p. 266; *Complete Peerage*, VI (London, 1926) 585.

[74] John Bakeless, *op. cit.*, I, 131 (following the *Dict. Nat. Biog.*, s.v. Sir Walter Ralegh, and its reference to Harleian MS 7042, fol. 401) writes that the Commission was "specifically instructed" to examine Sir Walter Ralegh, his older brother Carew, and others. But the manuscript cited (which I have checked in microfilm) contains notes by Thomas Baker, an eighteenth-century antiquary, on the original report of the investigation (Harleian MS 6849, fols.

figure in the investigation, grave suspicion was cast on Carew Ralegh, Thomas Harriot, and Thomas Allen, Lieutenant of Portland Castle, which was under Sir Walter's command. At the time, following the stern edict against Jesuits and recusants in 1591 and the stringent measures appended to enforce the edict, there was a high degree of sensitivity to any deviation from the path of orthodoxy. The Commission for Causes Ecclesiastical, functioning through regular county committees and committees appointed for special inquiries, cast a large net with a close mesh, and some very small fish were caught along with the large ones. According to the testimony at Cerne Abbas, Thomas Allen was indeed a godless person. But typical of the inconsequentialities into which some inquiries drifted is the comedy in which one Oliver, servant to Thomas Allen, is the hero. Oliver's offenses were his statements that the preacher was somewhat long-winded one Sunday, and that the preacher had praised Moses excessively but had neglected to mention his fifty-two concubines. The good housewives who heard these scandalous remarks reported to the Reverend Francis Scarlett that "their ears did glow." One of the ladies corrected Oliver's confusion of Moses and Solomon, and perceiving that he was "gone with drink" told him to go home and sleep. Of the same stamp is a shoemaker's report of a sect of atheists in the neighborhood; on examination the report breaks down into what the shoemaker heard his brother say concerning a sermon in which the preacher delivered "in the pulpit that there was such a sect which he did there seem to confute." [75] These trivia are

---

183–90). Baker simply refused to believe the accusations against Ralegh and did not transcribe them. The commission's instructions do not name the persons to be investigated, although several of the "interrogatories," especially numbers 5 and 6, point to individuals who had been quoted (or misquoted) in country gossip.

[75] The stories about Oliver and the shoemaker were deemed of sufficient importance to be the subject of further examinations by two of the commissioners in the week following the principal inquiry. Commenting on the shoemaker's report, G. T. Buckley, *Atheism in the English Renaissance*, p. 141, note 4, notes that the clergy themselves may have been responsible for spreading the idea that atheism was prevalent in England.

The Record

worthy of mention only as a counterpoise to interpretations of the Cerne Abbas inquiry which would make of it something exceptional. Although conditions varied from shire to shire, in the South one finds an alertness to details which today appear insignificant. In Surrey, for example, Sir George More, following in his father's steps, employed his office as he later employed his pen to defend the true religion. During the years when Sir William More and Sir George were prominent in the administration of county affairs, the opinions of a schoolmaster on preaching as the *sine qua non* of church service and a book dropped by a stranger received about equal attention.[76]

A third caution to be applied to the examinations at Cerne Abbas is that, so far as we know, they resulted in no formal charges and no formal action. This is not the place to discuss the meaning of Sir Walter's remarks, which are best understood in connection with his own commentaries on the nature of God and the soul. The fact of importance for this record is that we cannot read the questions addressed to Ironside as part of an "impious dialogue" [77] or as utterances to which "Horsey listened in scandalized amazement" [78] and then find no action taken. If "no capital charge could be framed from the hearsay evidence of country parsons and churchwardens," [79] could one have been framed from the sworn testimony of Ironside and the personal knowledge of the commissioner Sir Ralph Horsey? In 1593–1594 Ralegh's position at court, following his marriage, was not so strong, nor his enemies so weak, as to give him an extraordinary immunity. Nor is it consistent with the religious situation in those years to read Ralegh's speeches, in Ironside's report, as reflections of free thought but as insufficient to warrant further official action. Three

---

[76] Loseley MSS (Case 5, items 234 and 235, undated) in the Folger Shakespeare Library. Both Sir William More and his son George were appointed to the commission for Surrey under the proclamation of 1591 against the Jesuits and recusants; see Hist. MSS Comm., *Seventh Report*, p. 649. Sir George More is the author of *A Demonstration of God in His Works* (1597), an attack on atheism praised by John Dove. [77] Bakeless, *op. cit.*, I, 133.
[78] G. B. Harrison, ed., *Willobie His Avisa*, pp. 212–13. [79] *Ibid.*

weeks after the inquiry at Cerne Abbas, Sir Walter Ralegh, with an epistolary "tally-ho" to Sir Robert Cecil, rode off to join his host of the preceding summer and one of the commissioners at Cerne Abbas in a normal and customary occupation: the pursuit of Jesuits and a close watch upon recusants.

IV

The wide circulation of Parsons' *Responsio* very probably helped to spread rumors of Ralegh's "atheism," and how quickly rumor could spread—and how easily facts could be distorted—is clearly shown by the contrast between firsthand and hearsay testimony at Cerne Abbas. It is not surprising that from the time of the inquiry till his imprisonment one finds allusions to Ralegh's lack of faith ranging from the mildly ironical to the savagely vituperative, the latter especially in connection with the fall of Essex. A few illustrations will show the drift of popular opinion about Ralegh during the last years of Elizabeth's reign.

On October 15, 1595, Rowland Whyte wrote from London to Sir Robert Sidney: "Sir Walter Ralegh is here, and goes daily to hear sermons, because he hath seen the wonders of the Lord in the deep; 'tis much commended and spoken of." [80] The works of the Lord and his wonders in the deep (Psalms 107:23 and 24) are frequently cited by or for Elizabethan seafarers: Hakluyt, writing in the dedication of *The Principal Navigations* (1589) about his early interest in geography, tells how his cousin first explained a map to him and then opened the Bible at Psalm 107; and the verses are on the title page of William Barlow's *The Navigator's Supply* (1597). The "book of God's works" was a prime argument against atheism, especially by those who sought to convince the unfaithful by "reasonable" arguments alone. The report on Sir Walter, therefore, may be marked by a touch of irony which makes it unnecessary for Rowland Whyte to

---

[80] Hist. MSS Comm., *Report on the MSS at Penshurst Place*, II (1934), 173; quoted by G. B. Harrison, *A Second Elizabethan Journal* (New York, 1931), p. 52.

explain why the "Shepherd of the Ocean" waited so many years to marvel at the maritime wonders of the Lord.

Of all the criticisms of Ralegh, probably the most damaging in their practical consequences were those made by Sir Robert Cecil and Henry Howard in letters written to King James VI of Scotland in anticipation of his accession to the throne of England. In these letters, the purpose of which was to discredit Ralegh and his associates politically, religion is a distinctly subordinate but not unimportant topic. Cecil carefully left to his lieutenant Howard the task of making open and unguarded accusations; his own words are tempered by a note of caution. Ralegh is described as one of a group who view unhappily the prospect of the Scottish succession, "though they confess (Ralegh especially) that (*rebus sic stantibus*) natural policy forceth them to keep on foot such a trade against the great day of mart." Even if Ralegh writes anything in commendation of Cecil, James will do well to consider that the probable motive is "to keep me from any humor of imanity [*sic*], when, I thank God, my greatest adversaries and my own soul have ever acquitted me from that of all other vices. Would God I were as free from offense towards God, in seeking for private affection to support a person whom religious men do hold anathema." Having skillfully presented himself as the one loyal subject of Elizabeth who is competent to guard the interests of James, Cecil dismisses the unpleasant subject of Ralegh by leaving to Henry Howard "the best and worst of him and other things." [81] Very little of the "best" of Ralegh reached James by way of Howard's "ample Asiatic and endless volumes" (as James happily described his style). In Howard's letters on the succession, Ralegh, Cobham, and Northumberland are the "diabolical triplicity," and "hell cannot afford such a like triplicity that denies the Trinity." When Northumberland enjoys a brief respite from invective, Ralegh and Cobham become "that ac-

---

[81] *Correspondence of King James VI of Scotland with Sir Robert Cecil and Others*, ed. John Bruce, "Camden Society Publications," LXXVIII (1861), 18–19.

cursed duality." According to Howard, the problem of the succession figured in the disputes of Northumberland and his wife (the younger sister of the Earl of Essex): he describes one of their quarrels and separations as a parting "by the distemper of an atheist, that, besides Ralegh's Alcoran, admits no principles." [82] With phrases such as these the letters of Cecil and Howard planted in the mind of King James suspicions of Ralegh's religious as well as of his political soundness.

Ralegh reached a new low in popular esteem after the trial and death of Essex in 1601, for which the people held him largely responsible. Although Ralegh was not alone to blame for his rival's downfall, the extent of his opposition to Essex is attested today by a letter to Cecil which, however interpreted, is clearly hostile to Essex and may be read as urging his death.[83] But hatred of Ralegh at this time had other grounds than the popularity of Essex: there were long-standing grievances arising from Ralegh's exercise of monopolistic privileges and from his own "damnably proud" and sometimes arrogant bearing. In consequence Ralegh is the target of a number of verse libels and lampoons, some of them obviously written in the brief period between the execution of Essex and his own trial in 1603, which paradoxically turned the tide of public opinion in his favor.

The contrast between Essex and Ralegh is emphasized in some

---

[82] *Secret Correspondence of Sir Robert Cecil with James VI*, ed. Edmund Goldsmid, 3 vols. (Edinburgh, 1887), I, 26. For the other quotations from Howard's letters, see I, 24, 31; II, 6. For James's comment on Howard's style, see II, 38.

[83] Edwards, *Life*, I, 258–60; II, 213–23, is more partial to Ralegh in this matter than are biographers of Essex. He considers the letter "ungenerous" and "of an obviously immoral tendency"; but argues, on the grounds of date and of the terms used in referring to Essex's heir, that the letter is "not an incitement to the raising of a political scaffold."

According to a former servant, Essex on the day of his rebellion "told the people that he acted for the good of the Queen, city, and crown, which certain atheists, meaning Raleigh, had betrayed to the Infanta of Spain" (*Cal. State Papers, Dom.*, *1598–1601*, p. 547). At his trial Essex declared that he was acting against Ralegh, Cobham, and Cecil, not against the Queen.

anonymous stanzas written after Ralegh's conviction. The poem is distinguished from other verse libels by a greater literary sophistication, manifest in form and style and in lines which echo Spenser and possibly Shakespeare. The writer regrets that "the summer's nightingale, Immortal Cynthia's sometime dear delight" has fallen to evil courses and that "So rare a wit should be so ill employed." Such acknowledgment of any good parts in Ralegh is unusual in verses which appeared around 1603. The humility of Essex, who "would vail his bonnet to any oyster wife," earned him the love of the common people, as the pride of Ralegh earned their disdain. The writer sees revenge for Essex in his rival's fate, and concludes his poem with a metaphor likening the alleged treason of Ralegh to a stage tragedy, planned but not acted, in which "Ralegh should play the devil by his art." [84]

Other verses by partisans of Essex the less restrained:

> Essex for vengeance cries
> His blood upon thee lies,
> Mounting above the skies,
>   Damnable fiend of hell,
>   Mischievous Matchivel! [85]

Even more germane is the device which plays upon the syllables of Ralegh's name:

> *Water* thy plants with grace divine,
>   And hope to live for aye;
> Then to thy Saviour Christ incline;
>   In Him make steadfast stay;
> *Raw* is the reason that doth *lie*

---

[84] *Poetical Miscellanies*, ed. J. O. Halliwell, "Publications of the Percy Society," XV (1848), 15–17; Brushfield, *Bibliography*, No. 299-c. Folger Shakespeare Library MS 2071.7 contains a longer version of this poem which seems to me superior to the text published by Halliwell. "Vail his bonnet to an oyster wife" may echo *Richard II*, I, iv, 31; for discussion see *Times Lit. Supp.*, Oct. 15, 1931, p. 803; Dec. 10, 1931, p. 1006.

[85] *Poetical Miscellanies*, ed. Halliwell, pp. 13–14; Brushfield, *Bibliography*, No. 299-a.

56   The Record

> Within an atheist's head,
> Which saith the soul of man doth die,
> When that the body's dead.[86]

One follower of Essex, in prose reflections upon Ralegh's attempted suicide in 1603, concludes that his "stab was ungentle, savoring of barbarism, and too much tasting of desperation, together it had a spice of atheism; for he that denies himself, denies him that made him, and he that kills himself kills him in himself that redeemed him." [87] A more general indictment is found in the answers to Ralegh's "The Lie," especially to his stanza on the court and the church, which shows "What's good, and doth no good." On the contrary:

> The Court hath settled sureness
> In banishing such boldness;
> The Church retains her pureness,
>   Though Atheists show their coldness:
> The Court and Church, though base,
> Turn lies into thy face.[88]

---

[86] *The Courtly Poets from Raleigh to Montrose*, ed. J. Hannah (London, 1870), p. xxiv; Brushfield, *Bibliography*, No. 299-b. According to Aubrey (*Brief Lives* [1898], II, 182, 186) the syllables of Ralegh's name figured in a popular rebus, and King James himself could not resist punning on them. A more complimentary wording than Aubrey's is found in *Gabriel Harvey's Marginalia*, ed. G. C. Moore Smith (Stratford, 1913), p. 171. "Water," of course, was a common pronunciation of "Walter"; see *2 Henry VI*, I, iv, 33 and IV, i: Suffolk, told that he should die by water, is killed by Walter Whitmore.

[87] "Sir Walter Ralegh's Stab," in John Hutchins, *History of Dorset*, 4 vols. (Westminster, 1861–70), IV, 217–19; Brushfield, *Bibliography*, No. 163. King James made known his desire that at the examination of Ralegh "you would have some good preacher with you, that he may make him know that it is his soul that he must wound and not his body" (*Cal. Hatfield MSS*, XV, 212, quoted by Agnes M. C. Latham, "Sir Walter Ralegh's Farewell Letter," *Essays and Studies by Members of the English Association*, XXV [1940], 43–44).

[88] *Courtly Poets*, ed. Hannah, pp. xxvii–xxviii. Other replies are printed by Hannah and by Miss Agnes M. C. Latham in *The Poems of Sir Walter Ralegh* (London, 1929). Amid this general abuse, Henry Lok addressed to Ralegh one of the many complimentary sonnets attached to the religious poem *Ecclesiastes* (1597); and in 1603 Thomas Winter dedicated to Ralegh, in conventional terms, his translation of Du Bartas' *Second Day of the First Week*.

The Record

All this random evidence of a fixed popular belief in Ralegh's "atheism" culminates in some of the exchanges between prosecutor and accused at his trial for treason, which marks a turning point in reputation no less than in his career. The details of this notorious trial need no repetition here, and even Attorney-General Coke's charge of "atheism" might be dismissed as simply another pleasantry (such as his "Thou hast a Spanish heart, and thyself art a spider of hell"), if it were not for the publicity attendant upon the occasion and for the further implications of Coke's remark. Discoursing upon a letter which Ralegh wrote to Cobham, his fellow prisoner and accuser, Coke exclaimed:

> Further, he wrote thus, "Do not as my Lord Essex did; take heed of a preacher; for by his persuasion he confessed, and made himself guilty." I doubt not but this day God shall have as great a conquest by this traitor, and the Son of God shall be as much glorified, as when it was said, *Vicisti, Galilæe;* you know my meaning.[89]

Coke knew full well that his audience would know his meaning: Julian the Apostate, whose words are quoted, was for the Elizabethan one of the prototypes of the atheist. But after Cobham's letter had been read, Coke underscored his meaning:

> Oh, damnable atheist! He hath learned some text of Scripture to serve his own purpose, but falsely alleged. He counsels him not to be counselled by preachers as Essex was: he died the child of God, God honored him at his death. . . .[90]

Coke proceeded to charge Ralegh with gloating attendance at the Earl's death, and then abruptly checked himself before going too far: Essex *had* been guilty of treason, he hastened to add. Actually Ralegh's advice to Cobham was well-founded if indiscreet: the ministers who attended Essex in his last days were working for

---

[89] T. B. Howell, *State Trials*, II (London, 1816), 27. Accounts of Ralegh's trial differ in some particulars: see Edwards, *Life*, I, 383-439, and 385, note; and David Jardine, *Criminal Trials*, 2 vols. (London, 1832-35), I, 37-38, 400 and note.

[90] Howell, *State Trials*, II, 28. At his own trial, Essex, that "child of God," had objected to the offensiveness of Coke's manner and tactics; see Howell, *State Trials*, I (London, 1816), 1339, 1343.

the Privy Council, and they used the confessional as a political instrument, to strengthen the position of the government before the people, no less than as a means of spiritual salvation for the doomed man.[91]

In pronouncing sentence upon Ralegh, Chief Justice Popham not only was indulging in the severity for which he was notorious but also was summarizing what by the foregoing illustrations appears to have been a widely held opinion of Ralegh's "atheism":

You have been taxed by the world, Sir Walter Ralegh, with holding heathenish, blasphemous, atheistical, and profane opinions, which I list not to repeat, because Christian ears cannot endure to hear them; but the authors and maintainers of such opinions cannot be suffered to live in any Christian commonwealth. If these opinions be not yours, you shall do well, before you leave the world, to protest against them, and not to die with these imputations upon you; but if you do hold such opinions, then I beseech you renounce them, and ask God forgiveness for them as you hope for another life; and let not Heriott, nor any such Doctor, persuade you there is no eternity in Heaven, lest you find an eternity of hell-torments! [92]

And Popham repeated the censure of Ralegh's advice to Cobham not to confide in a priest: "You have shown a fearful sign of denying God, by advising a man not to confess the truth."

Popham's words are a fitting conclusion to this part of the "record" of Ralegh's reputation. Reprieved, never abandoning hope for a pardon, Ralegh turned more and more to the scholarly pursuits which culminated in the publication of *The History of the World* (1614). Although his life in the Tower varied from

---

[91] W. B. Devereux, *Lives and Letters of the Devereux, Earls of Essex*, 2 vols. (London, 1853), II, 164–72; G. B. Harrison, *The Life and Death of Robert Devereux, Earl of Essex* (London, 1937), pp. 315–25.

[92] Jardine, *Criminal Trials*, I, 450–51. Other reports of this speech do not mention Harriot's name. In Howell, *State Trials*, II, 30–31, this passage reads in part: "You know what men said of Harpool. . . . Let not any devil persuade you to think there is no eternity in Heaven. . . ." It is extremely unlikely that "Harpool" is a corrupted reference to Marlowe, as some writers have conjectured; the context of Popham's speech, in the several versions extant, seems to point to Harriot (Edwards, *Life*, I, 436).

time to time in the degree of restraint and inconvenience imposed upon him, during the greater part of his imprisonment he enjoyed the company of his wife and friends, and beginning in 1606 he had as a fellow prisoner his old friend, Henry Percy, Ninth Earl of Northumberland. The "Wizard Earl" and his "Three Magi"—Harriot, Hues, and Warner—enlarged the opportunity for scholarly pursuits, and the Earl maintained in the Tower an excellent library.

The unfairness of Ralegh's trial occasioned a violent shift in public opinion, a change epitomized in the words of the Scot who reported to King James that, "whereas when he saw him first, he was so led with the common hatred that he would have gone a hundred miles to have seen him hanged, he would, ere he parted, have gone a thousand to have saved his life." [93] Similarly, when this record of opinions about Ralegh's religious infidelity is extended beyond 1603 it becomes less one-sided; and in Ralegh's posthumous reputation (sometimes as an authority on such matters as the adequacy of Noah's Ark) the whirligigs of time bring in further revenges. Just as Popham's sentence summarizes hostile opinion, so do the words of Sir John Harington, written before the trial to his good friend Dr. John Still, Bishop of Bath and Wells, anticipate the change to a considered and temperate judgment of Ralegh:

I wist not that he hath evil design in point of faith or religion. As he hath oft discoursed to me with much learning, wisdom, and freedom, I know he doth somewhat differ in opinion from some others; but I think also his heart is well fixed in every honest thing, as far as I can look into him. He seemeth wondrously fitted, both by art and nature, to serve the state, especially as he is versed in foreign matters, his skill therein being always estimable and praiseworthy. In religion, he hath shown, in private talk, great depth and good reading, as I once ex-

---

[93] Dudley Carleton to John Chamberlain, in Howell, *State Trials*, II, 48. At one time after his arrest Ralegh was actually in danger of mob violence: see *Cal. State Papers, Dom.*, *1603–10*, p. 53. In a letter to Sir Robert Carr (1609?) Ralegh himself refers to the Scotsman's favorable report on the trial and to the shift in popular opinion (Edwards, *Life*, II, 327).

perienced at his own house, before many learned men. In good troth, I pity his state, and doubt the dice not fairly thrown, if his life be the losing stake. . . .[94]

But the story of Ralegh's reputation after 1603 must wait upon problems of interpretation and the discussion of his own writings. This chapter records, in the context of Elizabethan religious strife and personal and political rivalries, some popular opinions about Ralegh's beliefs. Next let us see what meanings can be found in the invectives so freely used.

[94] *Nugae Antiquae*, 3 vols. (London, 1779), II, 151–52. In the notes to Book XVI of *Orlando Furioso* (1591), Harington commends in passing Ralegh's epitaph on Sidney. In his *Brief View of the State of the Church*, telling how Ralegh secured possession of church lands, he is critical but not hostile, and he acknowledges that Ralegh had done him "some kindness" (*Nugae Antiquae*, I, 103–9, 130). The identification of "Paulus" in Harington's epigrams as Ralegh is difficult to reconcile with his acknowledged references to Ralegh by name. See *The Letters and Epigrams of Sir John Harington*, ed. Norman E. McClure (Philadelphia, 1930), p. 51, and the references cited (p. 52, note 1).

Chapter 3

Elizabethan Meanings of "Atheism"

Certainly as all the rivers in the world, though they have diverse risings and diverse runnings, . . . do at last find and fall into the great ocean: so after all the searches that human capacity hath, and after all philosophical contemplation and curiosity, in the necessity of this infinite power all the reason of man ends and dissolves itself

History, Preface, sig. D3

OF THE MANY MEANINGS which Elizabethans attached to the word "atheism" and its derivatives, its usage as a "snarl word," to be thrown indiscriminately at religious or political opponents for the slightest differences of opinion, is most easily dismissed. Queen Elizabeth was called an atheist by an Englishman in Germany; John Caius, Master of Gonville and Caius College, was simultaneously accused of Romanism and atheism; members of the Privy Council were unbelievers to the extreme Puritan "Left" as well as to the extreme Catholic "Right"; and the term appeared even in quarrels among the Catholics.[1] It would be idle to multiply examples of the abusive use of "atheism" in circumstances to which its present-day meaning could not apply. Ralegh himself, who in his *History of the*

---

[1] Queen Elizabeth: see John Bakeless, *The Tragicall History of Christopher Marlowe*, 2 vols. (Cambridge, Mass., 1942), I, 109; John Caius: see J. B. Mullinger, *The University of Cambridge, 1535–1625* (Cambridge, England, 1884), pp. 200–202, and *Dict. Nat. Biog.*, s.v. John Caius; for charges against the Council and the quarrels among the Catholics, see above, chap. ii.

62 Elizabethan Meanings of "Atheism"

World is extremely chary of the word, comments unfavorably on this controversial usage in words which suggest a personal application:

> But such indiscretion [as that of Bozius] is usually found among men of his humor: who, having once either foolishly embraced the dreams of others or vainly fashioned in their own brains any strange chimeras of divinity, condemn all such in the pride of their zeal, as atheists and infidels, that are not transported with the like intemperate ignorance. Great pity it is that such mad dogs are oftentimes encouraged by those who, having the command of many tongues, when they themselves cannot touch a man in open and generous opposition, will wound him secretly by the malicious virtue of a hypocrite.[2]

Moreover, it is not only in controversy that the term is common; digressions on "atheism" and "atheists," frequent in sermons and devotional books, are as likely to be found in epigram or character, in narrative poem or personal letter, in drama or essay—in short, in almost any context. Such materials, if they were presented in detail, would demonstrate the unanimity with which the Elizabethans, like the preacher of Calvin Coolidge's youth, were "against sin." However, the purpose of this chapter as an essay in semantics is not to survey for the independent interest of the subject Elizabethan opinion on religious unbelief,[3]

---

[2] *The History of the World* (1614), Bk. II, chap. viii, sec. 3, pp. 367–68.

[3] For descriptive accounts of Elizabethan atheism see J. M. Robertson, *A Short History of Freethought*, 2 vols. (London, 1906); Friedrich Brie, "Deismus und Atheismus in der englischen Renaissance," *Anglia*, XLVIII (1924), 54–98, 105–68; and G. T. Buckley, *Atheism in the English Renaissance* (Chicago, 1932). Brie's long article has useful bibliographical notes, sometimes in error on books which he was unable to examine (e.g., p. 163, the author of *St. Peter's Prophecy* is John Hull, not Hill, and the quotation is from Jeremy Corderoy's *Warning for Worldlings*, not from Hull). Brie's thesis, that English deism had its roots in native sources, has led to some misreading of the evidence as it applies to the sixteenth century. Without making clear the reasons for his distinctions, he sometimes accepts as valid (p. 111, Oxford and Ralegh) and otherwise rejects (p. 107) popular charges of atheism against prominent men. Buckley's work is a valuable survey, especially of the Continental influences on Elizabethan unbelief. He emphasizes, somewhat at the expense of other aspects of the subject, the opinions on immortality of the soul, and his survey stops at

Elizabethan Meanings of "Atheism" 63

but to provide the background of definition and language necessary to explain the inconsistency of Ralegh's reputation with the content and spirit of his published writings. Careless usage in controversy and the frequent references to atheism in works of all kinds have obscured the fact that the area of meaning of "atheism" in the Elizabethan Age, though extensive, had its boundaries and subdivisions. The definitions could be stated briefly, but for a better understanding of the climate of opinion in which such topics as God, immortality, and the truth of Scripture were discussed illustrations are quite as necessary as categorical distinctions, and phrase is almost as important as content. A cross section of Elizabethan opinion on atheism is presented in this chapter by summarizing two popular treatises on the subject to show the method of refutation, by reviewing more briefly other influential treatises, by illustrating from such specialized works and from general literature as well "atheistic" opinions and attitudes which were considered typical, and by citing causes popularly held to be responsible for the spread of atheism. Such a survey yields not only workable definitions but also suggestive analogues to the language and logic of Ralegh's published works and of his conversation with the Reverend Ralph Ironside.

Of the treatises against atheism, probably the most frequently cited by Elizabethans are the work by Robert Parsons popularly known as "The Books of Resolution" and Philip Mornay's *A Work Concerning the Trueness of the Christian Religion* (1587) in the translation begun by Sir Philip Sidney and completed by Arthur Golding. Parsons' book has a special claim upon our attention for more reasons than that it went through many editions, in Catholic and Protestant versions. Robert Greene, in his day considered an atheist, credits it first with arousing him to a despairing sense of his spiritual peril and then with bringing him com-

---

about 1600. His judicious chapter on Ralegh contains new material but strangely neglects *The History of the World*. To these works, and to Henri Busson, *Les Sources et le développement du rationalisme dans la littérature française de la renaissance* (Paris, 1922), I am indebted for guidance and suggestions in my study of the Elizabethan discussion of atheism.

fort, in his fear and torment, by its account of God's mercy.[4] Thomas Nashe turns from his own summary of arguments against atheism to refer the reader to the *Resolution:*

> O why should I but squintingly glance at these matters, when they are so admirably expatiated by ancient writers? In the *Resolution* most notably is this tractate enlarged. He which peruseth that, and yet is Diagorized, will never be Christianized.[5]

In other words, there is no hope for an atheist who can read the *Resolution* without being converted. Later, in the same context, Nashe returns inferentially to praise of the *Resolution* when he writes: "I am at my wits' end, when I view how coldly, in comparison of other countrymen, our Englishmen write. How in their books of confutation they show no wit or courage, as well as learning." [6] Just this point was made by the Jesuits and by Parsons himself in their comments on the Protestant adaptation of the *Resolution,* and the Protestants were somewhat more sensitive to the criticism than they need have been. Sir Edwin Sandys acknowledges the merits of Parsons' "books of Christian Resolution," but wishes that they "had been the fruits of conscience, rather than of the wits of those that made them"; and he finds the actions of Father Parsons not in harmony with his

---

[4] *The Repentance of Robert Greene,* in *Works,* ed. A. B. Grosart, 15 vols. (London, 1881–86), XII, 165–70. Richard Baxter as a boy read the book in an old, torn copy lent to his father by a poor laborer and was moved as profoundly as the reprobate Greene. See Helen C. White, *English Devotional Literature 1600–1640,* "University of Wisconsin Studies in Language and Literature," No. 29 (Madison, 1931), p. 143. My discussion of Parsons' book is adapted from my article, "Robert Parsons' Essay on Atheism" (*Joseph Quincy Adams Memorial Studies* [Washington, 1948], pp. 665–81), which contains additional bibliographical details concerning the book and the Catholic-Protestant dispute about it.

[5] *Christ's Tears over Jerusalem,* in *Works,* ed. R. B. McKerrow, 5 vols. (London, 1904–10), II, 121. Here, as commonly in the Renaissance, Diagoras is the prototype of the atheist; Nashe adds a marginal note: "Diagoras primus Deos negans."

[6] *Works,* ed. McKerrow, II, 122. Nashe's familiarity with the book is indicated further by his reference in *Strange News* (*Works,* I, 327) to the quarrel between Parsons and his Protestant adapter, Edmund Bunny.

teachings.[7] Even parenthetically, in a discourse on the excellency of poetry, William Vaughan asks "whether the books of Resolution be blameworthy, for that R. P. a fugitive papist wrote them?" and answers his own question, "O monstrous absurdity."[8] Along with a popularity attested by the number of editions, the frequency of allusion, and its acknowledged effectiveness, the book has an additional fillip in its authorship. Parsons, who wrote persuasively of Christian resolution, belabored his adversaries as atheists, and he in turn evoked such descriptions as William Watson's string of epithets: ". . . there is not a Jesuit in all England this day, but hath a bitter smack of Father Parsons' impiety, irreligiosity, treachery, treason, and Machiavellian atheism."[9]

Both book and author are of sufficient importance to merit a bibliographical digression, partly because it is necessary to distinguish the sections of the book which discourse on atheism and partly because its several titles have caused some confusion. Robert Parsons began his work as an enlargement of the English translation of Gaspar Loarte's *The Exercise of a Christian Life* (1579?), but, finding that the new material did not fit the old, proceeded to publish it as the first installment of a projected work in three books. This installment, in two parts, was entitled *The First Book of the Christian Exercise, Appertaining to Resolution* (1582), and on the verso of the title page was printed "The Summary of the Christian Exercise, as It Is Intended." In addition to the first book on "resolution," the second book was to "treat of the way how to begin well," and the third book was to "handle the means of perseverance." There followed in 1584 a second edition, unauthorized but also Catholic, which Parsons dismissed briefly as "disorderly" and incorrect. In the same year, however, appeared a Protestant adaptation by Edmund Bunny which aroused Parsons' wrath and set off a long-lived controversy.

[7] *A Relation of the State of Religion* (1605), sig. H2r.
[8] *The Golden Grove* (1600), sig. Y2r.
[9] *A Decacordon of Ten Quodlibetical Questions* (1602), p. 112; see above, chap. ii.

66 Elizabethan Meanings of "Atheism"

The work is well described by its title: *A Book of Christian Exercise, Appertaining to Resolution, . . . Perused, and Accompanied Now with a Treatise Tending to Pacification.* In this form alone the book went through twenty editions by 1640.[10] Parsons responded immediately to this appropriation of his work: he already had under way a revised edition—still Book One only in two parts—which included new material bearing on atheism and which was published under a new title, *A Christian Directory Guiding Men to Their Salvation* (1585). In a sharply worded preface he rejected the intended conciliation of Bunny's "Treatise of Pacification," rebuked him for his alterations of the text, jibed at the Protestants' inability to produce their own works of devotion, and, characteristically, labeled as "atheism" Bunny's attempts to minimize the differences between the Catholic and Protestant religions. At the end of Chapter V of Part I Parsons notes that he has become aware of Bunny's publication, and thenceforward duly indicates in the margin the corruptions of the text by his Protestant editor.[11] For our purposes the chief interest of this edition is in the well-written and carefully reasoned chapters on atheism. The new Catholic version left the Protestant adaptation incomplete, but the defect was supplied by an anonymous publication which combines both the titles used by Parsons: *The Second Part of the Book of Christian Exercise, Appertaining to Resolution, or, a Christian Directory* (1590). The book in fact is made up of the first five chapters, including those on atheism, from *Part I* of Parsons' enlarged edition of 1585, and a sixth and last chapter which corresponds to Part II, Chap-

[10] The total may be greater: the Folger Shakespeare Library has five variant copies of the editions of Bunny's work listed in the *Short-Title Catalogue*, and some of these variants may prove to be independent editions.

[11] Without actual collation of all the editions which followed, it is difficult to say how many editions of this particular enlargement of the book were printed. The edition of 1633 is labeled the seventh, but the publisher may be including in his count still another revision of the work by Parsons (in 1607) described below. Bunny replied to Parsons in a work entitled *A Brief Answer, unto Those Idle and Frivolous Quarrels of R.P. against the Late Edition of the Resolution* (1589), a work quite free of further attempts at "pacification."

ter I, of Parsons' edition. This "second part," therefore, has no relation to Parsons' division of his work in two parts, and is "second" only in the sense that it is an addition to the first Protestant version; it is not unusual to find joined in an early binding a copy of Bunny's adaptation and a copy of the Protestant "Second Part." [12] As late as 1607, Parsons still hoped to complete the work according to his original plan for three books; once more revising it, he reduced its size by eliminating some of the chapters added in 1585 and explained in a preface the history of the several editions. The *Resolution* therefore was available to Elizabethans in three versions authorized by Parsons, in two Protestant versions which together make a practically complete book, in one unauthorized Catholic version—and in one late edition in Welsh! The Protestant editions outnumber the Catholic by three to one: a conservative count, with copies that may be only variant issues excluded, totals forty editions of this work in all its forms, of which almost half contain the chapters on atheism. At the time of Greene's and Nashe's allusions to the book, both Bunny's revision and the Protestant addition known as the "Second Part" were accessible in several editions. The popularity of the book continued into the eighteenth century: a new Protestant revision by George Stanhope was published in a "fifth edition" in 1727, and occasional editions appeared thereafter.[13]

Of the material which Parsons added in the 1585 edition and which forms the Protestant *Second Part of the Book of Christian Exercise*, only Chapter II is directly concerned with atheism, although Chapter IV is a closely related defense of Christianity,[14]

[12] E.g., the Folger Shakespeare Library has copies of *STC* 19357 bound with 19380; of *STC* 19367 bound with 19384a (dated 1599); and of *STC* 19374 bound with 19387. Both parts of the last volume were printed in 1615.

[13] To summarize: the first editions of the versions authorized by Parsons appeared in 1582, 1585, and 1607; the first editions of the Protestant versions appeared in 1584 and 1590. *The British Museum Catalogue* lists editions as late as 1754 and 1861.

[14] In my summary of chap. ii, I have used the 1598 ed. of *A Christian Directory*, which has the same content as the 1585 edition but differs in pagination.

68 Elizabethan Meanings of "Atheism"

and the purpose of the entire book is to confirm the Christian in his faith and to save the wayward. Chapter II, "That There is a God, Which Rewardeth Good and Evil, against All Atheists of Old, and of Our Time," draws its proof not from Christian writers but from gentiles and Jews. It begins disarmingly with the statement that all arts and sciences rest on principles already known or conceded to be self-evident, and the thesis is illustrated from chivalry, from handicrafts, and from the branches of philosophy. Likewise divinity has its principles: were it not for the extreme wickedness of the time, these principles would be accepted, and we could proceed forthwith to our main subject, "resolution." But iniquity being ascendant in the world, Parsons finds it necessary to demonstrate the first principle, "That there is a God," on which the second, "That the same God is just to reward every man that seeketh him according to his deserts," necessarily depends.

The first argument proceeds from the created to the creator: "The works of the world do declare the workman," just as the presence of a fine building in a strange land would persuade a traveler that men lived there, though he saw none. Heavens, earth, sea, and man himself declare the existence and the glory of God. All wise men in all ages have acknowledged God; of ancient "atheists," such as Diagoras, Protagoras, and Epicurus, some were "utterly unlearned" and others denied not God but pagan idols. Section 2 of the chapter tells "How the heathens proved there was a God," and summarizes the traditional arguments of natural philosophy, metaphysics, and moral philosophy. Mathematics, be it noted, does not apply, "for that it hath no consideration at all of the efficient or final cause of things (under which two respects and considerations only God may be known, and declared to men in this world); therefore this science hath

---

Chap. ii (pp. 20–89) and chap. iv (pp. 108–243) are the longest in the book; together they are equal in length to several of the independent treatises and are longer than some. I have not cited page references for the brief quotations from Parsons because his liberal use of marginal headings makes them easy to find; I follow the order of his argument, with only slight changes.

no proper mean peculiar to itself, for proving this verity. . . ."
Natural philosophy has "infinite arguments to prove by the creatures" that there is a God, but Parsons reduces them to three heads, "arguments drawn from the motions, from the ends, and from the cause efficient of creatures that we behold," which he defines and illustrates largely out of Aristotle. On the third argument, from the efficient cause, only Aristotle of the "excellent philosophers" held for a time that the world was eternal, but even he recanted in his old age.

Metaphysics offers five proofs of God: (1) that the finite and limited things of this world must be referred to a higher cause, infinite and perfect, which is God; (2) that "every multitude or distinction of things proceedeth from some unity," as the complex structure and functions of the "little world" or microcosm, man, proceed from "one most simple unity and indivisible substance called the soul"; (3) that no creature in the world lives for itself alone, but in "subordination" to some other good—a thesis expounded in terms of the doctrine of degree; (4) that the "marvelous providence" apparent in the form and function of the least creature must proceed from an omnipotent Creator, and not from chance as "foolish Lucretius" supposed; and (5) that the soul, "a spirit and immaterial substance, whose nature dependeth not of the state of our mortal body," is by the "consent of all learned men" immortal. The fourth argument of metaphysics convinced even the anatomist Galen, "a profane and very irreligious physician." The immortality of the soul, the fifth metaphysical argument, is further proved by the conclusions of moral philosophy on the "last end" and "supreme felicity" of man, whose reason gives him "an appetite of some more high and excellent object" than the sensory satisfaction of the beast. Although Marcus Varro (as St. Augustine notes) collected two hundred and eighty-eight opinions on the felicity of man, "Plato found that nothing which might be named or imagined in this life could be the felicity or *summum bonum* of man, for that it could not satisfy the desire of our mind." That desire must be satisfied by a "spiritual and immaterial object"; thus Plato and Plotinus conclude that the final end of man is union with God. Further, the inequity of rewards and punishments in this world argues a better justice in the world to come, and therefore immortality. On the fundamental question of the existence of God, the principal argument (and first in Parsons' discussion) of moral philosophy rests on "the very natural inclination of man . . . to confess some God or deity." Even atheists, when they come to die, show fear of God. The next step of the ancient moral philosophers was to conclude that God is one, and therefore infinite. On this point there was general agreement; only the later "academics" by disputing about everything came to believe nothing. A marginal note, "So in this time of variety of sects," points the moral for the sixteenth century: Catholic and Protestant alike found in the bitter controversies of the sects a principal cause of religious doubt. Indeed, that is the reason given by Parsons, in the instructions to the reader which conclude his preface, for adding to the 1585 edition the chapters on faith.

Turning from the gentiles' philosophical demonstrations of God's existence to the additional proofs offered by the Jews, Parsons acknowledges at once that only by appeal to the Scriptures could a Jew say more than a gentile for the proof of God. But for an infidel not already moved by the appeal to philosophy and reason the Jewish Scriptures would be effective only in so far as their "truth and certainty" could be made manifest. The section on the Jews, therefore, is devoted to arguments [15] in support of the authenticity of the Scriptures: their antiquity, antedating not only heathen histories but the pagan gods themselves; the unique care displayed in the composition, authorization, and transcription of the Scriptures; the integrity and sincerity of the writers, especially the greatness of Moses, whose

[15] For a similar but not identical list of arguments see John Dove, *A Confutation of Atheism* (1605), chap. vii, "That the Books of the Bible Are the Word of God." This is likely to be an important topic in any extended treatise on atheism.

Elizabethan Meanings of "Atheism"

miracles are acknowledged by such hostile critics as Appio and Porphyry, though they mistakenly say that the miracles were performed by art magic; and the consent of the Scriptures, in which one writer's testimony supports another's. These four arguments, however, are merely "external"; even more persuasive are four "internal" considerations. Unlike heathen writings concerned with the deeds of men, the subject of the Scriptures "is nothing else but the acts and gests of one eternal God," to whom, and not to human leadership, is credited victory in battle. Their style—simple but profound, majestic and moving—is unique; note but the contrast between a story in the Scriptures and the same story told with much adornment by Josephus. In content too they are set apart from other writings, first in

> high and hidden doctrines, which are above the reach and capacity of human reason, and consequently could never fall into man's brain to invent them. As for example; that all this wonderful frame of the world was created of nothing, whereas philosophy saith, that of nothing, nothing can be made.[16]

The other remarkable part of their content is the prophecies, not made by observation of natural causes, not contingent as are the prophecies of soothsayers, astrologers, or oracles, but genuine foretellings of detailed events many years before their occurrence. Finally, although the Scriptures do not take their proof from man, "God hath so provided" that the principal contents of the Scriptures are confirmed by heathen writers; for example, the creation, Noah's flood, the long life of the first fathers, the career of Moses. With many details to support the major heads of the arguments for the divine origin of the Scriptures, Parsons closes his long chapter with a brief section to point the moral: if the ancient philosophers were blameworthy, as St. Paul says, because knowing God they did not glorify Him, how much more to blame are we who have not only the light of nature but God's own word to guide us? [17]

---

[16] P. 65.
[17] In a brief passage which occurs in all of his own and Bunny's editions (Part

72 Elizabethan Meanings of "Atheism"

The special duty of a Christian, even more than of a gentile, to lead a good life is the theme of Chapter III, which expounds the thesis that man was created to serve God. The service required, according to Chapter IV, is religion, specifically the Christian religion; the running title of the chapter is "Proofs of Christianity." Again confirming evidence is sought in unfriendly quarters, and Hebrew and gentile writers are cited in support of elements in Christian faith. Porphyry, an enemy of Jesus, testifies to his piety and sanctity, although, he writes, "these Christians are deceived in calling him God." Jewish writers and Mohammed himself concede his miracles, and Jewish and gentile prophets had written that the Messiah would be a worker of miracles.

In Parsons' discussion may be noted topics, phrases—and clichés—suggestive of correspondences in Ralegh's utterances or writings: such matters as opinions on the creation of the world and the "consent" of the Scriptures figure prominently in *The History of the World;* the appeal to principles and the nature of the soul were at issue in the conversation with Ironside; and the miracles of Moses and of Christ form an important item in the Baines note on Marlowe and are vigorously defended in the *History*. That these topics and phrases are by no means peculiar to Parsons will become apparent as soon as we turn to any other treatise on atheism. Nor are they original: although the question of "sources" lies outside this study, the traditional elements in Parsons' arguments are apparent even in this brief analysis of his refutation of atheism.

The method used by Parsons in his argument against atheism is in harmony with a major thesis of the Elizabethan writers on the subject: that the "atheist" must be convinced out of his own writers by the force of reason, not by appeals to revelation. The thesis is better expounded by Philip Mornay, who faces the prob-

---

II, chap. viii), Parsons discusses as an impediment to resolution "a secret kind of atheism" which denies God not in word but in deed. The two principal causes of such atheism are schism and heresy which "wearieth out a man's wit, and in the end bringeth him to care for no part, but rather to contemn all," and inordinate love of the world.

Elizabethan Meanings of "Atheism"

lem squarely in the preface to *A Work Concerning the Trueness of the Christian Religion* (1587).[18] He answers two kinds of objectors to the use of reason in persuading unbelievers of the truth of religion: those who say that it is impossible to convert infidels by the use of reason, and those who concede that reason can aid religion but hold that its use for such a purpose is "neither lawful nor expedient." People in the first category say, "It is to no purpose to dispute against such as deny grounded principles"; that is, if a person is so far gone as to reject the first principle of divinity—the fact of God's existence—reason and argument can do no good. Mornay agrees that "it is to no purpose to dispute against such as deny grounded principles, by the same principles which they deny"; the proper approach is to find principles common to both sides, as the Old Testament is common to Christian and Jew, though the latter denies the Gospel; and as the gentile and Jew agree on principles of philosophy, though the gentile rejects the Old Testament. From commonly accepted principles, it is possible to proceed by reason to more comprehensive conclusions—as the principle of Euclid, if equals are subtracted from equals the results are equal, may lead through other propositions to the more complicated, and less evident, theorem of Pythagoras. So may principles acceptable to the atheists be used against them; although this is the purpose of his entire book, Mornay illustrates the point briefly in his preface:

> Such are these proofs against the atheists: nothing hath moving of itself. It is nature that sayeth so. The world turneth about, and heavenly bodies have a moving: and that doth man himself see. Therefore they must needs be moved by some other power and that is the Godhead; which our eye seeth not, and yet by means of the eye, our reason conceiveth and perceiveth it in all things. Against them which deny Christ's Godhead, we allege this principle of their own. That naturally of

---

[18] First French edition, 1581. The book was far more influential than the four English editions before 1640 would indicate; references to it in Elizabethan literature are frequent. The *Catalogue général de la bibliothèque nationale* lists nine editions in French before the first English edition, and the book was available also in Latin and Italian.

nothing nothing is made. It is the saying of Aristotle, and the schools would have him by the ears that should deny it. Jesus Christ hath of nothing made very great things, yea even contraries by contraries. The heathen wonder at it, all ages cry it out, our eyes do still behold it. He that will deny this, must deny the world, he must deny all things, he must deny himself. It followeth then that Christ wrought by a power, that is mistress of nature. Aristotle himself saw it not, and yet Aristotle maketh us to see it.

Objectors of the second kind, who concede the possibility but question the lawfulness of using reason in support of religion, maintain that many things in Christian doctrine are beyond the capacity of man, and to measure them by reason would impair their dignity. Mornay concedes that and more: man is too ignorant to understand nature, let alone things above nature. The mistake of these people is to think that the use of reason on the side of faith means "that we should believe no further than reason can measure and comprehend." On the contrary, the function of reason is to persuade us "that we ought to believe even beyond reason." The processes of reason can lead us to the word of God in the "Old and New Testament, which contain things that cannot proceed from creatures. Here reason stayeth and holdeth itself contented. For seeing that God speaketh, it becometh man to hold his peace: and seeing that he vouchsafeth to teach us, it becometh us to believe." Similarly reason can be used to vindicate the Gospel against the unbelief of the gentiles. By the use of reason, therefore, Mornay undertakes to convince the unbelievers by two kinds of proof, arguments and records; against the atheists, he "will bring themselves, the world, and the creatures therein for witness," and he will cite as his authorities those writers who have founded their philosophies on nature and who are in highest credit with unbelievers.

Mornay's exposition of the fundamental truths of religion parallels that of Parsons; or, in chronological order, Parsons reads like a condensation of Mornay. Not that one is necessarily indebted to the other: this chapter is limited to works roughly contemporaneous with Ralegh, but if the limits were extended either backward or forward by a few years the uniformity of the arguments set forth in these summaries would not be seriously impaired. Like Parsons, Mornay at the beginning of his book asserts the necessity of believing propositions evident to common sense and cites by way of illustration the one which Ralegh used against Ironside in a different context of argument: "the whole is greater than his part." The truth of such propositions is so plain that it is a "common saying of the Schools, that there is no reasoning against those which deny the principles." But, like Parsons, Mornay finds it necessary to "bestow this [first] chapter upon the wickedness of our age" and to demonstrate what should be the self-evident principles of divinity. He advances the usual arguments: from the creature to the creator; the universal consent of mankind; the hostility of ancient "atheists" to idols and false gods, not the true God. Approximately the first half of the book, set off by a summary at the end of the fifteenth chapter, treats of such essentials of belief as God, the Trinity, the creation of the world, God's providence, and the immortality of the soul. The second half of the book, treating of the necessary beliefs of the Hebraic-Christian tradition, is written not simply against "atheists" and "epicures," but also, in the words of the title page, against "Paynims, Jews, Mahumetists, and other Infidels." Mornay's method throughout is to establish each major point by reasoning which he considers convincing, and then to buttress it by a separate chapter citing and quoting in its support the "wisdom of the world," that is, non-Christian writers and even enemies of the Christian faith.

Since a detailed summary of all the arguments advanced in *A Work Concerning the Trueness of the Christian Religion* would merely duplicate much of what has been said about the books of *Resolution,* a brief account of Mornay's treatment of three major topics—our knowledge of God, the creation of the world, and the immortality of the soul—will suffice to illustrate his method. Chapter IV expounds "What it is that we can comprehend concerning God"; in short, very little: "He is a thing which cannot be found, nor ought to be sought." Because "men are not able to attain to God's substance, they have gone about to betoken it by the excellentest names that they could devise." Mornay states clearly the philosophical difficulty of naming the attributes of God and resorts to a summary of negative qualities and of superlative phrases in a manner not unlike that of the first page of Ralegh's *History*.

In Chapters VII–IX Mornay argues from the temporal limitations of natural phenomena that the world was created. The interrelations of the elements are in time, "and time is a measuring of moving, and where measure is, there can be no eternity." [19] Examples of this variability—seasons, winds, tides, movements of the sun and moon—are cited liberally to prove that the world had a beginning. Further, that beginning is of recent date, because no human knowledge, art, or craft and no historical records can be shown to be of long duration. The fantastic records of the Chaldees, tracing 43,000 years of history before Alexander, are rejected as "month years." [20] Only a hundred years ago we were ignorant of half the world! Man, who lives in time, has an imperfect understanding of eternity: suppose for argument's sake that the world has lasted a hundred thousand, or ten hundred thousand, years—"what is all that in comparison of infiniteness?" To the question "What did God do before and out of the world?" Mornay foregoes the conventional answer (He was preparing Hell to receive fools who ask that question) and enjoins the doubter: "Once again amend thy plea. For in God there is neither afore nor after, within nor without." [21] The final authority on the creation is Moses. The usual chapter on the "wisdom of the world" as it bears on the creation again rejects an ancient record, this time the Egyptian,[22] as based on a shorter year, and inevitably Aristotle's ideas on the eternity of the world are presented for refutation. All of Chapter X is given over to prove that God made the world of nothing, "that is to say, with-

---

[19] Ed. 1587, p. 97.   [20] P. 115.   [21] P. 127.   [22] P. 136.

out any matter or stuff whereof to make it," and in support of the argument Porphyry, "the sorest and learnedest enemy that ever Christians had," is quoted at length.

On the immortality of the soul, its functions, its relations to the body, its immateriality, Mornay writes with great confidence.[23] He follows the accepted classification of "souls": quickening (or, as others call it, vegetative); sensitive; and reasonable. Plants have the first; animals the first and second; only men have all three. But man does not have three souls; the higher contains the lower, and the "three degrees of souls are three degrees of life."[24] It is a mistake to argue that the souls cannot be one because the growing and sensitive powers corrupt and perish, whereas the soul of man is immortal. Some of the powers of the soul are exercised through the instrumentality of the body, and other powers, the highest, are exercised quite independently of the body; therefore the soul, through infirmity of the body, may lose the power to exercise certain functions without losing the skill to exercise them. A lute-player whose instrument is broken still knows how to play the lute.[25] The reason of man raises him above the animals, who may surpass him in keenness of sense perception; and the reasonable soul of man may correct the false information of the senses, as, for example, that parallel lines converge. Throughout the chapter Mornay argues that the very concept of immortality is proof of immortality, and the ability of man to reason about it is a refutation of those who deny immortality. But with all this wisdom and lore about the soul, Mornay cheerfully admits defeat on one fundamental question, what the soul is: "And soothly if I should say, I cannot tell what it is, I should not belie myself a whit; for I should but confess my own ignorance, as many great learned men have done afore me."[26] Earlier in the book he had quoted with approval a like statement by "the most heathenish of all

---

[23] Chap. xiv. For further discussion of Elizabethan ideas about the soul, see below, chap. iv.
[24] P. 227.   [25] Pp. 252–53.   [26] P. 230.

writers," Galen: "I confess that I know not what the soul is, notwithstanding that I have sought very narrowly for it."[27]

Other English books against atheism follow the pattern and method of argument used by Parsons and Mornay, but differ in their emphasis on specific topics. Sir George More, vigilant in Surrey against religious irregularities in general and recusancy in particular, added theory to practice in a book entitled *A Demonstration of God in His Works* (1597). The promise of the title is not fulfilled by the book, in which the second chapter is given over to the premise "That the fool which denieth there is a God, may in some respect be denied to be a man"; here argument is liberally interspersed with assertion. Nevertheless, the book is highly praised by John Dove in dedicating to King James his own *Confutation of Atheism* (1605). Despite this deference, Dove is more comprehensive than Sir George in his arguments and more explicit in the definitions by which he distinguishes the "kinds" of atheism. Like his better-known predecessors Dove maintains that the principles of human arts are not to be proved by those same arts, and he makes the usual appeal to reason and to the authority of heathen writers.

> I cannot find any way to disprove the atheists better than that which the Apostles used to disprove the infidels, that is, by the testimony and witness of heathen authors. For, if they will neither stand to arguments drawn from reason, neither yet to authority, neither divine, nor human, then they reject all the topics of Aristotle and places whereby they should be confuted, they renounce the laws of schools, and order of disputation, and by a consequent, they show themselves merely ignorant, and *contra indoctos non est disputandum*, disputations are not to be held and maintained against them which know not the laws of disputation.[28]

---

[27] Pp. 153–54 (mispaged 144). The apologists seized eagerly upon such statements by the natural philosophers. Late in the next century, with its important discoveries for modern science, Edward Stillingfleet (*Origenes Sacrae*, 8th ed. [1709], "Addition," p. 17) quotes the remarks of "our sagacious Dr. Harvey" on the power and providence of God manifested in the formation of animals.

[28] P. 54; for citations of pagan authorities, cf. pp. 30–32.

Dove is singled out by Robert Burton as one of the able defenders of the faith, among whom Corderoy, Jackson, Abernethy, and Fotherby are also named in what may be called a contemporary "guide to the best books" on atheism.[29] Jeremy Corderoy's *Warning for Worldlings* (1608), a dialogue between an atheistic traveler and a poor but pious student, is remarkable for the fact that the traveler departs unconverted and angry [30] because the student discredits a repentance for wrongdoing which does not restore the profits of wrongdoing. The dialogue touches clearly and with comparative brevity on the major topics of atheism, and by assigning to a traveler the role of atheist points to what was generally considered a source of infidelity—foreign travel, especially in Italy. Incidentally, the traveler is given the modern advantage of roman type for his speeches, while the student's persuasions are buried in black letter. No doubt Abernethy and Jackson found special favor with Burton because they consider atheism a mental disorder; Abernethy's book especially may have appealed to Burton more for its method than for its specific but extremely limited chapters on atheism.[31] On the other hand, Thomas Jackson in his *Treatise of Unbelief* (1625), which is full enough in its treatment of atheism, makes some interesting departures from the arguments hitherto sum-

[29] These are the authors who "have written well of this subject in our mother tongue"; but Burton has praise also for a number of Latin works, several of them quite close to his own time. These recommendations conclude his own short but effective section on atheism in *The Anatomy of Melancholy*, ed. Floyd Dell and Paul Jordan-Smith (New York, 1927), Part III, sec. iv, memb. 2, subsec. 1, pp. 925-36. Burton does not give the titles of the English books, but they are easily identifiable.

[30] Unlike John Lyly's "Atheos," who is a push-over for Euphues. See "Euphues and Atheos," in *Works*, ed. R. W. Bond, 3 vols. (Oxford, 1902), I, 291-305.

[31] John Abernethy, *A Christian and Heavenly Treatise*, 3d ed. (1630); 1st ed., 1615. The book, which follows a method something like Burton's own, contains thirty-four chapters on spiritual ills, each chapter following the same outline: description, part affected, causes, signs and symptoms, prognostics, curation and remedies. Atheism is discussed chiefly in chap. iii, "Blindness of Mind," and chap. vi, "Hardness of Heart." Abernethy is more careful than many of his fellows in defining terms; e.g., pp. 45, 59-60.

marized. He does not share his predecessors' confidence in disputation as a cure for atheism, first because the method is illogical:

> To dispute with such as deny manifest and received principles, were to violate a fundamental law of the schools; which in matters of faith and sacred morality, is to be religiously kept, as in other respects, so chiefly in this: That general maxims, whence particular truths, and conclusions of best use must be derived, can hardly be proved by arguments more clear and evident than themselves. Now to interpose proofs of less truth or perspicuity than is the matter to be proved, is but to eclipse the evidence of it (which, of itself, would in due season shine to calm and purified meditations), or to provoke such as delight in trying masteries of strength or skill in arguing, to assault truths otherwise safe enough from all attempts, did they not see them so weakly guarded upon preparation.

Jackson belongs to the first of Mornay's two kinds of objectors who question the use of reason against atheists. His statement on the use of principles, a point at issue between Ralegh and Ironside, therefore varies from the customary one, found in Parsons and Mornay, which makes a concession to the wickedness of the times and permits discussion of what should be accepted principles. If forthright argument is not to be used, Jackson continues:

> The best method, in my opinion, to prevent atheism, or cure an atheist, would be to hold the mean betwixt the contemplative philosopher and the practical physician. . . . And he that would cure an ordinary atheist, should, as not sooth him in his impiety, so not directly or fiercely encounter him with syllogistical proofs, or discourses metaphysical; for so (*aegrescit medendo*) he will grow sicker by seeing the medicine: but labor rather, secretly to undermine the internal disposition whence such unhallowed imaginations spring. Atheism in grain is but a spiritual madness, arising from the abundance of such distemper in the soul, as in proportion answers to melancholy in the body.[32]

---

[32] Quotations pp. 8, 9-10. Jackson does not say that atheism is a form of melancholy, but makes an analogy between spiritual distemper and bodily melancholy. The distinction is noteworthy because some atheists professed to regard conscience as merely a bodily disorder. (See Timothy Bright, *A Treatise of*

Bishop Martin Fotherby's *Atheomastix* (1622), although published a few years earlier than Jackson's *Treatise*, is a fit conclusion to this selected list of English books on atheism. The good bishop, contemplating the mass of Continental and English writing on atheism, found this branch of learning deficient.[33] He set out to rectify the deficiency in a work dealing only with four fundamental propositions: in summary, that there is only one God, Jehovah, and that the Holy Scripture is His Word. The first of four parts was to have eight books, but as Fotherby completed the second book and approached the third (on the proof of God's existence from the structure of man's body), he was forced by illness to break off with the comment, "But the hand of Almighty God, at this present on mine own body, here stayeth my hand." What we have from his pen is a sizable fragment published posthumously; had he lived to continue his work on the scale on which it was begun, the three hundred and sixty-two pages in small folio that make up the printed fragment would represent only one sixteenth of the whole! Though he does not neglect the simple reader, Fotherby addresses his work primarily to the learned reader, who because of his learning and his sharpness of wit is especially prone to error proceeding from an overfondness for disputation. The writer's purpose is "to show unto those acute naturalists, who hold it a servility to

Melancholy [1586], pp. 187-88.) Jackson does distinguish (pp. 14-17) between speculative or abstract principles, like "every whole is greater than its part," which have their seat in the brain and are exempt from perturbation, and practical or moral principles which are seated in the heart and conscience and are therefore subject to eclipse by the "smoke of noisome lust, the streams of bloody and revengeful thoughts, the uncessant exhalations of other unclean and vast desires, which reign in the atheist's heart."

[33] In his preface Fotherby praises the work of a number of his predecessors, among them Mornay, Parsons, and an earlier writer not discussed in this chapter, Ludovicus Vives, whose *De Veritate Fidei Christianae* went through a number of editions in the sixteenth century. The title given for Parsons' book, *The Second Part of the Book of Resolution*, indicates the Protestant version which contains the chapters on atheism. Fotherby's complaint about his predecessors is that they treat too sketchily the fundamental principles to which he proposes to devote his entire treatise.

be led with brutish-believing, and will therefore entertain no more of religion than they find to be consonant unto reason; that here they may find reason for their religion." It cannot be denied, writes Fotherby, that the age surpasses all others in subtlety of wit and in learning, but "the greatness of men's wits sharpeneth many of them on, to see all things proved by arguments, and demonstrated unto sense. The Scriptures (with many) have lost their authority: and are thought only fit for the ignorant and idiot." [34] Despite the pretensions of *Atheomastix*, it adds little to the confutation of atheism with the possible exception that Fotherby is not content to let the argument from mathematics rest merely on the illustration of accepted principles. He extends the conventional analogies by finding parallels in application as well as in principle between mathematical truths and the natural truths which lead to the proof of God's existence.[35] Like Sir George More, Fotherby weakens his elaborate structure of "rational" argument by begging the question: in Chapter XIV of the first book he asserts that "there is no reckoning to be made of [the atheists'] opinion, because, in the opinion of all wise and learned men, they are esteemed no better than either fools, or madmen, or monsters of men."

From these treatises alone, without recourse to an even more extensive discussion of atheism in the literature of the courtier and citizen alike, it is possible to formulate the principles which led to such a variety of Elizabethan meanings of atheism. Disbelief in any one of these principles was equivalent—in sober Elizabethan opinion and not merely in the zeal of controversy —to "atheism": (1) there is a God, one God, in whose substance

---

[34] Pref., sigs. B2ʳ–B3ᵛ. Thomas Jackson devotes chap. vi of his *Treatise of Unbelief* to "disputative atheism"; and Mornay applies to some errors concerning the nature of the soul the ancient saying, "That there be certain follies which none but wise men can commit, and certain errors which none but learned men can fall into: because . . . learning is required in a man that he may conceive and hold a wrong opinion." Accordingly, "to fall into heresy by misconceiving some high and deep point, befalleth not an ignorant person" (*Trueness of the Christian Religion*, p. 255).

[35] Bk. II, chaps. ix and x.

Elizabethan Meanings of "Atheism" 83

are the three Persons called the Trinity; (2) God created the world, which is not eternal but had a beginning and therefore will have an end; (3) the world is governed by God's providence, not by fate or chance, and God is not tied to necessity; (4) the soul of man is immortal; (5) the Scriptures are the Word of God, and are therefore the final authority on such disputed problems as the chronology of the world and the miracles of Moses and of Christ; (6) man must believe in God in his heart, and not outwardly alone by words and ceremonies.[36] The first four principles are described as interdependent; Mornay, who lists them as three, says that they are so interlocked that if one is proved all three are proved.[37] There was well-nigh universal agreement that man has a soul—the atheist in Corderoy's *Warning for Worldlings* calls a question about that absurd; [38] but the immortality of the soul was debated, and its essence was freely conceded to be indefinable. The fifth principle, although valid in argument against an unbeliever only if by reason and heathen authority he could be persuaded of its truth, is essential to faith. The importance of the fifth principle is manifest in the extensive discussion of its illustrative subtopics: here the argument, in an early battle of the war between science and theology, takes

---

[36] In another context loyalty to the reigning monarch would be a necessary addition to this list. On the authority of Romans 13, sedition is one of the many synonyms of atheism. Thus John Hooker in dedicating to Ralegh his *Irish History* quotes the Epistle against the Irish traitors. The idea finds popular expression in the plays of Shakespeare and in the pages of *The Play of Sir Thomas More* which Shakespeare may have written. See A. W. Pollard and others, *Shakespeare's Hand in the Play of Sir Thomas More* (Cambridge, 1923), pp. 142–56, and More's speech, p. 212. For the background of the idea in political theory see J. W. Allen, *A History of Political Thought in the Sixteenth Century* (London, 1928), Pt. II, chap. x; Pt. III, chap. vii.

[37] *Op. cit.*, p. 287.

[38] P. 41. General agreement was possible because of the vegetative and sensitive functions of the soul, and because the soul was frequently discussed as synonymous with mind. John Dove observes that the "ambiguity of the word" may be a cause of religious error in opinions about the soul, and accordingly, before presenting his arguments for the immortality of the soul, he lists eight definitions of the term (*Confutation of Atheism*, pp. 68–69).

84 Elizabethan Meanings of "Atheism"

the form of human history and natural philosophy against Scripture. The sixth and last principle, perhaps more than any other in this formulation, explains the latitude with which the terms "atheist" and "atheism" were used. The argument runs simply enough: if a man believes in immortality and in God's justice, he will live righteously: if he lives as if there were no judgment to fear in the life to come—if, in Burton's words, he is one of "that impious and carnal crew of worldly-minded men, impenitent sinners, that go to Hell in a lethargy, or in a dream, who though they be professed Christians, yet they will make a conscience of nothing they do" [39]—then conversely he must not believe sincerely in immortality and in God. Misconduct as a sign of atheism could be personal, which the Elizabethans commonly called "Epicurism" or "libertinism," or political, often called Machiavellian atheism. In Burton's simplified description of three kinds of atheists, "some deny there is any God, some confess, yet believe it not; a third sort confess and believe, but will not live after his laws." [40]

The short step from insistence on fundamental principles to insistence on doctrinal points was taken readily by the religious partisans of the sixteenth and seventeenth centuries, but we need not follow the zealous on that path. With all their faults and with all their inequalities in applying reason to the support of religion, the writers whose motive was persuasion were necessarily more restrained in their terminology than were their controversial brethren. For example, Jackson begins the *Treatise of Unbelief* with a set of definitions, by which infidels are those who deny or do not believe the articles of the Creed concerning Christ, for example, Jews, Turks, Mohammedans, "whom no man calls atheists." On that point Jackson's confidence is sorely misplaced: a popular minister like William Perkins had no difficulty at all in proving Jews and Mohammedans to be "atheists," and

---

[39] *Anatomy of Melancholy*, ed. Dell and Jordan-Smith, p. 933.
[40] *Ibid.*, p. 935. This ethical definition of "atheism" is illustrated also in John Bate, *The Portraiture of Hypocrisy* (1589), which has as its running title "A Dialogue between a Christian and an Atheist."

with a little squirming he manages to bring papists into their company.⁴¹ In *The Unmasking of the Politic Atheist* (1602) John Hull devotes an entire book to demonstrating that papists are "atheists." And Parsons the Jesuit polemist turns the tables on the Protestants with violence and skill, no matter how judicious and reasonable Parsons the able Christian teacher may have been. The processes of reciprocal name-calling were continued down through the radical sects, like the Anabaptists and the Family of Love. Fortunately the usages of religious controversy, even in works ostensibly dealing with "atheism," need not detain us; they bring little to an understanding of Ralegh's position or of the skeptical trends in the thought of his time—except to enjoin the caution about meanings which makes this chapter necessary.

On the other hand, a set of general principles drawn from relatively calm and philosophical works of persuasion appears rather remote from the vitality of religious belief, the sense of reality which faith enjoyed in a world of hierarchical order. Although an extension of our survey to include additional discussions of atheism would not change materially the picture already presented, it is possible to fill in the foreground of the picture with interesting detail from the general literature of the time as well as from the formal treatises to which our discussion thus far has been limited. Writers of the court like John Lyly and Sir Philip Sidney, poets like Du Bartas and the philosophical Sir John Davies, scholars like Roger Ascham and Richard Hooker, "University Wits" like Robert Greene and Thomas Nashe—all had their say on atheism, some on one topic and some on another, some briefly and some discursively.⁴² Indeed, the distinction between the apologists and the men of letters whose works are only in part concerned with atheism is an arbitrary one, for they tell essentially the same story. In the treatises

---

[41] *A Treatise of Man's Imaginations* (1607), pp. 42–49.
[42] For digests of the opinions of these and other men of letters see G. T. Buckley, *Atheism in the English Renaissance*.

86 Elizabethan Meanings of "Atheism"

directly concerned with atheism are defined, more fully and perhaps more authoritatively than elsewhere, the principles fundamental to belief; and the treatises are the obvious source for illustrations of the ways in which the atheist revealed his infidelity and of the causes which led him into his enormous error. But such illustrations may be found also in the varied works, literary as well as theological, which reflect Elizabethan interest in atheism.

It is taken for granted that the atheist denies the existence of God, but the form of the denial is more likely to be refusal to credit the manifestations of His power than flat negation. He believes the world eternal, or he follows Lucretius and Epicurus in holding the creation to be an operation of chance.[43] In applying to Omnipotent God the natural limitation "ex nihilo nihil fit" he draws a false conclusion "from a maxim most true in a sense most impertinent." [44] Taking another tack, he laughs to scorn the Biblical chronology, for "there be mathematicians abroad that will prove men before Adam," and "the late discovered Indians are able to show antiquities thousands before Adam." [45] If this is his argument, then he may be found among the "politic atheists"; those "English Italianate and devils incarnate do hold these damnable opinions: that there was no creation of the world, that there shall be no day of judgment, no resurrection, no immortality of the soul, no hell: they dispute against the Bible, reckon up genealogies more ancient than Adam, allege arguments to prove that the story of Noah his Ark and the Deluge were fables." [46] With Epicurus the atheist believes providence faulty or nonexistent. If God made the world for man and controls its processes, why did He cover most of it with water,

---

[43] An idea fiercely attacked by Pamela in Sidney's *Arcadia*, Bk. III, chap. x; see Edwin Greenlaw, "The Captivity Episode in Sidney's *Arcadia*," *Manly Anniversary Studies* (1923), pp. 54–63. Cf. Du Bartas, *Divine Weeks*, "First Day."

[44] Jackson, *Treatise of Unbelief*, p. 46.

[45] Nashe, *Works*, ed. McKerrow, I, 172; II, 116.

[46] Dove, *Confutation*, pp. 4–5.

Elizabethan Meanings of "Atheism" 87

make half the land uninhabitable, and multiply such inconveniences as unseasonable storms, killing frosts, and creatures dangerous to man?[47] Why do the righteous perish and the wicked prosper? The atheist follows "the Pyrrhonics, whose position and opinion it is that there is no hell or misery but opinion."[48] With few exceptions, he denies the immortality of the soul. He makes his point by blowing out a lighted candle: there, says he, is your soul at death.[49] D'Amville and Borachio, the villains of Cyril Tourneur's *The Atheist's Tragedy* (1611), agree in the first twenty lines of the play that man is no different from a beast, except that he is indebted to his nature (not God) "for the better composition of the two." Because some books of the Bible have been declared uncanonical, the atheist considers all of it a "fabulous legend."[50] It is not only the Biblical chronology which he finds faulty; favorite points of attack on the Scriptures are the miracles of Moses and (less commonly) of Christ, which are attributed to human skill not supernatural power; the story of Noah and his Ark, which is found impossible; and the destruction of Sodom, which is explained by natural causes.[51] In general, the atheist attributes to nature what belongs to God.

By opinions such as these the "outward atheist" of Nashe's classification[52] makes himself known. If he is an "inward atheist," he may be content to conform in religious observances and keep his disbelief to himself. More likely the inward atheist will fall into the general pattern of Burton's "third sort" who "confess and believe but will not live after His laws." Believing or not, the inward atheist is distinguishable by his bad conduct: "if the tree may be judged of by the fruits, and the outward effects of men's lives do show the inward affections of their hearts, he that hath but half an eye may see that there are a great many amongst us of

---

[47] Mornay, *Trueness of the Christian Religion*, p. 175.
[48] Nashe, *Works*, ed. McKerrow, II, 116. [49] Dove, *Confutation*, p. 68.
[50] Nashe, *loc. cit.* [51] See below, chap. vi.
[52] *Works*, ed. McKerrow, II, 117. This distinction is a commonplace in discussions of atheism; it is used also by William Vaughan, *The Golden Grove* (1600), chap. iii, and by Bacon, Dove, and Burton.

those foolish men of whom David speaketh, who say in their hearts that there is no God." [53] For D'Amville in *The Atheist's Tragedy* incest has no bar in nature and therefore cannot be wrong.[54] The inward atheist is a religious hypocrite who "devours widows' houses under pretence of long prayers"; and a description of his character is fittingly entitled "a bad man or atheist." [55] He is John Dove's politic atheist, who has "turned Moses into Machiavel" and holds "that the Scriptures were devised by men, only for policy sake, to maintain peace in states and kingdoms, to keep subjects in obedience to laws and loyalty to magistrates, by thus terrifying them from enormities when their consciences are possessed with an opinion of hell fire, and alluring them to subjection by hope of eternal life." [56] This, indeed, is the inward atheist in his most terrible form, the Machiavellian atheist, who holds, along with his belief that religion is merely an instrument of government, that the pagan religion made men strong and the Christian religion makes them weak, that Moses took Judea by force, and that a prince should seem religious even if he is not. Machiavelli's "atheism" has spread from Florence over "most countries in Christendom, insomuch as few places but are so well acquainted with his doctrine, that the whole course of men's lives almost everywhere is nothing else but a continual practice of his precepts." [57]

Of these atheistic notions, the principal ones are summarized by Samuel Rowlands, who manages to compress into twelve lines

[53] La Primaudaye, *The Second Part of the French Academy* (1594), trans. by T. B[owes], the translator's "Epistle to the Reader," sig. b3ᵛ.

[54] Act IV, sc. iii; in *The Works of Cyril Tourneur*, ed. Allardyce Nicoll (London, 1929), p. 233.

[55] The hypocrisy is alleged by Nashe, *loc. cit.* A "character" with the title quoted is found in Alexander Garden, *Characters and Essays* (1625), No. 27. The atheist appears also in other character books, e.g., John Stephens, *Essays and Characters* (1615), pp. 258-63.

[56] *Confutation*, p. 5.

[57] La Primaudaye, *The Second Part of the French Academy* (1594), dedication to Sir John Puckering by the translator, T. B[owes]. This is the first English edition of the second part; the third English edition of the first part appeared in the same year. Edward Meyer, *Machiavelli and the Elizabethan Drama*

Elizabethan Meanings of "Atheism" 89

of verse the atheist's denial of God and immortality, his villainy, his scorn of Scripture, and his epicurean mode of life:

> Thou damned atheist, thou incarnate devil,
> That dost deny His power which did create thee:
> A villain apt for every kind of evil,
> And all the eyes in heaven and earth do hate thee.
> That mak'st account when thou shalt breathless lie,
> Thy soul and body like a beast do die.
>
> That Pharaoh-like dar'st ask what fellow's God?
> Esteeming sacred Scriptures to be vain:
> And that the dead in earth shall make abode,
> And never rise from out their graves again:
> That say'st; eat, drink, be merry, take delight:
> Swagger out day, and revel all the night.[58]

Leaving our anonymous atheist and returning to his censurers, we find them fairly well agreed on the causes of atheism, among which division in religion holds first place. Looking abroad, the thoughtful Christian found that he was in a minority: that the Mohammedans, who encroached upon Western Europe from the east and from the south, held another faith; that the Jews denied Christ to be the Messiah; that the pagans of antiquity and the savages in newly discovered lands held still other opinions on religion. Looking about him at home, the thoughtful Christian witnessed the acrimonious debates of the sects, each claiming an exclusive proprietorship in truth. Often the result of these observations was atheism,[59] or at least what we call agnosticism (a

---

(Weimar, 1897), pp. 77–78, mistakenly places T. B.'s remarks on Machiavellian atheism in the third edition of part one and regards it as an addition occasioned by the lively discussion of atheism in the years 1590–94. Actually T.B.'s prefaces are in harmony with the content of *The Second Part*, now published in translation for the first time, and are designed to show the relevance to English life of this new installment of the French work.

[58] *Look to It: for I'll Stab Ye* (1604), sig. C4ʳ. This is one of a number of poems of equal length addressed to offenders of all kinds; the lines are spoken by Death and each poem ends "I'll stab thee."

[59] The opinion, for example, of Parsons in the preface explaining the additions to *The Christian Directory* (1585); of Nashe, *Works*, ed. McKerrow, I,

distinction of which the Elizabethans knew something in Pyrrhonism). Also high on the list of causes are peace and prosperity, which lead men to exalt their own prowess.[60] Some men, desiring an easeful life, find it restful to their consciences to deny a belief in God and thus to free themselves from apprehensions about future punishment.[61] A third important cause is a lively intelligence. The apologists, especially Fotherby, frankly acknowledge that the atheists are numbered among the best wits of the day, and for that reason Nashe bewails the cold writing of an ill-prepared clergy who attempt to overcome atheism by the liberal citation of Scripture (already rejected by the atheist) and by a feeble smattering of ignorance in theology and philosophy.[62] The acknowledged intelligence of the adversary also explains the heavy reliance on pagan philosophy in the refutation of atheism. The keen-witted atheist, however, was in danger from his own subtlety and was likely to wrest to his purposes innocent meanings in ancient writings.[63] But above all he was likely to be a "naturalist," who, through overmuch study of nature, was inclined to exalt her, only the agent of creation, to the role of creator. Un-

---

171–72; of Bacon, in his essay "Of Atheism"; of Richard Hooker, *Of the Laws of Ecclesiastical Polity*, Bk. V, chap. ii. Ralegh, too, although he opposed legislation repressing the Brownists, criticized the spread of sects as impairing the dignity of religious ceremony and confusing true believers (*History*, II, v, 1, pp. 296–97).

[60] Dove, *Confutation*, pp. 7–8; Bacon, "Of Atheism."

[61] The Elizabethans firmly believed that the atheist, try as he would, could not stifle completely his conscience; that he was at heart fearful; and that he rarely maintained his atheism on his deathbed. William Vaughan, following Calvin, observes that atheists laugh but "from the teeth outward" when they ridicule the idea that the "feeling of God's nature" is engraved in the hearts of men (*Golden Grove* [1600], sig. C2r). Bacon in his essay "Of Atheism" finds in the constant proselytizing by atheists proof "that atheism is rather in the lip than in the heart of man." Jeremy Corderoy's traveler impiously asserts that he will avoid Scripture reading and church service, since ignorance of God may excuse his sins (*Warning for Worldlings*, p. 275); but his search for justification of his unethical conduct (pp. 302–41) reveals an uneasy conscience which he thinks he has salved by false prayer. [62] *Works*, ed. McKerrow, II, 121–29.

[63] John Dove, *Confutation*, chap. ii, "Of the Causes of Atheism," cites as an example what he considers a misreading of Cicero.

less we follow David in acknowledging that we are fearfully and wonderfully made, we will become engrossed in the mere matter and form of our bodies, as most men do, "so that many of them become mere naturalists and very atheists." [64] According to William Alexander,

> Of known effects grounds too precisely sought,
> Young naturalists oft atheists old do prove.[65]

Best known of such opinions is Bacon's dictum:

It is true that a little philosophy inclineth man's mind to atheism, but depth in philosophy bringeth men's minds about to religion; for while the mind of man looketh upon second causes scattered, it may sometimes rest in them, and go no further; but when it beholdeth the chain of them confederate, and linked together, it must needs fly to Providence and Deity. Nay, even that school which is most accused of atheism doth most demonstrate religion: that is, the school of Leucippus, and Democritus, and Epicurus: for it is a thousand times more credible that four mutable elements, and one immutable fifth essence, duly and eternally placed, need no God, than that an army of infinite small portions, or seeds unplaced, should have produced this order and beauty without a divine marshal.[66]

Pliny the elder was deservedly choked to death by poisonous fumes near Vesuvius because he was "over-curious in searching the causes of nature." [67] These are but a few of many citations on the impiety and danger of prying too closely into the secrets of nature, a doctrine which was to receive its classic expression in Raphael's advice to Adam, "Solicit not thy thoughts with matters hid." [68] Hence such works as *The Wonderful Workmanship of the*

[64] La Primaudaye, *The Second Part of the French Academy* (1594), "Epistle to the Reader," sig. b1ʳ. The reference is to Psalms 139:14.
[65] Commendatory verse in John Abernethy, *A Christian and Heavenly Treatise* (1630), sig. A7ᵛ.
[66] "Of Atheism," first published as an essay in 1612, is a revision of "De Atheismo" in Bacon's *Meditationes sacrae*, which was published with the first edition of the essays in 1597 and translated the year following. Epicurus fares better in the essay than in the earlier "meditation," and the essay stresses a little more than the "meditation" the desire of the atheist to win converts.
[67] Vaughan, *Golden Grove*, Bk. I, chap. iii.   [68] *Paradise Lost*, VIII, 167.

World (1578), designed to found scientific study on the Scriptures rather than on heathen writers like Plato and Aristotle.[69]

The confusion of sects, peace and prosperity, and pride of intellect are the chief causes of atheism, but there are others only a little less important. From the days of Roger Ascham foreign travel was considered dangerous to the faith of an Englishman. Nor was the atheist always given sole blame for his dereliction; poor preaching and an indolent clergy were held responsible in part for religious defection. Worse still, personal misconduct of the clergy was alleged as a cause of disillusionment. In Tourneur's play, D'Amville, already an atheist, is confirmed in his disbelief by the hypocrisy of his chaplain.[70] Certain authors, notably Machiavelli, were considered well springs of unbelief, especially among courtiers. Robert Greene asks the "famous gracer of tragedians" (most probably Marlowe) with whom Greene shared his atheism whether it is "pestilent Machiavelian policy that thou hast studied," and denounces such a course as "peevish folly." [71] Other writers besides Machiavelli were suspect, as Lucretius for his ideas on the creation, Lucian for his scoffing. The relatively judicious and fair-minded Thomas Jackson is certain that some passages in Paracelsus "are so plainly impious, that no man, which understands the principles of Christian religion, will undertake to make any orthodoxal construction of them." And he desires that none be admitted to the study of Paracelsian theories "without public approbation, not only of their sufficiency in learning,

---

[69] Thomas Twyne's translation of Lambert Daneau, *Physica Christiana* (1576); see F. R. Johnson, *Astronomical Thought in Renaissance England* (Baltimore, 1937), pp. 185–86.

[70] Act I, sc. ii; in *Works*, ed. Nicoll, pp. 184–85. Jeremy Corderoy (*Warning for Worldlings*, sig. A9) lists the causes of atheism given by Richard Hooker (*Of the Laws of Ecclesiastical Polity*, Bk. V, chap. ii) and adds another: "the corrupt life of some who have consecrated themselves to the service of God, yet dare not open their mouths against corruption in manners, but only busy themselves in matters of doctrine, lest they should hear *Medice cura teipsum*." See also Burton, *Anatomy*, ed. Dell and Jordan-Smith, p. 928.

[71] *Groatsworth of Wit* (1592), quoted by C. F. Tucker Brooke, *Life of Marlowe* (New York, 1930), p. 97.

but of their sincerity in religion." [72] Court life itself was a danger: Bowes, Nashe, and Dove agree that atheists are numerous at court, and John Donne asks, as one of his *Paradoxes and Problems*, "Why are courtiers sooner atheists than men of other conditions?" [73]

Before reducing this extensive folklore of atheism to terms useful in the study of Ralegh, two other considerations call for brief attention. The omission, from this essay in definition, of specific charges of atheism against named persons is deliberate, but it is by no means intended to minimize the importance of such charges. Indeed, one of the difficulties confronted in a study of Elizabethan atheism is that the apologists, visiting their wrath upon the ancients and upon anonymous whipping boys, are exceedingly wary of naming contemporary and (they say) numerous atheists. Although the omission is frequently vexatious in the study of individual writers, the impersonality of the discussion has its advantages for an understanding of the age. Formal and specific accusations of atheism, as distinct from the vocabulary of invective on the one hand and from philosophical discussions on the other, have acquired by reason of the personalities involved shadows which may obscure and highlights which may falsify. For purposes of definition, therefore, what was said of Oxford, or of Marlowe, or of Ralegh, has been put aside temporarily in favor of what was said of the anonymous atheist.

A second consideration is that unorthodox and even atheistical opinions were accessible to the Elizabethans in *print* to a greater

---

[72] *Treatise of Unbelief*, pp. 182-83. T. B[owes] laments the free circulation of the "lascivious pamphlets" of Robert Greene (identified by the quotation from his *Repentance*) and of similar works which "have mustered themselves of late years in Paul's Churchyard" to support atheism, no less than *Huon of Bourdeaux* and *King Arthur* once maintained popery (La Primaudaye, *The Second Part of the French Academy*, "Epistle to the Reader," sig. b4).

[73] First printed in 1652, but extant in a number of manuscripts. See E. M. Simpson, "More Manuscripts of Donne's *Paradoxes and Problems*," *Review of English Studies*, X (1934), 288-300, 412-16. Curiously enough, in several manuscripts the problem quoted is next to "Why did Sir Walter Ralegh write the history of these times?"

extent than an intentional dependence on apologetical works for the materials of definition might indicate. Naturally, in an age when massacre, burning at the stake, or the brutal punishment reserved for traitors might be invoked to settle doctrinal differences, "atheists" did not publish treatises on their unbelief, however persuasive they may have been in private conversation. The fuss made over the "Arian" document found in Kyd's possession is one of innumerable demonstrations of the danger of any contact with heresy. But the works of refutation themselves provided from both ancient and nearly contemporary authors a generous selection of atheist and anti-Christian writings.[74] This ironic situation is not peculiar to the Renaissance: the arguments of some of the earliest opponents of Christianity are known today only because the early church fathers quoted them *in extenso*. Some dubious works, like Pliny's *Natural History*, were reprinted with no other purification than a cautionary preface and possibly marginal comments to guard the unwary reader. The familiarity of the Elizabethans with this early anti-religious literature is demonstrated not only by frequent citation but even more clearly by the casual use of the names of ancient foes of Christianity, like Lucian and Julian the Apostate, as synonyms for "atheist." Thus Gabriel Harvey can write, with more intelligibility than Harvey could always muster, "Though Greene were a Julian, and Marlow a Lucian: yet I would be loath, he [Nashe] should be an Aretin"; and further, "Pliny's and Lucian's religion may ruffle and scoff a while: but extreme vanity is the best beginning of that bravery, and extreme misery the best end of that felicity."[75] Chief Justice Popham was sure of being understood

---

[74] Note that the document found among Kyd's papers consisted of heretical statements extracted originally from the work in which they were refuted. See W. D. Briggs, "On a Document Concerning Christopher Marlowe," *Studies in Philology*, XX (1923), 153–59. John Orr, *English Deism: Its Roots and Its Fruits* (Grand Rapids, 1934), pp. 37–45, cites some notable instances of anti-Christian writings, e.g., of Celsus and Porphyry, preserved in the refutations of the church fathers.

[75] *A New Letter of Notable Contents* (1593), quoted by C. F. Tucker Brooke, *op. cit.*, p. 112.

when he used against Ralegh Julian's oft-quoted sentence, "Vicisti, Galilæe."

Certain of the ancients symbolize particular aspects of atheism: Aristotle rejects the creation of the world, but believes in providence; Epicurus holds that the world was created, but rejects providence. Ancient writers who, like Cicero, questioned the existence of the gods were often drafted to serve in the cause of true religion because they rejected false gods, not God—although some apologists recognized that a wayward reader might transfer to the Christian faith the arguments used against pagan gods. Two powerful anti-Christian writers, Celsus and Porphyry, known through extensive quotation by the church fathers, are frequently cited by the Elizabethans. The attack of Celsus on Jesus is like that attributed to Marlowe; and Porphyry is quoted triumphantly whenever he is on the side of the angels in philosophical arguments on the existence of God.[76] Freedom of words rather than freedom of thought is illustrated by William Watson's example of a thesis permissible for debate: "For if that by way of a quodlibet or thesis proposed, a man may without blasphemy, sin, scandal, or any offence in the world, ask whether God or the Devil be to be honored: whether our Savior Christ could sin or no: whether our Blessed Lady were an adultress or common woman or not, etc." then surely it is not reprehensible to debate the relative merits of secular priests and Jesuits.[77] Constant reference to the early enemies of Christianity continues well into

---

[76] Mornay and Parsons quote and cite Celsus and Porphyry with some frequency; and references to Origen, *Contra Celsum*, the source of information about Celsus' attack on Christ, occur in the works of such writers as Thomas Nashe and Francis Meres as well as in the apologetical treatises. Ralegh refers to the *Contra Celsum* (*History*, I, vi, 7, p. 93) and to Porphyry (*ibid.*, III, i, 2, p. 3). For correspondences between the opinions of Celsus and those attributed to Marlowe see Paul H. Kocher, *Christopher Marlowe* (Chapel Hill, N.C., 1946), pp. 63–66.

[77] *A Decacordon of Ten Quodlibetical Questions* (1602), sig. A5ᵛ. Robert Parsons in his *Manifestation* (1602), fol. 104, promptly misconstrued this statement by his adversary, who was defended by W. C., *A Reply unto a Certain Libel* (1603), fol. 102.

the seventeenth century; in Edward Stillingfleet's *Letter to a Deist* (1677) four of the best known of the ancient detractors are still joined in symbolic unity: "And neither Julian, nor Celsus, nor Porphyry, nor Lucian did ever question the truth of the story itself, but only upbraided the Christians for attributing too much to Christ." [78] The wide circulation, even at second hand, of the opinions of ancient atheists and foes of Christianity, helps to explain the freedom with which radical opinions could be discussed while minor heresies, actively propagated, were punished with imprisonment, or torture, or death.

This interpretation of the Elizabethan meanings of "atheism" yields no simple, unique formula for judging Ralegh's alleged atheism. With so many opinions and actions quite properly labeled atheism, the reader may be excused for impatiently accepting the popular Elizabethan meaning, that an atheist is a dubious character or an intractable opponent. But the problem of definition, of definitions rather, cannot be ignored. The word "atheism" for the Elizabethans covered a large area of meaning which later generations have divided into unequal and sometimes overlapping sections by such terms as "atheism" (in a limited meaning), "religious skepticism," "agnosticism," "unitarianism," "deism," "unethical conduct." It is frequently possible, however, through an author's own definitions and classifications of the term or through the context in which it is used, to discern his special meaning. A number of such special meanings have been presented in this chapter, first by summarizing the principles essential to faith and secondly by giving a cross section of Elizabethan opinion on the atheist's ideas and actions. Aside from the content of the discussion of atheism, several conclusions about the conduct of the debate are valuable for understanding Ralegh's position. First, the emphasis upon reason in persuading unbelievers immediately enlarges the field of discussion to include philosophy as well as theology, even though divinity continues its rule as queen of the sciences. A by-product of the emphasis on reason is

---

[78] Pp. 57-58.

Elizabethan Meanings of "Atheism"

the fondness for intellectual disputation which Thomas Jackson deplored as a regrettable consequence of arguing about first principles. Quite clearly, however, debate on fundamental religious questions, beyond and above the constant warfare of the sects, was commonplace; against the background of the apologetical works, the conversation of Ralegh and Ironside loses something of its esoteric quality. Secondly, the very number of the apologetical works encouraged circulation of the anti-religious and anti-Christian arguments which were presented for refutation. Finally, although the rationalism of the debate often breaks down and although it draws its analogies from errors in natural philosophy long since exploded, the discussion is frequently on a level of philosophical sophistication which we shall find at least equal to that of *The History of the World*.

The Elizabethan meanings of atheism provide the semantic context in which we may interpret the charges of atheism against Ralegh, presented in their historical context in Chapter II. The historical record specifies the derelictions concerning which we should seek evidence in Ralegh's own works, and the general discussion of atheism will be helpful in reconciling the apparently contradictory evidence of what Ralegh said and what was said about him. In the chapters which follow, some major topics in the apologetical literature will be combined, for the interpretation of Ralegh's works, with the principal charges of unbelief made against him in his lifetime: in Chapter IV, Ralegh's opinions on God and the soul, the subject of conversation at Sir George Trenchard's table; in Chapter V, the loosely defined "inward atheism" or Machiavellianism to which the courtier was ever exposed and of which Ralegh was at one time easily convicted in the court of popular opinion; and in Chapter VI, Ralegh's ideas on the authority of the Scriptures, especially on miracles and the creation of the world—the Scriptures which, by report, were mocked in his "school of atheism."

Chapter 4

Of God and the Soul

... such a Nature cannot be said to be God, that can be in all conceived by man

History, Preface, sig. E3^r

UNLIKE the scant survivals of his table talk, Ralegh's works provide abundant records of his views on all the topics controverted in the books on atheism and on all the questions raised in his lifetime concerning his religious beliefs. *The History of the World* alone, with its moralistic intent and digressive method, contains a commentary on the problems of religion extensive enough to make a passable work of Christian apologetics; and the opinions expressed in the *History* are frequently supplemented by comment in miscellaneous writings—poems, letters, essays, and treatises. Following an order customary in the confutations of atheism discussed in Chapter III and adopting some questions [1] of the Cerne Abbas inquiry which seem to concern Ralegh, let us review his closely related beliefs about God's being, the creation of the world, and God's providence; about the soul; and about the Scriptures and salvation. It will then be possible to reexamine, with some hope of getting at its meaning, the Reverend Ralph Ironside's report of his brief encounter with Carew and Sir Walter Ralegh.

---

[1] For a complete list of the questions see *Willobie His Avisa*, ed. G. B. Harrison (London, 1926), App. III; or F. C. Danchin in *Revue-Germanique*, IX (1913), 578–87. The investigating committee at Cerne Abbas put to each witness nine "interrogatories," groups of questions, obviously framed to sift rumors of specific departures from orthodoxy not only by Sir Walter Ralegh but also by members of his retinue. These interrogatories will introduce appropriately Ralegh's own answers to the kind of questions raised with personal intent at Cerne Abbas and in general terms, as we have seen, in all extended discussions of atheism.

Of God and the Soul

I

The Being of God

> Whom do you know, or have heard, that have argued, or spoken against, or as doubting, the being of any God? Or what or where God is?

One of Parsons' libels was that in Ralegh's "school of atheism" the scholars were "taught among other things to spell God backward." Years later John Aubrey recalled Lord Scudamour's remark, "Twas basely said of Sir W. R. to talk of the anagram of Dog." [2] No trace of such levity or irreverence appears in the stately periods which begin *The History of the World*:

> God, whom the wisest men acknowledge to be a power uneffable and virtue infinite, a light by abundant clarity invisible, an understanding which itself can only comprehend, an essence eternal and spiritual, of absolute pureness and simplicity, was and is pleased to make himself known by the work of the world: in the wonderful magnitude whereof (all which he embraceth, filleth, and sustaineth), we behold the image of that glory, which cannot be measured, and withall that one, and yet universal nature, which cannot be defined.

In the first section of his book Ralegh develops the thesis, conventional in thought however distinguished in style, "That the invisible God is seen in his creatures." He quotes St. John, St. Paul, and the church fathers on man's inability to see God with corporal eyes, and he names a dozen authorities [3] in support of St. Augustine's words: "That nature, or that substance, by whatsoever name that is to be called which is God, whatsoever that be, the same cannot be corporally perceived." Man, who cannot see God, does have other means of knowing Him—by His works and word:

---

[2] *Brief Lives*, ed. Andrew Clark, 2 vols. (Oxford, 1898), II, 188. It is impossible to determine whether this observation has independent value or is merely an echo of Parsons' widely circulated libel.

[3] Such a clubbing of authorities, far from being evidence that Ralegh has consulted them at first hand, is often a sign that he is following a convenient commentary. See below, note 41.

For he of whom there is no higher cause cannot be known by any knowledge of cause or beginning (saith Montanus), but either by the observing and conferring of things, which he hath, or doth create and govern, or else by the word of God himself.[4]

When he comes to discuss "the image of God, according to which man was first created," Ralegh instructs us "to know and consider that God, who is eternal and infinite, hath not any bodily shape or composition, for it is both against his nature and his word; an error of the Anthropomorphitae, against the very essence and majesty of God." Man's resemblance to God is "chiefly in respect of the habit of original righteousness, most perfectly infused by God into the mind and soul of man in his first creation."[5]

Like Mornay and other apologetical writers, Ralegh finds the knowledge of God in the wise of all ages, though he holds with some of the church fathers and other authorities that such heathen knowledge derived from Moses.

And this is certain, that if we look into the wisdom of all ages, we shall find that there never was man of solid understanding or excellent judgment: never any man whose mind the art of education hath not bended; whose eyes a foolish superstition hath not afterward blinded; whose apprehensions are sober, and by a pensive inspection advised; but that he hath found by an unresistable necessity one true God and everlasting being, all for ever causing and all for ever sustaining.[6]

Unfortunately this wisdom became perverted in some quarters, as in Egypt, where the true knowledge of God reverently expressed by Hermes was "at length by devilish policy of the Egyptian priests purposely obscured; who invented new gods, and those innumerable, best sorting (as the Devil persuaded them) with vulgar capacities, and fittest to keep in awe and order their common people."[7] It is to false teaching, therefore, that Ralegh assigns the Machiavellian idea of religion as an instrument of civil policy; a noble concept of God, whether derived by

---

[4] *History of the World* (1614), I, i, 1, pp. 1-2. Man's inability to comprehend God is restated a number of times in the sections immediately following.
[5] I, ii, 1, and 2, pp. 24, 27.   [6] I, vi, 7, p. 96.   [7] *Ibid.*

Of God and the Soul

reason from the wonders of the created universe or learned by revelation or gathered at second hand from philosophers who knew the writings of Moses, is the heritage of all wise men.

The power of God is as limitless as it is incomprehensible. A witness at Cerne Abbas, William Arnold, testified that "he heard Mr. Carew Ralegh say at Gillingham that there was a god in nature." The record does not show that Arnold was pressed for details, and the remark as it stands, without an explanatory context, is certainly a heretical opinion, but one which Sir Walter vigorously rejects.

For the rest, I do also account it not the meanest, but an impiety monstrous, to confound God and nature, be it but in terms. For it is God that only disposeth of all things according to his own will, and maketh of one earth vessels of "honor and dishonor." It is nature that can dispose of nothing, but according to the will of the matter wherein it worketh. It is God that commandeth all; it is nature that is obedient to all.

Wonder and worship are due not to "the faculty that worketh, nor the creature wherein it worketh," but to Him who endowed nature with the power "to work all things to their last and uttermost perfection." In closing the paragraph Ralegh manages to get into one sentence three related arguments commonly used by the apologists: that all great philosophers have acknowledged an infinite power, that reason can prove the existence of such a power, and that once such a power is accepted the teachings of Scriptures follow naturally.

And therefore every reasonable man, taking to himself for a ground that which is granted by all antiquity and by all men truly learned that ever the world had; to wit, that there is a power infinite and eternal (which also necessity doth prove unto us, without the help of faith; and reason, without the force of authority) all things do as easily follow which have been delivered by divine letters, as the waters of a running river do successively pursue each other from the first fountains.[8]

God's power over all nature is further expounded in a section en-

---

[8] The quotations are from Pref., sig. E2^v.

titled, "That nature is no *principium per se,* nor form the giver of being; and of our ignorance how second causes should have any proportion with their effects." The powers of nature are no more self-operative than are the works of a clock which has been wound. Or one might as well consider that the helm and rudder which steer a ship possess an "absolute virtue," and not look further to the hand that guides the helm or the judgment that directs the hand. "All second and instrumental causes, together with nature itself, without that operative faculty which God gave them, would become altogether silent, virtueless, and dead." [9]

But if man's reason can achieve the knowledge of the existence of God, it is utterly incapable of comprehending His essence or "the manner and first operation of his divine power." [10] In so far as Ralegh's ideas on the limitations of reason apply to man's knowledge of God, they can best be stated by quoting an emphatic passage from the preface to the *History:*

I confess it, that to inquire further, as of the essence of God, of His power, of His art, and by what mean He created the world, or of His secret judgment and the causes, is not an effect of reason; *sed cum ratione insaniunt,* but they grow mad with reason, that inquire after it. For as it is no shame nor dishonor (saith a French author) "de faire

[9] I, i, 10, p. 13. Ralegh's statements on the relation of nature to God are in line with those of Du Bartas and other popular expounders of the orthodox position. For a doubly appropriate example see "The Argument" prefixed to *The Second Day of the First Week* (1603), translated by Thomas Winter and dedicated to Ralegh. Winter summarizes the "First Day," in which our poet "judiciously declared that the world had a beginning, against the absurd paradoxes of some doting philosophers, which held that it was from all eternity," and also "taxed and answered their atheistical curiosity, which busy their . . . brains, about inquiring what God did before the creation." Winter then proceeds to the argument of the "Second Day," chiefly about astronomical and meteorological phenomena, and concludes: "But albeit [Du Bartas] shows himself a philosopher in producing these natural reasons, yet he would have every man to show himself a Christian, in not wholly resting satisfied with these second causes; but ever so to acknowledge the wisdom of the Almighty, that he rather admire the creator, than adore the creature: . . . And that [Du Bartas] may clip the wings of man's pride, which is wont to soar beyond itself in self-conceits, he demonstrates how it is impossible for the most cunning naturalist, to render sound reasons of all accidents." [10] I, i, 6, p. 6.

Of God and the Soul

arrest au but qu'on nasceu surpasser," for a man to rest himself there, where he finds it impossible to pass on further: so whatsoever is beyond and out of the reach of true reason, it acknowledgeth it to be so, as understanding itself not to be infinite, but according to the name and nature it hath, to be a teacher that best knows the end of his own art. For seeing both reason and necessity teach us (reason, which is *pars divini spiritus in corpus humanum mersi*) that the world was made by a power infinite, and yet how it was made it cannot teach us; and seeing the same reason and necessity make us know that the same infinite power is everywhere in the world, and yet how everywhere it cannot inform us: our belief hereof is not weakened, but greatly strengthened, by our ignorance; because it is the same reason that tells us, that such a nature cannot be said to be God, that can be in all conceived by man.[11]

In describing God in idealized and abstract terms and in asserting that God's nature cannot be fully comprehended by man, Ralegh is in harmony with conservative religious writers of his time. In addition to the relevant quotations from the apologetical writers in Chapter III, evidence of that harmony may be found in books of widely varying purposes. For Thomas Morton of Berwick, God is in His nature infinite and incomprehensible to men and angels; "the shallowness of our brains and the weakness of our capacity" make it impossible for God to reveal himself to us in His true form. We should be grateful for whatever limited insight we may attain, "for in this case the least glimpse of truth is to be esteemed knowledge." [12] Thomas Milles begins his encyclopedic work of translation, *The Treasury of Ancient and Modern Times* (1613), with a consideration of the nature of God, according to the ancient philosophers and the church fathers. Again we have abstract superlatives, the story how the philos-

---

[11] Pref., sig. E3^r. In a marginal note Ralegh quotes an applicable principle from Aristotle's *Posteriora:* "Quod est infinitum et non secundum naturam terminatum, non continetur a scientia."

[12] *A Treatise of the Nature of God* (London, 1599), pp. 36, 44; quotations pp. 65, 67. Pages 1–35 of this work are in effect a tract against atheism; Morton calls his book "rather a philosophical than theological discourse, of the nature of God in general," wherein Christians, Jews, Turks, and all other infidels agree (Dedicatory Epistle, sig. A3^v).

opher Simonides wrestled in vain with the problem of definition, and, at the end of Chapter I, the cause of the difficulty:

> The philosophers say that definition may wholly specify the proportion of a thing; or his kind, quality, difference, or some peculiar accident: all which several things are not to be found in God, which is the reason that he cannot be defined or comprehended. . . .

Even in the brief catechisms of the time phrases like Ralegh's appear:

> Q. What is God?
> A. God is a spirit, eternal, infinite, almighty, only wise, most just, and most merciful.[13]

Or another answer to the same question:

> No man is able to define fully what God is in his essence. But we must content ourselves to know him by his attributes, namely that he is strong, mighty, merciful, wise, slow to anger, of great goodness, and so forth, as he is described unto us by himself in his word.[14]

In short, the philosophical tenor of the first pages of *The History of the World* on the being of God finds its origin in the religious thought of an age, not in the intellectual independence of an individual.

The Creation

> Whom do you know or have heard that hath spoken against God His providence over the world? or of the world's beginning or ending? or of predestination? or of heaven or of hell? or of the resurrection in a doubtful or contentious manner?

It was probably through his association with Thomas Harriot that Ralegh's soundness on the creation came to be questioned. Despite its internal contradiction, Anthony à Wood's brief reference to the subject has been widely quoted and often accepted:

---

[13] John Rogers, *The Sum of Christianity* (n.d.), p. 1; another edition of this work is dated 1579.

[14] Gervase Babington, *A Very Fruitful Exposition of the Commandments* (London, 1583), p. 26.

Of God and the Soul 105

But notwithstanding his great skill in mathematics, he [Harriot] had strange thoughts of the Scripture, and always undervalued the old story of the creation of the world, and could never believe that trite position, *Ex nihilo nihil fit*. He made a philosophical theology, wherein he cast off the Old Testament, so that consequently the New would have no foundation. He was a deist, and his doctrine he did impart to the said count [Northumberland] and to Sir Walt. Ralegh when he was compiling the *History of the World*, and would controvert the matter with eminent divines of those times; who therefore having no good opinion of him, did look on the manner of his death . . . as a judgment upon him for those matters, and for nullifying the Scripture.[15]

So far as an opinion on the creation of the world is involved, no position could be more orthodox than refusal to accept the principle "nothing is made of nothing." Aside from this internal contradiction, Wood's statement does not accord with the external facts, for Ralegh's *History* reflects no such tutelage—as this chapter demonstrates in part. The first error can be explained by reference to Wood's source, the notes of John Aubrey, whose labors Wood compensated with ungrateful abuse. Even if his facts are unsupported by any evidence now available, Aubrey at least tells a coherent story.

The bishop of Sarum (Seth Ward) told me that one Mr. Haggar (a countryman of his), a gentleman and good mathematician, was well acquainted with Mr. Thomas Hariot, and was wont to say, that he did not like (or valued not) the old story of the creation of the world. He could not believe the old position; he would say *ex nihilo nihil fit*.[16]

This at least makes sense: Mr. Haggar's story has Harriot advancing against the Biblical story of the creation a familiar argument out of Aristotle—applying, in Thomas Jackson's words, "a maxim most true in a sense most impertinent."[17] In copying

---

[15] *Athenae Oxonienses*, II (Oxford, 1815), 300–301. Quoted from the 1691 edition by Henry Stevens, *Thomas Hariot and His Associates* (London, 1900), pp. 146–47. Stevens rejects the passage as an account of Harriot's views, and cites in opposition the heavy use of Scripture in Ralegh's *History*. See below, sec. iii of this chapter.

[16] *Brief Lives*, I, 286.   [17] See above, p. 86.

Aubrey's note, Wood omitted the words "he would say," and thus made nonsense of the passage. The story came to Aubrey at third hand, and its ending makes one suspect that Mr. Haggar told the anecdote more for its clumsy jest about the cause of Harriot's death than for information about his philosophy: "But said Mr. Haggar, a *nihilum* killed him at last: for in the top of his nose came a little red speck (exceedingly small), which grew bigger and bigger and at last killed him."

Only the wide circulation of the story in Wood's mangled version justifies even this brief notice, for Ralegh repudiates emphatically Aristotle's argument for the eternity of the world. He begins his history with the creation because examples of divine providence are "everywhere found (the first divine histories being nothing else but a continuation of such examples)." Providence and the creation are inseparably linked: providence presupposes the creation, and the creation "infers" providence—"for what father forsaketh the child that he hath begotten?"

Yet many of those that have seemed to excel in worldly wisdom have gone about to disjoin this coherence; the Epicure denying both creation and providence, but granting that the world had a beginning; the Aristotelian granting providence, but denying both the creation and the beginning.

This doctrine of faith, that the world was created in time, is "too weighty a work for Aristotle's rotten ground to bear up"; yet it is remarkable that natural reason alone did not lead him to recognize "the necessity of infinite power, and the world's beginning." As Ralegh warms to his subject he digresses into an attack on blind following of "the positions of heathen philosophers" as if they were "undoubted grounds and principles indeed"; and he calls for greater independence in study within the limits of man's reason, incapable as that reason is of explaining God's manner of working and presumptuous as it is in its attempts at explanation. After quoting with approval the citation by Lactantius of many learned pagans who acknowledged in one way or another a divine power, Ralegh concludes his scornful

Of God and the Soul

rejection of limits upon God's creative power by asserting vigorously the philosophical necessity of divine omnipotence. As all rivers are ultimately lost in the great ocean, "in the necessity of this infinite power all the reason of man ends and dissolves itself." [18]

Returning to the immediate subject, the creation, he regards the supposition that God did not create the world from nothing, but from preexistent matter, as "so weak as is hardly worth the answering." [19] Nevertheless, he argues the logical fallacies of that position, and then, having disposed of the arguments for the eternity of matter, he rejects the application to God's power of a principle operative only in natural and finite processes. The principle, of course, is that familiar bone of contention, *Ex nihilo*:

> But now for those who from that ground, "That out of nothing nothing is made," infer the world's eternity, and yet not so salvage therein as those are which give an eternal being to dead matter: it is true, if the word "nothing" be taken in the affirmative, and the "making" imposed upon natural agents and finite power, that out of nothing, nothing is made. But seeing their great doctor Aristotle himself confesseth, . . . "That all the ancient decree a kind of beginning, and the same to be infinite": . . . it is strange that this philosopher with his followers should rather make choice out of falsehood to conclude falsely, than out of truth to resolve truly.

It is a mockery, says Ralegh, for Aristotle "to confess a sufficient and effectual cause of the world (to wit an almighty God) in his antecedent, and the same God to be a God restrained in his conclusion." The result of such philosophical thinking is "to resolve of God as of natural necessity, which hath neither choice, nor will, nor understanding." Ralegh rejects also the Aristotelian argument that, because God is immovable and always the same, He is forever the cause of the world and the world is therefore eternal. The answer is that God could perform in due time "that

---

[18] The quotations in this paragraph are from Pref., sig. D2^r–sig. D3^v. Ralegh makes a passing reference to the distinction between Epicurean and Peripatetic beliefs about the creation, in II, xiii, 7, p. 435.

[19] Pref., sig. D3^v.

which he ever determined at length to perform.... For the same action of his will, which made the world forever, did also withhold the effect to the time ordained." Although he considers this explanation sufficient in itself, Ralegh quotes approvingly, with necessary Christian adaptation, the Platonic distinction made by Ficino between the "spiritual world" or "idea" which was the first work of God and the "creation in time" which was His second work.

That representative, or the intentional world (say they) the sampler of this visible world, the first work of God, was equally ancient with the Architect; for it was forever with Him, and ever shall be. This material world, the second work or creature of God, doth differ from the worker in this, that it was not from everlasting, and in this it doth agree, that it shall be forever to come.

Christians agree, says Ralegh, that the world has not existed forever; the second point, that the world will endure forever, Christians apply to "a new heaven and a new earth," which will follow after the consummation of this world. He cites as worthy of speculation the opinions of Proclus the Platonist concerning "an eternal and unchangeable cause, producing a changeable and temporal effect," and the means whereby a finite world is knit to the Divine Being by an infinite virtue. Ralegh then turns from his Platonizing to refute those who say that the world will have no end.[20]

Robert Parsons cited the doctrine of the world's creation from nothing as an example of the "high and hidden doctrine," beyond human capacity, found in Scriptures; Philip Mornay had applied the principle "ex nihilo nihil fit" to prove the divinity of Christ, who exercised supernatural powers. Ralegh, too, denies that a natural principle can bind an omnipotent God, and he makes belief in the creation of the world a matter of faith; but he is not loath to argue the point on philosophical grounds. On no other issue does he more clearly belong with the Christian apologists.

[20] The quotations bearing on Aristotelian and Platonic views on the creation are from Pref., sig. D4^r–sig. E1^r.

Of God and the Soul

Providence

In the writings of the apologists, in the questions at Cerne Abbas quoted above, and in the preface to the *History*, God's providence and the creation of the world are inextricably linked. But belief in providence has a special importance in Ralegh's work because his *History* is designed to show that an omnipotent God visits upon sinful men and nations just and inevitable punishments. This moral purpose, which is in accord with the ideas of a major school of Renaissance historiography,[21] finds pictorial illustration in the engraved frontispiece to *The History of the World* (1614). The central figure is History, the "mistress of life," represented by a female who radiates light. She treads upon Death and Oblivion and holds aloft a globe of the world to the clear, white figure of Good Fame and the spotted figure of Evil Fame, who stand trumpeting as they point to the globe between them. The watchful eye of Providence at the top of the design surveys all. History is flanked by figures representing Truth and Experience, who guide her; and in her labor of holding up the world to good or bad report she relies upon her peculiar strengths, represented by four pillars bearing the names by which History is known:

> Time's witness, herald of antiquity,
> The light of truth, and life of memory.

[21] For an account of sixteenth-century opinions on the purpose of history, see Lily B. Campbell, *Tudor Conceptions of History and Tragedy in "A Mirror for Magistrates"* (Berkeley, Calif., 1936). In *Shakespeare's "Histories": Mirrors of Elizabethan Policy* (San Marino, Calif., 1947), pp. 79-84, Miss Campbell discusses the preface to Ralegh's *History* as the "culminating document of Renaissance historiography in England," wherein he "gathered all the theories of the Renaissance and the Reformation into a new whole, and as a great artist . . . fashioned a masterpiece which superseded all that went before." The frontispiece to Ralegh's *History*, reproduced in Miss Campbell's study of Shakespeare's history plays, may be found also in T. N. Brushfield, *Bibliography of Ralegh* (Exeter, England, 1908); *The Poems of Ben Jonson*, ed. B. H. Newdigate (Oxford, 1936); and G. W. Whiting, *Milton's Literary Milieu* (Chapel Hill, N.C., 1939).

This description, a favorite in the Renaissance, is from Cicero; the couplet completes a poem (attributed to Ben Jonson) which is printed facing the title page as an explanation of its symbolism. Ralegh would not have understood a nineteenth-century criticism of his didactic purpose on the ground that "it is the part of the moral teacher rather than of the historian to point out these lessons. Ralegh confuses the two functions, and is too much of a preacher to be a historian." [22] For him, as for his contemporaries, "the end and scope of all history" is "to teach by example of times past, such wisdom as may guide our desires and actions," [23] and the instruction is at all times cognizant of God's love and God's wrath. Full recognition of this theory of history is essential for a valuation of Ralegh's statements on other matters of faith; his narrative is so permeated by the belief in divine justice that one cannot dismiss lightly his declarations concerning God, the creation, and the soul, on which his orthodoxy was questioned.

Since the creation and God's providence are inseparably linked, Ralegh goes back to the earliest times for examples of the operation of divine justice: from the Bible, for him the oldest of all records, the writings of "those happy hands which the Holy Ghost hath guided"; but also from the secular writings of those "who have gathered the acts and ends of men mighty and remarkable in the world." The examples are in no wise invalidated by their antiquity, because

> the judgments of God are forever unchangeable; neither is he wearied by the long process of time, and won to give his blessing in one age to that which he hath cursed in another. Wherefore those that are wise, or whose wisdom, if it be not great, yet is true and well grounded, will be able to discern the bitter fruits of irreligious policy, as well among those examples that are found in ages removed far from the present as in those of latter times.[24]

Further, there is little variety in the actions of men, governed as they are by the same affections. But, lest the reader think that

---

[22] Louise Creighton, *Life of Sir Walter Ralegh* (London, 1877), p. 206.
[23] II, xxi, 6, p. 537. [24] Quotations from Pref., sigs. A2ᵛ, A3ʳ.

Of God and the Soul

recent examples of the "bitter fruits of irreligious policy" are wanting, Ralegh proceeds with a scathing review of the conduct of English and European monarchs down to Henry VIII, who is described as the pattern of a merciless prince—only James, it would appear, being exempt from the traditional misconduct of kings. As a soldier, courtier, and politician, Ralegh has a lively interest in the immediate causes of man's conduct, and his own varied experience lends vitality to his analyses of long-past events in court and field. Nevertheless, he insists upon the subordination of all explanations of causes and motives to a humble recognition of controlling Providence, which works its ends by diverse instruments and the frail "affections" of men. The peculiar merit of Biblical history is that events are referred unto the revealed will of God, even if the "concurrence of second causes with their effects is in these books nothing largely described." Yet it is not unlawful for the historian to gather from profane sources information about second causes, provided he does not "derogate from the first causes, by ascribing to the second more than was due." [25] The principle is kept constantly in mind: it may take the form of a brief conditional parenthesis, as when Ralegh begins a discussion of the decay of Alexander's army with "The causes whereof (under the divine ordinance) . . ."; [26] or it may conclude an awful lesson:

So also hath God punished the same and the like sins in all after-times, and in these our days by the same famine, plagues, war, loss, vexation, death, sickness, and calamities, howsoever the wise men of the world raise these effects no higher than to second causes, and such other accidents, which, as being next their eyes and ears, seem to them to work every alteration that happeneth.[27]

Ralegh is not content with perfunctory illustration of the working of divine Providence, and divine judgment; examples are

---

[25] Quotations from II, xxi, 6, pp. 536, 538: a section entitled "A digression, wherein is maintained the liberty of using conjecture in histories." In the Preface (sig. A3ʳ), Ralegh comments upon the diversity of opinion that arises when men seek to explain by second causes the decay of nations.

[26] IV, iii, 1, p. 212.   [27] II, xix, 3, p. 509.

numerous and diversified. On the story of the early life of Moses, he comments:

> There is not therefore the smallest accident, which may seem unto men as falling out by chance and of no consequence, but that the same is caused by God to effect somewhat else by; yea, and oftentimes to effect things of greatest worldly importance, either presently, or in many years after, when the occasions are either not considered, or forgotten.[28]

God's promises to His chosen people are conditional on their obedience and worship; the conditions not observed, it is irreligious to accuse Him of failure to keep promises.[29] He is merciful but just, and angry in justice; His wrath is severe on both places and men; divine Providence, in the unspeakable greatness of sovereignty, is just and majestical, "not (as Herodotus falsely terms it, and like an atheist) envious or malicious." [30] God may use evil spirits as the ministers of His vengeance; the corrupt affections of men accomplish His hidden purposes by the self-defeat of their own worldly wisdom; He allows the wicked to run their evil courses before visiting upon them the fruits of their iniquities, but the suffering of the righteous works to their own good.[31] God is the giver of victories; if success comes from individual labor and skillful planning, then thanks are due "both for the victory and for those virtues by which the victory was gotten." [32] In Books III, IV, and V, concerned largely with pagan history, Ralegh has less to say on the subject of God's control of human affairs than in Books I and II, wherein the unquestionable words of the prophets point the moral of a narrative based upon

---

[28] II, v, 10, p. 310.   [29] II, vii, 2, p. 332.

[30] II, v, 3, p. 299; II, xii, 3, p. 413, and II, xiii, 5, p. 427; V, iii, 12, p. 485. Ralegh very seldom is guilty of the practice he condemns—the casual use of "atheist."

[31] II, xxix, 7, pp. 516–17; II, xx, 4, pp. 524–25; II, xxii, 3, p. 543; IV, iii, 20, pt. 3, p. 243. Ralegh's discussion of the instruments of God's wrath, elsewhere uniformly dignified and often lofty in style, is in one instance worthy of Joshua Sylvester: God "hindered all, with a draught of cold water, which Cleomenes drank in a great heat" (V, ii, 6, p. 406).

[32] II, xxii, 8, pp. 550–51.

Of God and the Soul 113

the Old Testament. But even in pagan history references to God's judgments are not infrequent, though briefly stated.[33]

The centrality in the *History* of the theme of God's providence and justice is therefore more important than the direct exposition of the subject in the last five sections of the first chapter, wherein Ralegh considers the relation of fortune and fate to providence, and the meanings of prescience, providence, and predestination.[34] As God is above all nature, so is he not bound by fate; nor does he "bind us inevitably to the destinies, or influences of the stars, or subject our souls to any imposed necessity." The concept of fate as presented in the writings of learned men would be tolerable if the authors had not attached to it the idea of inevitable necessity and "dominion over the mind of man, and over his will." Prayer, especially the "lead us not into temptation" of the Lord's Prayer, is further warrant that God has tied neither man nor Himself to an immutable fate.

The inadequacy of Ralegh's three brief sections on prescience, providence, and predestination may be explained by the modesty of his purpose: because these three and destiny are often confounded, "I think it not impertinent to touch the difference in a word or two, for every man hath not observed it, though all learned men have." Prescience is infallible foreknowledge, but in God it is not "the cause of anything futurely succeeding; neither doth God's foreknowledge impose any necessity, or bind." Providence embraces foreknowledge and care and order as well; it not only beholds past, present, and future, but is also the cause of all that happens. Moses, the Prophets, Christ, and the Apostles teach us about providence; the learned pagans acknowledge it; and the

---

[33] E.g., Bk. III: viii, 8, p. 100; viii, 11, p. 104. Bk. IV: ii, 1 and 2, pp. 170, 171; iii, 20, pt. 2, p. 242; vi, 6, p. 285. Bk. V: i, 4, pt. 4, pp. 334, 341; ii, 6, p. 411; ii, 8, p. 416; iii, 9, p. 462; iii, 21, p. 580; v, 1, p. 642; vi, 7, p. 752. These illustrative references are merely brief clauses—usually such an expression as "But God had otherwise determined"—to remind the reader that second causes are not complete explanations of human affairs.

[34] I, i, 11–15, pp. 14–22; since my discussion of these pages follows Ralegh's order, further references for quotations are unnecessary. Ralegh's ideas on astrology in their relevance to his scientific thought are discussed below, chap. vi.

Turks believe in it so implicitly that they disregard the dangers of pestilence or other mortal risks. Providence is an "attribute and transcendent ability" belonging "to absolute power; to everywhere presence; to perfect goodness; to pure and divine love"; in short, to God.

Providence concerns all creatures, from angels to worms; predestination concerns men alone, and even for them not in general but their salvation or ("as some have used it") their perdition. Ralegh cites a few authorities on the subject, but having distinguished the term, as he promised, he is quick to drop it: ". . . as for the manifold questions hereof arising, I leave them to the Divines." He is willing to say with St. Augustine, "Hidden the cause of his predestination may be, unjust it cannot be"; but in the context of the discussion of fate, foreknowledge, and providence, his few sentences on predestination do not suggest even faintly the ironclad system of Calvin.

Since God's providence is supreme over fate and nature, it is inevitable that Ralegh should reject fortune as a "kind of idolatry, or god of fools." Fortune is an imaginary power to which we ascribe the variable success of human actions when no obvious cause can be found, whereas Scripture teaches us that what seems "most casual and subject to fortune is yet disposed by the ordinance of God, as all things else." The section on fortune is interesting more for its personal reflections on the working of "fortune" on the worldly stage than for any added information on Ralegh's ideas on providence. To those who would still ask why it is "that so many worthy and wise men depend upon so many unworthy and empty-headed fools; that riches and honor are given to external men, and without kernel: and so many learned, virtuous, and valiant men wear out their lives in poor and dejected estates," Ralegh answers that the "inferior or apparent cause" (that is, under God's ordinance) lies in the ability or inability, the willingness or unwillingness, to serve the time and change with the time. "That man which prizeth virtue for itself, and cannot endure to hoist and strike his sails as the diverse natures of calms and storms require, must cut his sails and his cloth of mean length and breadth, and content himself with a slow and sure navigation, (to wit) a mean and free estate." He ends the discussion of fortune, and the long first chapter on God, the creation, and providence, with a layman's declaration of faith that conditions his attitude in the *History* toward all questions of polity, of moral philosophy, and of natural philosophy:

> But of this dispute of fortune and the rest, or of whatsoever lords or gods, imaginary powers, or causes, the wit (or rather foolishness) of man hath found out: let us resolve with St. Paul, who hath taught us, that there is "but one God, the Father, of whom are all things, and we in him, and one Lord, Jesus Christ, by whom are all things, and we by him"; there are diversities of operations, but God is the same which worketh all in all.

II

> Whom do you know or have heard . . . that hath otherwise spoken against the being; or immortality of the soul of man? or that a man's soul should die and become like the soul of a beast, or such like; and when and where was the same?

Aside from numerous incidental references in his works, Ralegh made two quite unoriginal contributions to the vast literature on the soul. *A Treatise of the Soul,* a summary of conventional beliefs which includes brief statements and refutations of some of the principal heresies, has come down to us in a copy made by Elias Ashmole and has been printed only once, in the Oxford edition of Ralegh's *Works* (1829). Chapter II of the *History,* entitled "Of man's estate in his first creation, and of God's rest," deals primarily with theological questions: how we are to understand the creation of man in God's image; how the "intellectual mind of man" is distinguished from the soul which animates the body; what folly it is to neglect the care of the immortal soul; how man is a little world, a microcosm; how Adam was given freedom to direct his own nature. This discourse, as part of the widely read *History*, was far better known than the manuscript *Treatise*, which differs from it in many ways. The *Treatise* is a kind of survey, touching briefly on a number of questions; Chapter II discusses fewer problems in greater detail. For an answer in Ralegh's behalf to the questions posed at Cerne Abbas it is better to begin with the comprehensive *Treatise* than with the specialized Chapter II, important as the chapter is for its theological discussion.[35]

A prime source of trouble in discussions of the soul, for the Elizabethan as well as for the modern reader trying to understand him, is the broad meaning given the term "soul." Even in a brief and popular work like *The Confutation of Atheism* John Dove found it necessary to distinguish eight meanings of "soul," although he was concerned with only one aspect of the subject. Scrupulous attention to any scriptural usage of the word led to some hairsplitting and played a part in the distinctions made by Dove, who was content, however, with Aristotle's definition freely translated: the soul is "an act or perfection of the body which giveth unto the body life, sense, motion, vegetation, etc." [36] Far more troublesome than real or fancied scriptural distinctions, the difficult problems involved in a belief in immortality were complicated by the inclusion in treatises on the soul of questions of reproduction and growth now considered subject to investigation in the biological sciences. For example, the familiar distinction of three souls, or powers of the soul—vegetative, sensitive,

---

[35] There are enough differences in method and content in Ralegh's two discourses on the soul to warrant at least a scruple as to the authenticity of the *Treatise*, which reads like an abstract of a single work, rather than like an independent essay or even a compilation based on wide reading. For example, the authorities cited in the *Treatise* are all early: the Bible, the classical philosophers, the church fathers; chap. ii of the *History* leans heavily upon contemporary authorities. The "asides" in chap. ii have a personal ring which is missing from such comments as do appear in the *Treatise*. Nevertheless, in the absence of convincing evidence to the contrary, I have conformed to the general acceptance of the *Treatise* as Ralegh's. My principal thesis is not involved in the question of authorship, for chap. ii, authentic however unoriginal, is quite as orthodox as the *Treatise*. [36] *Confutation* (1605), pp. 68–69.

and rational [37]—answered one kind of question only to raise another. The vegetative and sensitive souls are shared by animals and in them are mortal; what, therefore, is their relationship to the third soul, or power, which is peculiar to man and is immortal? Although he does not answer this particular question as fully as some other writers do, Ralegh follows a well-beaten path and begins his *Treatise* with a description of the tripartite soul: "There are two kinds of souls, one void of reason, another endued with reason; and of those without reason there are two sorts, one which feedeth and nourisheth the body, the other which giveth sense and feeling." [38] Ralegh calls them "three kinds of souls" corresponding to three several operations of life; the "feeding soul" always attends the "feeling soul," and both accompany the rational soul. Animals have only the first two souls, which have their origin by nature, "of the seed." "Our souls are immortal and have an heavenly beginning; whereas theirs are mortal and do perish with the body, as of the body they have their beginning." Animals mind only things present, earthly, visible; men mind things absent as well as present, heavenly as well as earthly, hidden and secret as well as visible. "These things do prove that the souls of men and beasts be of diverse natures, have not a [that is, one] substance, are not to be comprehended under one kind." Thus compactly, in the less than two pages of section 1, Ralegh sets down the premises of his treatise. Section 2, equally brief, states that the reasonable soul is common to all mankind, women

---

[37] That part of Elizabethan psychology which deals with the functions of the soul in the body—in Ralegh's *Treatise* chiefly sections 1 and 5—has been explained in detail in a number of studies of the Elizabethan period and its major writers: e.g., R. L. Anderson, *Elizabethan Psychology and Shakespeare's Plays*, "University of Iowa Humanistic Studies," Vol. III, No. 4 (1927); L. B. Campbell, *Shakespeare's Tragic Heroes* (Cambridge, England, 1930); *The Works of Edmund Spenser*, Variorum Ed., Vol. II (Baltimore, Md., 1933), Appendices VIII-X; and Hardin Craig, *The Enchanted Glass* (New York, 1936), chap. v.

[38] *A Treatise of the Soul*, in *Works* (1829), VIII, 571–91, is short enough to make page references for quotations unnecessary in this summary of the essay section by section.

included, and that each has his own soul (a proposition more fully developed in explaining the origin of the soul). Scripture and the church fathers are liberally cited in support of the thesis that "women have souls eternal, endowed with reason, wise, sober, temperate, and holy, redeemed by Christ, sanctified by his Spirit, and chosen by the Father to the everlasting kingdom of heaven."

Section 3 covers a far more difficult problem, the nature of the soul, concerning which the wisest men confess ignorance:

The substance of the soul is hardly known; Lactantius denieth that men can attain to the knowledge of the nature of the soul; and Galen confesseth that he cannot tell what or where the substance of the soul is. And Athanasius saith, "that, while we live, there are three things whereof we cannot attain the knowledge: the substance of God, of angels, and of our souls." By the objects, we may come to the operation; and by the operation to the faculties; and by the faculties to the substance; but yet imperfectly and somewhat afar off.

Ralegh turns directly to the refutation of certain errors: of the Manichees, that man has two souls; of the Priscillianists, who, with Plato, have thought "that our souls are substance of the divine nature." Such a relationship of man to God, who is a simple substance, is impossible; it does not follow that because the soul is the image of God it therefore is of His substance. "There is a double image of God: one of the same substance, which is Christ, and no other creature; the soul of man is the other, which is the image of God, not in substance the same, but like in quality." Philosophical opinions which ascribe to it some kind of earthly, or even celestial, substance debase the soul, which had its origin in God's breath and is above all the elements. Ralegh continues the discussion of the substance of the soul, chiefly out of Augustine, who, also confessing an inability to name it, says that even by comparison with the finest earthly substances it can be but dimly comprehended; "for every bodily substance is great in greater places, and less in lesser places. The soul is all present wheresoever it is present."

Of God and the Soul

The origin of the soul is the subject of section 4, the longest in the *Treatise*. Ralegh disagrees with Rufinus, who said that he had learned from Scripture "no certainty of the original of souls"; it is unlikely that God, who revealed himself to us, should hide from us our own beginning. Certain ideas on the subject are stated only to be rejected. Origen's opinion that God created all souls in the beginning and kept them in heaven until they were sent into men's bodies is most unlikely; "if they had been created, they must have done somewhat, souls cannot sleep like dormice." [39] Since God creates nothing idle, why should He make the soul first and the body three thousand years later? Another idea on the origin is that the soul (the rational no less than the vegetative and the sensitive) is begotten of the soul as the body is begotten of the body. Ralegh devotes more than a page of his brief *Treatise* to stating the arguments supporting this opinion, which has its origin in the difficulties attendant upon the relationship of the three souls and in the doctrine of original sin. If God creates souls now, then He did not cease to create on the seventh day as the Scripture says. If each soul comes from God then God is sometimes a partner to adultery. Why do children resemble their parents in mind as well as in body; and why is not mention made of breathing a soul into Eve? Having presented quite fairly these traducianist arguments, Ralegh proceeds to a vigorous refutation. The vegetative and sensible souls may come from the seed, but the rational soul comes directly from God. In a passage which bears the marks of compact summary, Scripture, philosophy, and the writings of the fathers are cited against the idea that the soul is begotten. According to Jerome, for example, if the soul begins with the body it must end with the body. Not that either Jerome or Ralegh concedes the slightest possibility of such an end: so certain are they that the soul does *not* end with the body that the argument is cited as conclusive against any notion

---

[39] A like figure is used, in asserting God's providence, in "The Seventh Day of the First Week" of *Bartas: His Divine Weeks*, trans. by Joshua Sylvester (London, 1605), p. 235: God is not "a sleeping dormouse."

that the origin of the soul is one with the origin of the body. Further, the rational soul of man is capable of "action" outside the body, and in the body without the help of bodily instruments.

... as the fire moveth of itself upward and is carried round with the heavens, so the soul of man is led somewhat by the senses and doth many things in and out of the body without them; which shows that it must have some other beginning than this is. Is it not a manifest argument that it cometh from God, seeing in all things it resteth not till it come to God? The mind in searching causes is never quiet till it come to God, and the will never is satisfied with any good till it come to the immortal goodness.

Also against the idea that the soul is begotten is the fact that "there is no example in nature that a thing incorporate cometh of that which is corporal." Augustine as well as Jerome condemns vigorously this opinion of the soul's origin, and many passages in Scripture are against it. That God creates the souls of men is not contrary to the fact that "he ceased from creation the seventh day; for by this he createth no new kind, but multiplieth and preserveth that kind which he made before." Nor does it mean that God gives the sin because he gives the soul, "but the body doth communicate it to the soul, as the soul doth impart many things to the body." [40] The issue in brief is that one group of men would have the soul directly from God; the other would have it come from God, "but yet by means." The weight of Scripture favors the first idea, and our faith is helped thereby because "God toucheth our souls, and is joined to them in the creation; is joined likewise to them in our regeneration; and most of all will become one spirit with us, or rather we with him, in our glorification."

[40] R. W. Battenhouse, *Marlowe's "Tamburlaine"* (Nashville, Tenn., 1941), p. 62, reads this passage as further evidence of Ralegh's Platonism (see below, footnote 52) and contrasts Ralegh and St. Augustine on the relative guilt of soul and body. But Ralegh's emphasis seems to be on the unity of soul and body in one person, with the soul "straightway subject to the state of sin with the body by the just sentence of God" (*Works*, VIII, 584). Note also that the soul is free of [physical] corruption from the body and that sin corrupts the quality not the substance of our souls (*Works*, VIII, 590–91).

The argument is settled, therefore, by an appeal to Scripture in support of faith.

Section 5 elaborates upon the division and functions of the souls so briefly stated in the first paragraph of the *Treatise*. The vegetative faculty of the soul controls nourishment, growth, and reproduction. The sensitive faculty of the soul, by which we feel and move, works inwardly and outwardly. The outward senses are the familiar five (even this simple statement is accompanied by scriptural citation); the inward senses are three: "the common sense and imagination in the foreparts, and judgment or cogitation in the middle, and memory in the hinder part of the brain." The power of motion is communicated from the brain and the marrow of the back. The appetites, affections, and desires also proceed from the soul, and, although Ralegh does not make the point explicit, have an approximate correspondence to the three faculties of the soul. Desire is of three sorts: natural, which leads us to seek food, drink, and rest; that which proceeds from our endowment of sense, whereby we seek good and shun evil; and the will, "by which we desire that good which the understanding comprehendeth to be such indeed or in appearance, and flieth the contrary," and which "we use to stir us up to seek God and heaven, and heavenly things." The second kind of desire Ralegh distinguishes as of two kinds: on the one hand love or hate, desire or shunning, joy or sorrow; on the other hand hope, despair, boldness, fear, and anger. Though he does not use the words, Ralegh is here making the customary division of the appetitive part of the sensitive soul into concupiscible and irascible powers. The will and the understanding are "the proper and only faculties of the reasonable soul." The reasonable soul, especially the understanding, is man's highest glory. The *Treatise* reaches its climax in praise of the human understanding:

This is it wherein the glory and excellency of man especially standeth; this, together with the will, is that about the garnishing and perfecting whereof all our pain and labor is bestowed; this is proper, together with the will, the breath of life, which God breathed into the face of man;

this is the spirit which returneth unto God that gave it. This understanding hath two faculties; one by which it may know all things, and is like a clean paper, in which there is nothing written; but you may write in it any thing. The other is that by which it knoweth already, and discourseth and practiseth, and meditateth that it knoweth; they that learn not, nor will not learn anything, but continue not writing good knowledge in their souls, they are as if they had no souls; they are as the ass and mule, which have no understanding; for they have but the tables, they have nothing written in them.

The few remaining pages, section 6, are given over to the place of the soul in the body and to immortality. As usual, authorities differ widely on the location of the soul. Ralegh distinguishes two parts of the problem, the soul considered as a whole and the soul considered in its several faculties. Considered as a whole, the soul is in the body "as the form thereof, for it giveth life and motion to the whole, and is in it, not as a mariner in a ship, but being present everywhere." When we consider the soul in its faculties, then we may ask the principal location of the reason and understanding. Diverse arguments favor the brain as the seat of the understanding, and others favor the heart; Plato the brain, Christ the heart. Ralegh turns from this inconclusive discussion to a brief treatment of immortality, properly a separate section though printed as part of section 6. That the reasonable soul of man is immortal was held by all wise men to and including Plato; after his time a few foolish persons argued that the soul is mortal. The soul is exempt from physical corruption, either from anything within itself or from the body. So much we know from the soul's origin in the breath of God. Here follows in support of immortality the heaviest concentration of scriptural citations in the *Treatise*, which ends abruptly in an argument commonly used in the apologetical works described in Chapter III. Religion and the fear of God testify to immortality: religion is engrafted in all men's hearts by nature, and religion presupposes rewards; but rewards must be in the life hereafter, for the godly prosper little in this life.

Of God and the Soul 123

In comparison with the *Treatise*, Chapter II of the *History*, wherein Ralegh leans heavily on the Biblical commentaries of his own time,[41] is concerned more with theological questions than with psychology. He first attempts to explain what is meant by the "image of God" in which man is made, and in good Protestant fashion rejects the over-subtle distinctions which the school-men make between "image" and "similitude" in favor of an interpretation of Scripture which makes the terms synonymous. These distinctions of the term "image" lead to an examination of the meaning of "the intellectual mind of man" in relation to the soul: *mens*, or *animus*, is that "by which we will and make election"; it is not the *anima physica* which according to Aristotle is the form of man. The problem is complicated by other definitions of *mens;* but after pursuing the subject a little further Ralegh refers the befuddled reader who seeks more information on how the mind uses the body, especially in imagination, to the work of Thomas Bilson.[42] Ralegh's conclusion to the main problem, how man resembles God, is that it is "chiefly, in respect of the habit of original righteousness, most perfectly infused by God into the mind and soul of man in his first creation." Therefore it is not in the natural gifts of the soul, but in the supernatural gifts of

[41] Arnold Williams, "Commentaries on Genesis as a Basis for Hexaemeral Material in Literature of the Late Renaissance," *Studies in Philology*, XXXIV (1937), 191–208, demonstrates Ralegh's direct (and rarely acknowledged) borrowing from the commentaries, especially for the first four chapters of the *History*. Mr. Williams presents convincing parallels between passages in chap. ii and Benedict Pererius's *Commentariorum et disputationum in Genesin*. Even in this copying, however, Ralegh is not inhibited in his asides: thus he takes at second hand (see Mr. Williams' article, p. 202) an opinion of Aristotle on the place of the soul in the body, but so far as I can tell from the parallels adduced he adds his own tart comment on the difficulty of proof.

[42] I, ii, 2, p. 26. It is clear from Ralegh's reference that he has in mind *The Survey of Christ's Suffering for Man's Redemption* (London, 1604), and his page reference (185 ff.) is accurate enough to identify the passage he mentions. Just before his reference to Bilson, Ralegh quotes from Hieronymus Zanchius, *De operibus Dei* a passage which he seems to have taken from Bilson's work rather than directly from Zanchius (whom he quotes also in I, ii, 1, p. 24). From their page references, I judge that both Bilson and Ralegh used an edition of Zanchius other than the one accessible to me (Hanau, 1597).

"divine grace and heavenly glory," that the image of God in man is "wholly blotted out and destroyed by sin." This danger to the soul leads to some melancholy reflections on man's preoccupation with worldly prosperity and his neglect of his spiritual welfare until old age and imminent death recall him to a sense of his first responsibility, his debt to God.

Returning to questions of terminology, Ralegh follows good authority in rejecting "the beggarliness of carnal sense" which would conceive of God as using bodily hands and lips in the creation of man's body and soul. Soul and spirit are regarded as synonymous, and on the authority of Genesis, which differentiates the creation of animals and of man, that spirit which comes from God shall return to God. Section 5 of the chapter states briefly several ideas which are recognizable as Elizabethan commonplaces. God made man "an abstract or model, or brief story of the universal," the partaker of three kinds of living natures: he shares an intellectual being with the angels, a sensual nature with the animals, and he has peculiar to himself the capacity of reason. He is a microcosm, corresponding point by point to the macrocosm; in his body are similarities to earthly phenomena and his soul was made in the image of God; his seven ages are comparable to the seven planets—a reflection which ends in more chords on the theme *vanitas vanitatum*. The chapter concludes with the large freedom granted to Adam before the Fall to shape himself as he pleased, unlike the animals, who could not change their natures. This concept of man's freedom to develop by his own choice was expressed "enigmatically" by the ancients in the fable of Proteus and in stories of metamorphoses. But Adam fell; and "man having free will and liberal choice purchased by disobedience his own death and mortality."

Of the many references to the soul elsewhere in the *History*, two digressions in the Preface are noteworthy. In a passage on the futility of seeking wealth and honor for the sake of one's children, Ralegh quotes with approval the words of Augustine on the ignorance of the dead concerning the living. More significant

Of God and the Soul

for an understanding both of acknowledged opinions and of the opinions credited to him by others is his blunt statement on the narrow limits of man's self-knowledge:

"Man" (saith Solomon) "that can hardly discern the things that are upon the earth, and with great labor find out the things that are before us"; that hath so short a time in the world, as he no sooner begins to learn than to die; that hath in his memory but borrowed knowledge; in his understanding, nothing truly; that is ignorant of the essence of his own soul, and which the wisest of the naturalists (if Aristotle be he) could never so much as define but by the action and effect, telling us what it works (which all men know as well as he) but not what it is, which neither he, nor any else, doth know, but God that created it; ("for though I were perfect, yet I know not my soul," saith Job). Man I say, that is but an idiot in the next cause of his own life and in the cause of all the actions of his life, will (notwithstanding) examine the art of God in creating the world; . . .[43]

In short, all speculation on the nature of the soul is hemmed within the narrow pale of man's presumptuous ignorance.

There would be little profit, for this study, in attempting to trace all the connections of Ralegh's reflections on the soul with a centuries-old speculation. The conventionality of both the *Treatise* and Chapter II of the *History* is sufficiently apparent by comparison with one of many similar treatises and by a brief review of the provenance of some of the principal topics and ideas. If we turn to a popular work like the tenth sermon in the fourth of Henry Bullinger's *Decades*,[44] the very language shows

[43] Pref., sig. D3r.

[44] Ed. by T. Harding for the Parker Society (Cambridge, England, 1851), pp. 365–408; quotations from pp. 366, 368, 375. There are, of course, differences between Bullinger and Ralegh on some matters. Although he recognizes that many distinguished writers have concerned themselves about the distinction between *anima* and *animus* (which Ralegh discusses in chap. ii of the *History*), Bullinger dismisses the topic on the ground that most writers use the terms indiscriminately.

G. T. Buckley, *Atheism in the English Renaissance* (Chicago, 1932), p. 149, observes that Ralegh's *Treatise* was clearly "written under the influence of such works" as those of John Woolton, Philip Mornay, and Sir John Davies; i.e., written in the orthodox tradition. To these works and to the commentaries dis-

how commonplace some of Ralegh's statements are. "For who knoweth not," writes Bullinger, "that there are reckoned three kinds or parts (give me leave so to speak for instruction's sake) or three principal powers of the soul?" He recognizes a variety of meanings of soul, mind, and spirit, but holds that, whatever the terminology, man has one soul. What the reasonable soul is neither he nor the "wise heads of this world" can tell. The soul, although bodiless, is certainly a substance, not a quality. It cannot be a part of God, but it is made by God and by him "poured into the body when it is fashioned." Bullinger quotes Augustine on the powers of the soul, and of course holds that the soul is immortal, as the Scriptures and all wise men testify. Even so sketchy an index as this (Bullinger's sermon is longer than the *Treatise* and covers more topics) may serve to indicate that Ralegh's exposition would be quite acceptable in ecclesiastical company.

The traditional quality of his thought is apparent, too, when we seek to determine its place in relation to the ideas, often conflicting, which the eclecticism of the Renaissance had gathered from two thousand years of recorded speculation on the mystery of the human soul. The teachings of Plato, early naturalized in Christianity and in part incorporated in the writings of St. Augustine, and the philosophy of Aristotle, systematized in Christian thought by Thomas Aquinas, dominated the Renaissance discussion of the soul as they did other problems which philosophy and religion united to solve. In each of the classical philosophers there are ideas that harmonize and ideas that conflict with Christian teaching. The greater spirituality of Platonic philosophy with its faith in immortality was offset by its sharp dualism, which did not suit well with Christian belief in the resurrection of the body. The Aristotelian doctrine of the soul as the form of the body

---

cussed by Arnold Williams (*op. cit.*) I would add as another possible source of information the work of Zanchius (see note 42, above) which Ralegh cites in the *History*. The possibility that Ralegh in the *Treatise* is following a single authority, not yet identified, should not be dismissed.

presented no obstacles to faith in the resurrection, although Aristotle was himself inconsistent on immortality.[45] What we have called the vegetative and sensitive souls he described as inseparable from the body and therefore presumably perishable with the body. But he concedes that some parts of the soul may be separable "because they are not the actualities of any body at all." Still more significantly, "that in the soul which is called mind . . . is, before it thinks, not actually any real thing. For this reason it cannot reasonably be regarded as blended with the body: . . . while the faculty of sensation is dependent upon the body, mind is separable from it." [46]

By judicious interpretation, medieval and Renaissance writers had little difficulty in reconciling Aristotle's statements to a belief in immortality,[47] even though they continued to recognize the danger inherent in his conflicting remarks. When the atheistic traveler of Jeremy Corderoy's *A Warning for Worldlings* (1608) offers out of Aristotle four reasons against immortality, the student answers readily from the same source with four refu-

[45] Cf. Clement C. J. Webb, *Studies in the History of Natural Theology* (Oxford, 1915), pp. 259–63.

[46] *De Anima*, II, 1; III, 4, in *The Works of Aristotle*, ed. W. D. Ross, III (Oxford, 1931), 413^a, 429$^{a\text{-}b}$.

[47] A notable exception—and an excellent contrast to Ralegh—is Pietro Pomponazzi, who in his *Tractatus de immortalitate animae* (1516) argues with great skill and learning that "no natural reasons can be adduced proving that the soul is immortal, and less proving that the soul is mortal," and that the opinion of Aristotle as given in his own works does not support the concept of immortality. In his last chapter Pomponazzi rejects his philosophical demonstration as inapplicable to Christian belief in immortality, "which is an article of faith, as is plain by the Apostles' and the Athanasian Creed; therefore it ought to be proved by things proper to faith." Still more emphatically, "if those reasonings seem to prove the mortality of the soul, they are false and mere semblances, since the first light and the first truth show the opposite." The quotations are from the last chapter of a translation by William H. Hay II, published with a facsimile of the *editio princeps* (Haverford College, 1938). See also A. H. Douglas, *The Philosophy and Psychology of Pietro Pomponazzi* (Cambridge, England, 1910). Clement C. J. Webb, *op. cit.*, p. 329, considers Pomponazzi's concluding submission to the Holy See as "ironical," the means by which "Pomponazzi ever seeks to evade the heresy-hunters around him." But why should not a late medievalist quite sincerely give priority to faith over reason, however powerful?

tations and, to boot, four positive arguments for immortality.[48] An even better presentation of Aristotle's position than in Corderoy's confident dialogue is found in Mornay, who distinguishes between Plato's figurative description of the soul in terms of the pilot of a ship and Aristotle's relating the soul and body as form and matter. As in Ralegh's *Treatise,* Mornay resolves the difficulty by making the soul one whole, "immortal in power and ability," which, however, upon death suspends the exercise of those powers which depend upon bodily instruments.[49]

As might be expected, both the Platonic and Aristotelian traditions are represented in Ralegh's thought, more likely by indirect than by direct borrowing. With Plato, Ralegh argues the desires of the soul as evidence of its immortality; but he rejects, in the *Treatise,* the pilot-ship relationship for the soul and body. In his poem "The Lie," however, the soul is the "body's guest." With Aristotle, he makes the soul, in the *Treatise,* the form of the body, and in the *History,* too, he quotes Aristotle's opinion, "The soul is wholly in the whole body, and wholly in every part thereof"; but he adds the proviso, "that it is otherwise than potentially true, all the Aristotelians in the world shall never prove."[50] Not uncommonly he pools the contributions of Platonists and Aristotelians: in the course of his discussion of the intellectual mind of man, with its attempts to distinguish such terms as "animus" and "anima," he interjects, "This division and distinction out of the Platonics and Peripatetics, I leave to the reader to judge of."[51] In general Ralegh shows a decided preference for the teachings of Plato and the Platonists, indicated by approximately a score of

---

[48] Pp. 172–202. In this dialogue, which shows the adaptation of Aristotle on the popular level, the student is quite free in his interpretation of Aristotle's words.

[49] *The Trueness of the Christian Religion* (1587), p. 264. For other passages interpreting Plato and Aristotle and helpful to an understanding of Ralegh's *Treatise* see pp. 234, 239, 251, 272, and chap. xv, *passim.* Mornay reminds the reader that Aristotle's error about the creation may have led him into further error. For a brief summary of Mornay's chapters on the soul see above, chap. iii.

[50] I, ii, 1, p. 23. The definition is from a passage which Arnold Williams has shown to be taken from Pererius; see above note 41.   [51] I, ii, 2, p. 26.

Of God and the Soul

references in the Preface and Chapter I, alone. This preference, however, has a broader base than the subjects discussed in the early chapters of the *History* and cannot be explained simply in terms of Aristotelian and Platonic teachings concerning God and the soul.[52]

The transmission of the ideas of the classical philosophers, long since adapted to Christian teaching, lies outside the purpose of this sketchy survey, which is intended only to show that Ralegh is writing in the tradition. For even Ralegh's ideas on God and the soul, rooted as they are in the Christian apologetical literature of his own and earlier ages, have been read as evidence of thought advanced for his time. A few writers, although recognizing his strong religious bent, have overemphasized the philosophical content of his religious thought and have neglected the important role of natural theology in sixteenth-century thought. Another cause of "modernizing" Ralegh's beliefs is the application of some of his skeptical arguments to fields in which they were, for him, inoperative.

An example of the modernizing interpretation of Ralegh is found in remarks by Mr. V. T. Harlow,[53] who has assembled in

[52] In a chapter on "Ralegh's Religion," R. W. Battenhouse, *op. cit.*, pp. 50–68, rightly emphasizes Ralegh's Platonism; but here as elsewhere in his book, notably in the preceding chapter on "Elizabethan Religion and Atheism," Mr. Battenhouse exaggerates the dominance of natural theology over Christian revelation, of ethical teaching over salvation through Christ. The stress on rational proofs of God's existence is explained in part, as I have shown in chap. iii, by the desire to convince unbelievers out of their own favorite authors rather than out of Scripture. In discussing what he considers Ralegh's preference for humanistic philosophy over Christian doctrine, Mr. Battenhouse neglects Ralegh's heavy use of Scripture and occasionally falls into errors of fact: e.g., p. 64, "When arguing for the immortality of the soul [Ralegh] appeals not to Scripture but to the philosophers and to nature," whereas in *A Treatise of the Soul* the heaviest concentration of Scriptural references is in the brief discussion of immortality (*Works*, VIII, 590). For an excellent statement of the "marriage" of philosophy and religion in Renaissance thought see Arnold Williams, "The Two Matters: Classical and Christian in the Renaissance," *Studies in Philology,* XXXVIII (1941), 158–64.

[53] For the opinions here cited or quoted see his edition of *The Discovery of Guiana* (London, 1928), Introd., pp. xxxii–xxxviii.

two useful and well-edited volumes the principal materials dealing with Ralegh's voyages to Guiana. Following in part Miss U. M. Ellis-Fermor's acceptance of a close friendship between Marlowe and Ralegh, "well attested by documentary evidence," Mr. Harlowe finds in the two men a kinship of belief which in Marlowe's short lifetime remained negative but from which Ralegh evolved a great Neo-Platonic concept of God, stated in the famous opening lines of the *History*. A passage in Chapter II on the freedom of choice which God granted Adam *before the Fall* Mr. Harlow reads as expressive of man's hope, his freedom "to fashion himself after the Divine Image by a progressive discernment" of the reality of truth. As we have just seen, the sequel, in Ralegh's chapter, to God's gift of freedom is grimly orthodox: "For man having a free will and liberal choice purchased by disobedience his own death and mortality. . . ." This misinterpretation of Ralegh's words on man's freedom of choice leads to the most extreme statement in Mr. Harlow's analysis of Ralegh's religious beliefs:

In thus asserting that God was Light and man a rational being who, by virtue of that faculty, was capable of continuous progress by focussing within himself the beams which emanated from the Light, Ralegh was far removed from the current belief that truth could only be communicated to man by revelation in the Scriptures. Equally opposed are his views to the Calvinistic theory of predestination. He was, in fact, enunciating ideas that were identical with the teaching of the Cambridge Platonists some fifty years later. With him as with them the human faculty of reason was the ultimate authority and also the token of man's kinship with God.

But neither the Middle Ages nor the Renaissance regarded revelation as the "only" means by which truth, even God's truth, could be communicated to man, although the Scriptures were indeed believed the most certain revelation of truth ever vouchsafed to man. Ralegh, far from assigning "ultimate authority" to the faculty of reason, yielded that finality to the Scriptures, no

Of God and the Soul

matter what the tax on human credulity might be. Both the scope of natural theology in the Renaissance and the vitality of the Platonic tradition are seriously underrated when a distinguished amateur like Ralegh is praised because, unlike Bacon, "he extended the bounds of philosophy into the realm of religion. By so doing he became the greatest ethical philosopher of his time and one of the first teachers of Christian Platonism in England." To challenge these extravagant claims for his work one need not minimize at all the great esteem in which the *History* was held for more than two centuries, largely because of its ethical teaching.

A second cause of "modernizing" Ralegh's thought, the unwarranted linking of his essay *The Skeptic* to his speculations on religious problems, may be noted in passing. Miss U. M. Ellis-Fermor finds it "clear that the contents of the Baines libel [against Marlowe] has much in common with *The Skeptic*." Mr. Harlow writes that Ralegh and his circle "questioned and rejected many accepted tenets of Christian faith. The point of view is admirably expressed in Ralegh's treatise, *The Skeptic*. . . ." According to Miss M. C. Bradbrook, "The Preface to *The History of the World* reiterates the substance of *The Skeptic* in a condensed form." [54] For the first, I fail to see any connection between Marlowe's alleged anti-scriptural and anti-clerical utterances and Ralegh's reflections on the limitations of sensory knowledge. As we shall see, *The Skeptic* is strictly limited in origin and purpose; there is no evidence that Ralegh intended his incomplete summary of the skeptical tropes to be applied to religious problems. The fundamental error in all these statements is that when Ralegh himself brings skeptical arguments to bear upon religion, as in the preface to the *History*, it is to support the Christian faith,

[54] Ellis-Fermor, *Christopher Marlowe* (London, 1927), p. 163; Harlow, *op. cit.*, p. xxxiii; Bradbrook, *The School of Night* (Cambridge, England, 1936), p. 61. But a discussion of Ralegh's ideas on the limitations of human reason cannot be confined to the topical limits of this chapter; see below, chap. vii.

not to question its tenets. Here again he is one with the Christian apologists, who used the Pyrrhonic system to defend religion by attacking human learning.⁵⁵

III

> Whom do you know or have heard that hath spoken against the truth of God His Holy Word revealed to us in the Scriptures of the Old and New Testament? or of some places thereof? or have said those Scriptures are not to be believed and defended by Her Majesty for doctrine, and faith, and salvation, but only of policy, or civil government, and when and where was the same?

If the philosophical element in Ralegh's ideas on God and the soul lends itself to some misreading of Ralegh's position, the danger is eliminated when we turn to his forthright "answers" to the questions which the Cerne Abbas investigators asked about Scripture and salvation. One item in Parsons' bill of particulars against "Sir Walter Ralegh's school of atheism" is that therein "both Moses and our Savior, the Old and New Testament are jested at, and the scholars taught among other things to spell God backwards." A note by Aubrey, followed by Wood, specifically charges Harriot with undermining the Scriptures and teaching his doctrine to Ralegh:

> He made a philosophical theology, wherein he cast off the Old Testament, and then the New one would (consequently) have no foundation. He was a deist. His doctrine he taught to Sir Walter Ralegh, [to] Henry, Earl of Northumberland, and some others. The divines of those times looked on his manner of death as a judgment upon him for nullifying the Scripture.⁵⁶

Far from accepting this alleged nullification, Ralegh finds in

---

⁵⁵ G. T. Buckley, *op. cit.*, pp. 146–49, comments on this Christian use of skeptical arguments and shows Ralegh's indebtedness in *The Skeptic* to Sextus Empiricus. Although skepticism was thus enlisted in the cause of Christianity, there was some distrust of the ally; for example, Thomas Nashe blamed the "Pyrrhonics" for contributing to the atheists' disbelief in hell. See above, chap. iii, note 48. ⁵⁶ *Brief Lives*, I, 287.

Of God and the Soul 133

the Scriptures his one unquestionable authority, and devotes to the agreement of the Testaments an entire section, of which the following passage on authorship is typical:

In the Author they agree, because both are of God, and therefore both one Testament and will of God in substance of doctrine. For as there was ever one church, so was there one covenant, one adoption, and one doctrine. As the old law doth point at Christ so doth the new law teach Christ; the old proposing him as to come, the new as already come; one and the same thing being promised in both; both tending to one, and the same end; even the salvation of our souls: which according to St. Peter is the end of our faith.[57]

Even in "a matter but for the testimony of the Scriptures exceeding all belief" [58] the divinely inspired word is final. Again and again Ralegh turns for the solution of some debated point to the Bible, holding up to his readers the simplicity and finality of the scriptural text in contrast to the varying opinions found in profane writers and the commentaries.[59] But it is not amiss to cite profane writers, when there is agreement among them, to show their agreement with the Scriptures: St. Paul did so, and "Truth (saith St. Ambrose) by whomsoever uttered, is of the Holy Ghost." [60] Reason is second in authority to Holy Writ,[61] and Ralegh's God derides the wisdom of worldly men who "rely on the inventions of their own most feeble and altogether darkened understanding." [62] Nevertheless, the unquestioning acceptance of scriptural authority leaves a wide field for the operation of Ralegh's independence of mind; the historian's interest in second causes, whether in human actions or natural phenomena, is legitimate as long as the first cause is given priority. When

[57] II, iv, 11, p. 281.
[58] II, xvii, 9, p. 492. The comment is upon the amount of King David's treasure.
[59] E.g., I, i, 8, p. 12; I, vii, 10, pt. 15, p. 127; II, i, 7, p. 228; III, i, 5 and 6, pp. 9, 10, 13; III, i, 13, p. 23; III, ii, 3, p. 27.
[60] I, i, 2, p. 3; III, i, 4, pp. 6-7.
[61] I, vii, 10, pt. 2, p. 114; I, viii, 2 and 3, pp. 131, 133, 135.
[62] II, iii, 3, p. 250.

Scripture is silent, on a point not touching our salvation (the two provisions are stated frequently), one may in good conscience seek the answers to vexed questions by the use of reason.[63] Nor is there any harm in bringing reason to support a story related in Scripture, although admittedly man's faith should be sufficient without such merely human props.[64]

Finally, there remain the questions concerning Ralegh's religious faith in the specific terms of church doctrine and creed. Grouped in the Cerne Abbas interrogatory with inquiries about the creation and providence is the question, "Whom do you know or have heard that hath spoken . . . of the resurrection in a doubtful or contentious manner?" Did religion mean for Ralegh, as for Sir Thomas Browne, the Church of England? Aubrey credits a report of Ralegh's speech on the scaffold that omits all reference to Christ:

In his speech on the scaffold, I heard my cousin Whitney say (and I think 'tis printed) that he spake not one word of Christ, but of the great and incomprehensible God, with much zeal and adoration, so that he concluded he was an a-Christ, not an atheist.[65]

If Ralegh failed to satisfy "my cousin Whitney," he had better success with Dr. Robert Tounson, Dean of Westminster, who attended Ralegh in his last days and on the scaffold. At first afraid that the prisoner's cheerful contemplation of death was based upon pagan courage rather than Christian faith, Tounson found his admonitions answered "very Christianly, so that he satisfied me then, as I think he did all his spectators at his death." [66] The Dean's confidence is borne out by other observers, and his own comments were widely circulated. John Chamberlain, in a letter to Carleton, reports that Ralegh "died very religiously, and every way like a Christian, insomuch that the Dean of Westminster (they say) commends him exceedingly and says he was

---

[63] I, viii, 11, pt. 4, p. 157.

[64] E.g., I, viii, 15, pt. 6, p. 177; II, xxvii, 2, p. 615. Passages cited in note 61 are also relevant.

[65] *Brief Lives*, II, 188–89.   [66] Ralegh, *Works* (1829), VIII, 780–83.

Of God and the Soul

as ready and as able to give as take instruction." [67] One of the fullest accounts of Ralegh's execution survives in a manuscript in Archbishop's Sancroft's handwriting. According to this narration Ralegh denied by oath some of the charges against him, "as ever I hope to see God, or to have any benefit or comfort by the passion of my Savior." [68] A more circumstantial version has him concluding his address from the scaffold with a public profession of the faith already privately avowed in his counsels with the Dean:

> Then the Dean of Westminster asked him in what faith or religion he meant to die; he said, "In the faith professed by the Church of England, and that he hoped to be saved and to have his sins washed away by the precious blood and merits of our Savior Christ." [69]

The profound impression made by Ralegh lived on in tradition, fairly represented in the next generation by Francis Osborne's epigrammatic phrasing of the story: "His death was by him managed with so high and religious a resolution, as if a Roman had acted a Christian, or rather a Christian a Roman." [70]

Not that his last speech passed entirely without question; one man, at least, felt that nothing in Ralegh's life became him like the leaving of it. Sir Lewis Stukeley, popularly considered Ralegh's betrayer and rechristened "Sir Judas," tried to remove the effect of Ralegh's allegations against him. He offered to take the sacrament publicly and swear to the truth of his testimony against Ralegh, "but Sir Thomas Badger told him in good company, that all that would not serve his turn, unless he should

---

[67] *The Letters of John Chamberlain*, ed. N. E. McClure, 2 vols. (Philadelphia, 1939), II, 178. Similar reports appear in other letters of the time: cf. Sir Edward Harwood to Carleton, in *Cal. State Papers, Dom.*, *1611–18*, p. 588; Thomas Lorkin to Sir Thomas Puckering, in Arthur Cayley, *Life of Ralegh*, 2 vols. (London, 1805), I, App. XVII.   [68] Ralegh, *Works* (1829), VIII, 776.

[69] David Jardine, *Criminal Trials*, 2 vols. (London, 1832–35), I, 508. In his general introduction (I, 37–38), Jardine comments on the variations in the reports of state trials, and his observation holds good in some measure for contemporary accounts of executions.

[70] *Memoirs of Elizabeth and James*, in *Works* (1682), p. 429. Osborne was a young man at the time of Ralegh's execution.

be presently hanged and so seal it with his death." [71] In a "humble petition" to the King, Stukeley publicized his grievances, reproved Ralegh for lack of charity following upon a promise of forgiveness, and proclaimed him an angel of darkness who "did put on him the shape of an angel of light at his departure."

All men have long known that this man's whole life was a mere sophistication, and such was his death, in which he borrowed some tincture of holiness, which he was thought not to love in his life, therewith to cover his hatred of others in his death.[72]

King James and Sir Francis Bacon, embarrassed by the largeness of speech permitted the condemned Ralegh, could not afford such bluntness as Stukeley employed. Reluctantly they left to God Almighty the right to judge Ralegh's solemn oaths, "For sovereign princes cannot make a true judgment upon the bare speeches or asseverations of a delinquent at the time of his death, but their judgment must be founded upon examinations, reexaminations, and confrontments, and such like real proofs. . . ." [73]

One need not share the defensiveness of Stukeley and Bacon to pose a reasonable question about the relevance of Ralegh's last speech to the beliefs of a lifetime. The Archbishop of Canterbury, for example, regarded Ralegh's confession of faith as praiseworthy amends for his earlier doubts and questions:

Sir Walter Ralegh amongst us did question God's being and omnipotency, which that just Judge made good upon himself in over-humbling his estate, but last of all in bringing him to an execution by law, where he died a religious and Christian death, God testifying his power in this, that he raised up of a stone a child unto Abraham.[74]

---

[71] *Letters of John Chamberlain*, ed. McClure, II, 180.

[72] *The Humble Petition and Information of Sir Lewis Stucley* (London, 1618), p. 2. According to John Chamberlain (*Letters*, ed. McClure, II, 191), Stukeley's pamphlet was written by Dr. Lionel Sharpe. The same letter bears the news that Stukeley "is now most commonly known and called by the name of Sir Judas Stukeley."

[73] *A Declaration of the Demeanor and Carriage of Sir Walter Ralegh* (London, 1618), sig. I2^{r-v}.

[74] George Abbot, Archbishop of Canterbury, to Sir Thomas Roe, in *Cal. State Papers, Colonial, East Indies, 1617–21*, p. 247.

Of God and the Soul

The Archbishop's letter brings us back to the question in a modified form: if the "deism" alleged by Aubrey does not appear in Ralegh's speech on the scaffold, is it found in other speeches or in his works?

Some readers have remarked upon the lack of references to Christ in the *History*. But the omission appears noteworthy only in comparison with the frequent appeals to God's providence and justice. Allusions to Christ appear in two passages already quoted [75] in this chapter, and the phrasing of both these and like references indicates tacit acceptance of Christian doctrine rather than the grudging concessions of doubt. The words of Christ are quoted in a passage arguing man's inability to comprehend God; the New Testament is to be read as if Christ himself had set it down; the first commandment squares with human reason, for if men acknowledged many gods there would be far greater strife than that which we now have "even among those nations which acknowledge one God and one Christ"; man is saved not by the wood of the cross but by reverence of the Father and "the faith in his Son, which shed his blood" on the cross.[76] Such references and assumptions are found also in *A Treatise of the Soul*.

Up to this point illustrations of Ralegh's beliefs have been drawn chiefly from *The History of the World*, because it is Ralegh's major work and was published in his lifetime, and from *A Treatise of the Soul* because of its subject. This method, however, does not convey an adequate idea of the extent to which a religious point of view permeates many of Ralegh's writings and recorded utterances. His digressions on the ways of God, his advice to his son, several of his letters and poems, all bespeak a religious faith which Ralegh found compatible with the exercise of an inquiring mind. The point of view of the *History* is reflected in such works of "policy" as *The Cabinet-Council* and *The Maxims of State:* the first rule of policy is to observe

---

[75] See above, pp. 115, 118.

[76] These illustrative references are all from the *History:* I, i, 6, p. 6; I, vii, 10, pt. 15, p. 127; II, iv, 14, p. 287; II, xv, 2, 460–61. The list could be extended to more than a score of references in the first two books of the *History*.

the true worship of God; want of religion is the first cause of the decay of a state; God's providence protects good kings and is likewise the first cause of civil wars; as it is the greatest merit to introduce true religion into a country, so it is the greatest infamy to introduce atheism.[77] Formal advice to his son concludes with no less formal admonitions to serve God. The letter to his wife when he expected execution in 1603 became a minor classic in the seventeenth century, if one may judge from the frequency of printed and manuscript copies. Neither it nor the grief-stricken letter on the death of young Walter in Guiana fourteen years later reads like the work of a belated convert. In his letter of consolation to Sir Robert Cecil on the death of Lady Cecil a settled religious philosophy appears even through the conventions of Elizabethan moralizing.[78] Lastly, a few of his poems carry this note of religious conviction. The criticism of the church in *The Lie*,

> Say to the Church it shows
> What's good, and doth no good,

is aimed not at religion but at the failure of a human institution to attain its spiritual goals, a failure remarked by priests as well as by poets. In *The Passionate Man's Pilgrimage*, Ralegh looks forward to the justice of "heaven's bribeless hall" with greater confidence than his experience warranted him to place in earthly courts:

> For there Christ is the King's Attorney:
> Who pleads for all without degrees,
> For he hath angels, but no fees.

[77] These references, in the order cited, are from *Works* (1829), VIII, 10, 30, 62 and 82, 97.

[78] For the letter to Cecil see Edward Edwards, *Life of Ralegh*, 2 vols. (London, 1868), II, 161–63; for the letters to Lady Ralegh, II, 284–87 and 359–63. Religious expressions are quite common in the letters but often have no more significance than the conventional modes of salutation and farewell. The letters which I have singled out and a few others are in the highly personal vein of private communication.

Of God and the Soul

> When the grand twelve million jury,
> Of our sins with sinful fury,
> Gainst our souls black verdicts give,
> Christ pleads his death, and then we live, . . .

And the concluding couplet of what is probably his best-known stanza epitomizes Christian faith:

> And from which Earth, and Grave, and Dust,
> The Lord shall raise me up I trust.[79]

IV

A number of things about Ralegh's questions and the Reverend Ralph Ironside's answers on the nature of God and the soul are clearer in the context of the treatises discussed in Chapter III and of Ralegh's own writings than they are in isolation.[80] Ironside at first maintained a sound pastoral position in telling Carew Ralegh, who began the questioning, "better it were that we would be careful how the souls might be saved, than to be curious in finding out their essence." Then Sir Walter, giving a more serious turn to his brother's question—"Soul, . . . what is that?"—asked that the minister answer the question "for their instruction." Despite his Oxford training and his conversations with diverse, said Sir Walter, "in this point (to wit what the reason-

---

[79] For the poems quoted see the edition by Agnes M. C. Latham (London, 1929) pp. 43–47, 64, and notes. Virgil B. Heltzel, "Ralegh's 'Even Such Is Time,'" *Huntington Library Bulletin*, No. 10 (1936), pp. 185–88, notes the publication of Ralegh's "epitaph" in 1619, with the heading, "By Sir W. R. which he writ the night before his execution." This early publication brings close to the actual date of Ralegh's death the tradition that he composed his "epitaph" (in fact, the couplet added to an earlier stanza) the night before his execution.

[80] For the circumstances of the inquiry at Cerne Abbas, see above, chap. ii. As I have already indicated (chap. ii, note 70), I follow the report of the inquiry as published by G. B. Harrison, checked by F. C. Danchin's version and a microfilm of the manuscript. In the quotations which follow the MS reads *"imediatum principuum,"* with the last letters of *"principuum"* confused. Harrison incorrectly reads *"minus"* for *"maius"* in *"totum est maius quamlibet sua parte."*

able soul of man is) have I not by any been resolved. They tell us it is *primus motor* the first mover in a man, etc." Taking up this cue, Ironside left a safe theology for a debatable and academic psychology; he replied by distinguishing between the soul as the cause of motion and the brain or heart as the "first mover." Urged to explain further, and "hearing Sir Walter Ralegh tell of his dispute and scholarship some time in Oxford," Ironside had recourse to Aristotle, *De Anima,* Book II, first section, for a definition of the reasonable soul as "Actus primus corporis organici animantis humani vitam habentis in potentia." [81] Ralegh objected that the definition was obscure and intricate; Ironside demurred that it could not be to Sir Walter, who was learned, but since it must seem so to most of those present he would be content to say with divines (and here he returns to safe ground) "that the reasonable soul is a spiritual and immortal substance breathed into man by God, whereby he lives and moves and understandeth, and so is distinguished from other creatures."

At this point the issue was joined on what constitutes a definition.

"Yea but what is that spiritual and immortal substance breathed into man, etc.," sayeth Sir Walter.

"The soul," quoth I.

"Nay then," sayeth he, "you answer not like a scholar."

Hereupon I endeavored to prove that it was scholarlike, nay in such disputes as these, usual, and necessary to run *in circulum* partly because *definitio rei* was *primum et immediatum principium,* and seeing *primo non est prius,* a man must of necessity come backward and partly because *definitio* and *definitum* be *nature reciproce* the one convertibly answering unto the question made upon the other. As for example, if one ask what is a man? you will say he is a creature reasonable and mortal; but if you ask again, what is a creature reasonable and mortal, you must of force come backward, and answer, it is a man. *Et sic de ceteris.*

Now Ironside, who studied at Oxford when the curriculum

---

[81] In a modern text, "the first grade of actuality of a natural body having life potentially in it." *Works of Aristotle,* ed. W. D. Ross, III (Oxford, 1931), 412^a.

Of God and the Soul

was dominated by Aristotelianism,[82] may be faithful to his logic here, but again he is shifting the argument from the teachings of Scripture to the principles of contemporary philosophy. He is, with one important difference, in the position of the apologists who maintain that there is no disputing about principles and then proceed to rationalize them. Parsons, Mornay, and their fellows, however, first make it clear that they regard the principles as self-evident and that they concede a rational demonstration of the principles only because of the obstinate wickedness of the age. Ironside differs in his emphasis: he argues, for the moment, not from the principles as simply self-evident nor from philosophical demonstrations of the principles, but from logic. He is therefore vulnerable to a logical retort.

"But we have principles in our mathematics," sayeth Sir Walter, "as *totum est maius quamlibet sua parte*, and ask me of it, and I can show it in the table, in the window, in a man, the whole being bigger than the parts of it."

As we have seen, this axiom is the very analogue used by the apologists to claim an equal privilege for first principles in divinity. Although Ironside still does not make as strong a reply (in the natural theology of his day) as he might, he does bring the dialogue back to the original question, "what."

I replied first that he showed *quod est*, not, *quid est*, that it was but not what it was; secondly, that such demonstration as that was against the nature of man's soul being a spirit. For as his things being sensible were subject to the sense, so man's soul being insensible was to be discerned by the spirit. Nothing more certain in the world than that there is a God, yet being a spirit to subject him to the sense otherwise than perfected it is impossible.

All of which is sound sixteenth-century doctrine: the apologists and Ralegh himself agree that neither man's soul nor God can

[82] Some idea of the limitations of study at Oxford may be formed from an order, in 1585/86, calling upon the students in their disputations to "lay aside their various authors" and "only follow Aristotle and those that defend him." See Frances A. Yates, "Giordano Bruno's Conflict with Oxford," *Journal of the Warburg Institute*, II (1939), 227–42; quotation, p. 230.

be perceived directly, or otherwise than in the effects, by any human means. Ralegh cites man's ignorance of his own soul as evidence of his presumption in seeking to explain the creation; he asserts that "they go mad with reason that inquire" too curiously after the essence of God and the nature of his power; as Ironside distinguishes between "that" and "what" so Ralegh distinguishes between "that" and "how." [83] His language, indeed, is stronger than Ironside's. But on this occasion he is not satisfied and he pursues his quest of an answer to an unanswerable "what?"

"Marry," quoth Sir Walter, "these two [God and the Soul] be like for neither could I learn hitherto what God is." Mr. Fitzjames ventured something about Aristotle's saying that God is *"Ens entium."* Mr. Ironside willingly conceded that there might be some uncertainty in history about the manner of Aristotle's death and his last words; "but that God was *ens entium*, a thing of things, having being of himself and giving being to all creatures, it was most certain, and confirmed by God himself unto Moses."

"Yea but what is this *ens entium?*" sayeth Sir Walter.

I answered, "It is God."

And being disliked as before Sir Walter wished that grace might be said; "For that," quoth he, "is better than this disputation." Thus supper ended and grace said, I departed to Dorchester with my fellow minister, and this to my remembrance is the substance of that speech which Sir Walter Ralegh and I had at Wolveton.

Ironside's brief but vivid record has the authority of a factual report written by a man who had been counseled to eschew hearsay and to limit his remarks to what he knew at first hand. But this very quality has its defects: the document as it stands is an open invitation to read between the lines, and that process has led to a variety of interpretations, generally exaggerating the liberalism of the debate. Certain constructions put upon words of Ralegh are obviously not justified: notably, in the months

---

[83] See above, pp. 102–103.

Of God and the Soul

following the supper party, that Sir Walter had had "some reasoning against the deity of God and His omnipotency"; or that he had argued "touching the being, or immortality of the soul, or such like." Ironside tried to set that straight by cautioning the inquisitive John Davis that "the matter was not as the voice of the country reported thereof," and Davis repeated the correction along with the rumors. The brief debate, as reported, concerns solely the definition of God and of the soul; neither the deity of God nor the immortality of the soul is questioned.[84] In a different manner from the good people of Dorset, some modern scholars have misconstrued Ralegh's remarks by attributing to them an esoteric quality which they do not have. At Trenchard's supper table in 1593 and in formal writings two decades later Sir Walter said that he did not know what God is or what the soul is, and he was in good company in his ignorance. Then why, it may be fairly asked, did he refuse to accept Ironside's comparatively mild statement of the position? A ready answer, not infrequently given, is to find a difference between the religious beliefs of Ralegh in 1593 and 1614. An answer more consistent with Ironside's testimony and Ralegh's writings is forthcoming when we distinguish between the content, even the language, of the debate and Ironside's logical method.

As for the content, the uncertainty of man's knowledge of his own soul is no less a commonplace in Elizabethan literature than his corresponding ignorance of God's essence. Ignorance, however, was no bar to speculation, and the accumulations of two millennia continued to grow. In John Marston's *What You Will* the topic is a convenient symbol of profitless university studies when Lampatho reflects that long nights of poring over books produced no more wisdom than his spaniel acquired in a sound sleep:

[84] Not in the conversation of Ironside and Sir Walter. The only suggestion of doubt in the incident as reported by Ironside is in Carew Ralegh's question—"Soul, what is that?"—when the minister tells him that the wages of sin is the death of the soul and the body. Carew apparently attempted to turn aside flippantly a deserved reproof for his "loose speeches."

Of God and the Soul

>   . . . first *an sit anima,*
> Then, and it were mortal. O hold, hold! at that
> They're at brain-buffets, fell by the ears amain
> Pell-mell together; still my spaniel slept.
> Then whether 'twere corporeal, local, fix'd
> Extraduce; but whether 't had free will
> Or no, ho philosophers
> Stood banding factions all so strongly propp'd
> I stagger'd, knew not which was firmer part;
> But thought, quoted, read, observ'd and pried,
> Stuff'd noting-books: and still my spaniel slept.
> At length he waked and yawn'd and by yon sky,
> For ought I know he knew as much as I.[85]

At the opposite pole of popular literature, the righteous Owen Felltham gives an opinion which even in language resembles one of Ralegh's statements in the preface to the *History:*

'Tis certain, man hath a soul; and as certain, that it is immortal. But what and how it is, in the perfect nature and substance of it, I confess, my human reason could never so inform me as I could fully explain it to my own apprehension. O my God! what a clod of moving ignorance is man! when all his industry cannot instruct him, what himself is; when he knows not that, whereby he knows that he does not know it.[86]

On another intellectual plane the idea appears in Sir John Davies' much-admired poem on the soul, *Nosce Teipsum:*

> For how may we to others' things attain,
>   When none of us his own soul understands?
> For which the devil mocks our curious brain,
>   When, Know thyself, his oracle commands.

---

[85] *What You Will,* II, ii, 168-80, in *The Works of John Marston,* ed. A. H. Bullen, 3 vols. (London, 1887), II, 363-64. The lines quoted are part of an extended passage in which Lampatho traces his career through earnest study into the doubt engendered by too much learning—
  "The more I learnt the more I learnt to doubt:
   Knowledge and wit, faith's foes, turn faith about"—
until he reached a dubious state of Socratic wisdom:
  "I know I know naught but I naught do know."

[86] *Resolves* (London, 1628), pp. 183-84.

> For why should we the busy soul believe,
>   When boldly she concludes of that and this;
>   When of herself she can no judgment give,
>   Nor how, nor whence, nor where, nor what she is.[87]

There is nothing to shock his listeners in the language used by Ralegh. Indeed there are some rough analogues in Thomas Morton's *Treatise of the Nature of God* (1599) to Ralegh's disclaimer of benefits from his Oxford studies and conversations with "diverse." Morton's treatise is in the form of a dialogue between two travelers, a gentleman and a scholar, who improve the time with religious discourse. The gentleman, though a firm believer, asks leading questions in order to arm himself with better reasons for his beliefs; but he takes exception to the vagueness of the scholar's definition of God:

I have heard and read many discourses of this matter, yet never knew I any take such a course as to define one thing by another, and to jumble up into one definition things of diverse natures, as you do in defining God to be an infinite angel or a reasonable air; for thus you make a monster of him, as it were an hermaphrodite, half of one nature and half of another, half reasonable and half unreasonable.[88]

The clue to the significance of Ralegh's impatience with Ironside's definitions lies not in any fundamental disagreement in belief nor in any irreverence in speech. Ralegh was dissatisfied, both temperamentally and intellectually, with Ironside's logic. By shifting from faith to logical argument and back to faith again, Ironside weakened his case, all the more because Sir Walter was no respecter of Aristotle and even on the definition of the soul gave his opinions only a qualified acceptance. There could have been no disagreement had Ironside answered solely out of Scripture and maintained that one must accept on faith the evidence of things unseen. But granted the premises that the Bible is a

---

[87] *Poetry of the English Renaissance*, ed. H. W. Hebel and H. H. Hudson (New York, 1932), p. 360.

[88] Pp. 78–79. The passage is quoted only for its style. Actually the gentleman is quite content with a definition in the proper form; Ironside could have satisfied him.

Christian's adequate authority for belief in God and immortality, and that the human mind is too frail an instrument to penetrate such mysteries, speculation was still permissible—witness the countless words of Elizabethan divines who, professing to find God inexplicable in human terms, proceeded to explain him. There is good reason to believe that Ralegh found such speculation congenial (as many a passage from the *History* quoted in this chapter shows), but no good reason to infer that it exceeded the bounds of religious propriety.

Ralegh loved debate with friend or foe: with the Jesuit priest, Father Cornelius; with a captured navigator, Sarmiento; the captured Governor of El Dorado, Antonio de Berrio; in the groups which Sir John Harington mentions; even, for that matter, when his life was at stake.[89] Sir Dudley Carleton wrote of Ralegh at his trial in 1603: "He answered with that temper, wit, learning, courage and judgment, that save that it went with the hazard of his life, it was the happiest day that ever he spent."[90] More to the immediate point is the statement which, in Aubrey's disconnected style, seems to suggest cause and effect: "He was scandalized with atheism; but he was a bold man, and would venture at discourse which was unpleasant to the church-men."[91] If we are to interpret his remarks beyond the plain meaning of Ironside's text, Sir Walter on this occasion welcomed an opening for philosophical discussion on the nature of the soul even though he knew full well that such discourse could never be conclusive. But Ironside preferred his circular definitions, logical according to his instruction but not conducive to an enlightening discussion. Further, his definitions represented an authority and a logical method which Ralegh did not accept in their entirety. When his logic was rejected, Ironside fell back upon

---

[89] For Father Cornelius and Sir John Harington, see above, chap. ii. Ralegh himself tells of his entertainment of Sarmiento, in the *History*, II, xxiii, 4, p. 574; see also above, chap. ii, note 50. For Berrio, see *The Discovery of Guiana*, ed. V. T. Harlow (London, 1928), pp. lxxxvii–viii, 15, 34, 75, and *passim*.

[90] *State Trials*, ed. T. B. Howell, II (London, 1816), 47–48.

[91] *Brief Lives*, II, 188.

Of God and the Soul 147

faith and the Scriptures, which no one present questioned. Disappointed of his hope either for profitable conversation or for lively debate, Ralegh terminated the discussion by calling for grace to be said—an ironic conclusion if the conversation were as radical as it has sometimes been painted. If Ralegh were heretical in this colloquy, his heresy was philosophical, not religious; as Ironside presented his case, Ralegh was rebellious against Aristotle and school logic, not against Scripture or belief in immortality. In that rebellion, from which the word of God is specifically exempt, lies the key to much of Ralegh's thought, to his sometimes unhealthy reputation with the churchmen, and to his contemporary influence.

Chapter 5

Of the Architecture of Fortune

We profess that we know God, but by works we deny him. . . . We are all, in effect, become comedians in religion; and while we act in gesture and voice divine virtues, in all the course of our lives we renounce our persons and the parts we play

History, Preface, sig. C2ᵛ

THE MOST INCLUSIVE of Elizabethan definitions of "atheism" is that based upon wrongdoing. The reasoning is syllogistic: men who risk their immortal souls through evil deeds do not sincerely follow God's commands and do not believe in the life to come; this man is guilty of evil deeds; therefore he does not believe in God or immortality. By such reasoning few of the sons of Adam could escape the charge of atheism, and of those whose high office or prominence involved them in controversy few did escape. In this vein of wholesale condemnation, the Richard Cholmeley who figures prominently in the charges against Marlowe is reported to have said of the Queen's Counsellors that they "have profound wits, be sound atheists, and their lives and deeds show that they think their souls do end, vanish, and perish with their bodies." [1] The ease with which one could attach to human frailties this charge of "inward atheism" made it a popular weapon in irresponsible

---

[1] F. C. Danchin, "Études critiques sur Christophe Marlowe," *Revue-Germanique*, IX (1913), 577; from Harleian MS 6848. There is more than a suggestion of this "syllogism" in Robert Parsons' invective against the Council, especially Lord Burghley, described in chap. ii. See also Ralegh's note on the slanderous use of the epithet "atheist," quoted above, beginning of chap. iii.

Of the Architecture of Fortune

controversy. Further, the malicious discrediting of an opponent was recognized by the Elizabethans as a Machiavellian technique. But when due allowance is made for careless abuse and deliberate slander, there still remains (as a number of writers quoted in Chapter III bear witness) a large area of sincere belief in honest living as one measure of true religion.

Quite clearly, Ralegh was the victim of the "smear" technique as practiced by such adversaries as the Jesuits or the partisans of Essex. Just as clearly, even a less ambitious man than Ralegh could not have survived a long career at court without arousing —in this frame of reference—the suspicions of good citizens free of personal bias. Ralegh himself acknowledged on the scaffold this Elizabethan concept of the spiritual significance of one's course of life—his own, he confessed, one of "vanity." I have been, he said, "a sea-faring man, a soldier, and a courtier; the least of these were able to overthrow a good mind, and a good man." [2] In the face of such an acknowledgment and of such agreement in principle, it is enough merely to cite some of the most disputed actions of Ralegh's life to show how they could be judged, either in vindictive hostility or grave admonition, as evidence of inward atheism. A few have already figured in this story, among the criticisms recorded at the time of Ralegh's greatest unpopularity; for example, the ambiguous, but still sinister, letter to Cecil about Essex, and his attempt at suicide.[3]

---

[2] *Works of Sir Walter Ralegh* (Oxford, 1829), VIII, 779. This report of his words is corroborated by John Chamberlain in a letter to Carleton; see Chamberlain's *Letters*, ed. N. E. McClure (1939), II, 176–77.

[3] See above, chap. ii, footnotes 85 and 89. John Shirley, an early biographer of Ralegh, surmised that his seduction of Elizabeth Throckmorton may have earned him the title of "atheist"; see below, chap. viii. Some scurrilous anecdotes concerning Ralegh and his son Walter, reported by John Aubrey, are omitted from Andrew Clark's edition of the *Brief Lives*, 2 vols. (Oxford, 1898), because "the turbulence attributed to Sir Walter Raleigh seems to have made his name in the next age the centre of aggregation of quite a number of coarse stories" (Preface). Clark's explanation is probably correct: all ages have a way of fastening such stories upon notable persons. The anecdotes are included in more recent editions of Aubrey's papers: *The Scandals and Credulities of John Aubrey*, ed. John Collier (London, 1931); and *Aubrey's Brief Lives*, ed. O. L. Dick (London, 1949).

150 Of the Architecture of Fortune

Another is his wiliness with his captors in 1618, especially his feigned illness, which he justified on the scaffold by the precedent of King David.[4] More general and inclusive, his political maneuverings in the years before the accession of James were devious and intricate, though not, on any evidence known, treasonable. Ralegh was simply playing the game of court politics, and how sorry an enterprise that could be at a Tudor court has been attested by poet and dramatist, courtier and preacher, essayist and historian.

To rest the case with a "nolo contendere" is not to stigmatize Ralegh a court villain but to recognize how easily the omnibus charge of "inward atheism" could be brought against him and how much it may have contributed to his reputation as an "atheist." Although as prone to rationalize as any mortal, Ralegh can be dispassionate and objective about moral issues as they touch himself. When the subject is broadened to a general consideration of the moral basis of the "architecture of fortune," of the rights and wrongs of gaining wealth and position, his writings are more consistent than their diversity in content and occasion would lead one to expect. Such discussions, since they are linked to his skepticism only by the loose connection of Elizabethen "inward atheism," can be reviewed briefly and selectively. Worthy of special notice, again because of Elizabethan emphasis, is Ralegh's treatment of Machiavelli and his writings.

I

Underlying all of Ralegh's discourses on morality is his providential interpretation of history, manifest throughout his great work. A specific framework for his scattered remarks is found in a few pages of the Preface,[5] which balance nicely his sense of the vanity of human wishes and a prudential regard for the demands of life in this world. The passage follows a long and

[4] *Works*, VIII, 777. In his *History of the World* (1614), II, xvii, 1, p. 478, Ralegh had duly noted this incident in the story of King David.

[5] Sigs. C2^r–D2^r. Unless otherwise noted, the ensuing quotations are from this passage.

Of the Architecture of Fortune

well-known commentary on the self-defeating ambitions and evil practices of the world's monarchs. Of what use, asks Ralegh, is it to adduce these past examples, when humanity remains ever the same, when we carefully forget the lessons of our own personal experience? We are even capable of persuading ourselves that "God hath given us letters patents to pursue all our irreligious affections with a *non obstante*." Since we are made of earth and inhabit it, since "the heavens are high, far off, and unsearchable," there is little wonder that our thoughts are earthly, less that worldly men cannot teach us the lessons which we are unwilling to learn from the divinely inspired writers of the Scriptures. Ralegh then launches into a sharp statement of the wide gap between our professions and our performances.

For although religion and the truth thereof be in every man's mouth, yea in the discourse of every woman, who for the greatest number are but "idols of vanity," what is it other than an universal dissimulation? We profess that we know God, but by works we deny him. For beatitude doth not consist in the knowledge of divine things, but in a divine life; for the devils know them better than men. "Beatitudo non est divinorum cognitio, sed vita divina." [6]

Christians are so occupied with religious contention, even to the point of war, murder, and massacre, that their strife has well nigh driven the practice of religion out of the world. If one were to judge from the disputations of men, "and not of their lives which dispute," one would conclude that their thoughts were fixed solely on the attainment of heaven, and that they regarded the world as an inn for temporary repose.

When on the contrary, besides the discourse and outward profession, the soul hath nothing but hypocrisy. We are all (in effect) become comedians in religion; and while we act in gesture and voice divine

---

[6] This observation is a commonplace of Renaissance moral philosophy. For example, Agrippa phrased it well in *Of the Vanity and Uncertainty of Arts and Sciences* (1569), chap. i: "For the true felicity consisteth not in the knowledge of goodness, but in a good life; not in understanding, but in living with understanding. For not the good understanding, but the good will joineth men unto God."

virtues, in all the course of our lives we renounce our persons and the parts we play. For charity, justice, and truth have but their being in terms, like the philosophers' *materia prima*.

Ralegh's indictment would fit well into a preacher's warning against "inward atheism." Elsewhere he states the issue more bluntly; discoursing upon law in general and upon man's duty, in love of God, to keep His commandments, Ralegh concludes: "Certainly he is but a liar that professeth to love God and neglecteth to observe the word of His will with all his power." True, the special grace of God is needed to enable a man to obey the commandments; but if we examine ourselves honestly we find that our own self-indulgence, rather than the difficulties of the commandments, is the cause of our disobedience.[7]

Continuing his prefatory development of the theme, Ralegh exposes the futility of worldly aims and success. As wealth increases, so do the demands upon it by the self-seeking followers of the rich man. The honor due to great men is not without merit, if it includes a right esteem of their inward qualities; otherwise, "what is the applause of the multitude but as the outcry of an herd of animals, who without the knowledge of any true cause, please themselves with the noise they make?"[8] As the world judges, honor is more likely to attend prosperous rascality than unprosperous virtue, and such honor is at the mercy of fickle fortune. If we seek the perquisites of greatness to benefit our posterity we are likewise deceived, for after death we shall have no knowledge of their glory, and the heavenly bliss which

---

[7] *History*, II, iv, 12, pp. 283–84. Immediately following in the same chapter (sections 13 and 14, pp. 284–88) Ralegh develops his argument that obedience to the commandments is within the reach of human endeavor, compares the Tenth Commandment with the judgment of Aristotle on continence, and reasons that, even if religion did not require it, observance of the Decalogue is essential to man's preservation and well-being.

[8] Pref., sig. C3ʳ. The phrasing is remarkably suggestive of Milton's lines in *Paradise Regained*, III, 49–51:

> And what the people but a herd confused,
> A miscellaneous rabble, who extol
> Things vulgar, and well weighed, scarce worth the praise?

will follow "the long and dark night of death" will be supreme above any earthly concerns.

How, then, are we to regard riches and honor? At this point the moralizing takes a prudential turn, and the question receives an answer no less characteristically Elizabethan than the indictment of worldliness from which it springs. "Shall we therefore value honor and riches at nothing? and neglect them as unnecessary and vain? Certainly no." The justification for valuing them is found in the degrees which the infinite wisdom of God has ordained among men no less than in the heavenly bodies and the creatures of the earth. Since rank is hereditary and since titles without the means to support them are merely pitiable, "I accompt it foolishness to condemn such a care, provided that worldly goods be well gotten and that we raise not our own buildings out of other men's ruins." By thus invoking the Elizabethan doctrine of degree Ralegh attempts to harmonize with a primary concern for eternal values a reasonable and honest concern for earthly wealth. But he turns immediately to reemphasize the transitoriness of this life. One man's wealth is as nothing in proportion to the whole world, and the longest life is an insignificant period in comparison with time forepast and time to come. Again, *vanitas vanitatum.*

Worst of all vanities is that of the man who, having placed his peculiar worldly ends before faith and honesty, cries for God's mercy when death approaches. Such an appeal is an affront to God, and the Scripture tells us "That God will not be mocked." Ralegh vents his sarcasm upon the hollowness of such a deathbed repentance

For what do they otherwise, that die this kind of well-dying, but say unto God as followeth? We beseech thee, O God, that all the falsehoods, forswearings, and treacheries of our lives past may be pleasing unto thee; that thou wilt for our sakes (that have had no leisure to do anything for thine) change thy nature (though impossible) and forget to be a just God; that thou wilt love injuries and oppressions, call ambition wisdom, and charity foolishness. For I shall prejudice my son

154 Of the Architecture of Fortune

(which I am resolved not to do) if I make restitution, and confess myself to have been unjust (which I am too proud to do) if I deliver the oppressed.

Yet for all this worldly concern, prosperity and adversity are alike momentary and interchangeable. "For there is no man so assured of his honor, of his riches, health, or life, but that he may be deprived of either or all the very next hour or day to come." Good and bad fortune are alike perishable in memory. Since God, "who is the Author of all our tragedies," has been impartial in assigning roles even to the great ones of this world, who have suffered startling reversals of fortune, why should humbler men complain? We change fortunes as actors change clothes.

Certainly there is no other account to be made of this ridiculous world than to resolve that the change of fortune on the great theatre is but as the change of garments on the less. For when on the one and the other every man wears but his own skin, the players are all alike.[9]

In these few pages of his Preface, which could stand alone as an "essay," Ralegh has touched upon some major themes of Elizabethan moralizing: the inconsistency of our professions and our deeds; the insignificance of human concerns in the face of eternity; the doctrine of degree; the mutability of human fortunes. His "essay" might be summarized thus: our first duty is to God; while we are in the world we may pursue its lawful ends, always with regard to honesty and God's commandments; yet, even though we may have a rightful concern for worldly interests, let us not forget that they are ephemeral, nor let us be dismayed by the reversals of fortune. Ralegh's concession to the practical demands of life occupies only a small part of this discourse, but the prudential note recurs in the remarks and comments scattered through the *History* and other works, notably in the *Instructions to His Son and to Posterity*.[10] Even in

---

[9] Pref., sig. D2^r; this concludes the section of the Preface here abstracted. Some other remarks by Ralegh on Fortune are quoted in the preceding chapter, as part of his discussion of Providence.

[10] *Works*, VIII, 557–70. Anthony à Wood prints an interesting letter from

this hardheaded treatise, however, the pragmatic wisdom neither neglects nor obscures ethical considerations, and the advice to his son ends with an emphatic admonition to serve God first. Not infrequently in his writings Ralegh attempts to square the decisions required by a specific situation with the high standard of religious conduct. He has no illusions about human frailty, in himself or others, in making such adjustments; men who can consistently value worldly vanities at their true worth and who can approach death with the "comfortable memory of a well-acted life" are as rare as black swans.[11]

Let us see how Ralegh's attempted reconciliation of the demands of worldly position and the demands of our higher duty to God applies to specific problems. Reflecting upon the punishment of Nebuchadnezzar for his pride in his great works, Ralegh remarks: "Surely I not only hold it lawful to rejoice in those good things wherewith God hath blessed us, but a note of much unthankfulness to entertain them with a sullen and unfeeling disposition." Yet the overweening pride of man in his own imagined worth "make us to reflect our thoughts upon our seeming inherent greatness, forgetting the whilst him to whom we are indebted for our very being." [12] But what is tolerated in the *History* is encouraged in the *Instructions,* wherein Ralegh urges upon his son the conservation of his estate: "Believe thy father in this, and print it in thy thought, that what virtue soever thou hast, be it never so manifold, if thou be poor withal, thou and thy qualities shall be despised." [13] There follows more advice on the blessings of wealth and the evils of poverty, again with the warning found in the Preface to the *History:*

---

young Walter's tutor to Ralegh concerning the boy's education (*Athenae Oxonienses* [1817], III, 169). For comment on the *Instructions* in relation to its genre see Siegmund A. E. Betz, "Francis Osborn's *Advice to a Son,*" *Seventeenth Century Studies,* 2d ser., ed. Robert Shafer (Princeton, N.J., 1937), pp. 61–62, and *passim.*

[11] Pref., sig. D1^v.   [12] *History,* III, i, 77, p. 21.

[13] *Works,* VIII, 565. Cf. *History,* II, xviii, 1, p. 496, in comment on Solomon's choice of wisdom: ". . . the desire of private riches is an affection of covetousness which God abhorreth."

156   Of the Architecture of Fortune

On the other side, take heed that thou seek not riches basely, nor attain them by evil means; destroy no man for his wealth, nor take any thing from the poor, for the cry and complaint thereof will pierce the heavens. And it is most detestable before God, and most dishonorable before worthy men, to wrest any thing from the needy and laboring soul.[14]

And Ralegh further commands charity to the poor, not "vagabonds and beggars, but those that labor to live." The advice quoted above from the Preface—"that we raise not our own buildings out of other men's ruins"—echoes his own plea to Sir Robert Carr, when the King's favorite was granted Ralegh's Sherborne estate.

And for yourself, Sir, seeing your day is but now in dawn and mine come to the evening . . . I beseech you not to begin your first buildings upon the ruins of the innocent, and that their griefs and sorrows do not attend your first plantation.[15]

Far more dangerous than the honest pursuit and enjoyment of riches is ambition,

. . . a monster that neither feareth God (though all-powerful, and whose revenges are without date and forever lasting) neither hath it respect to nature. . . . All other passions and affections by which the souls of men are tormented are by their contraries oftentimes resisted or qualified. But ambition, which begetteth every vice and is itself the child and darling of Satan, looketh only towards the ends by itself set down. . . . It was the first sin that the world had and began in Angels, for which they were cast into hell without hope of redemption. It was more ancient than man and therefore no part of his natural corruption. The punishment also preceded his creation, yet hath the Devil, which felt the smart thereof, taught him to forget the one as out of

---

[14] *Works, VIII*, p. 567.
[15] Edward Edwards, *Life of Ralegh*, 2 vols. (London, 1868), II, 327; Edwards, assigns the letter to 1609. The passage is cited for the striking parallel to the phrasing of the Preface. In the complex operation of his monopolies and in his office of Lord Warden of the Stannaries, Ralegh himself had been charged with burdensome taxation of the poor, though he was not without defenders. The financial transactions of his busy lifetime were, like those of most Elizabethans of prominence, exceedingly involved.

Of the Architecture of Fortune 157

date and to practise the other as befitting every age and man's condition.[16]

Ambition knows neither trust nor gratitude, for "benefits bind not the ambitious, but the honest." There are similar indictments in the *History* of the ills sometimes attendant upon ambition: covetousness, which neglects a present good in quest of what it does not need; unchristian pursuit of revenge; and envy which can endure to see a country harmed rather than a rival gain glory. All such passages are brief commentaries upon the events narrated; for example, the remark upon covetousness, a "curse upon mortal men" since the Creation, occurs in an aside of two sentences, in a sustained account of a Roman campaign in Sicily.[17] In his *Instructions*, Ralegh's advice to his son on problems within this broad compass is phrased in positive, rather than negative, terms: the choice of friends and wife; the avoiding of quarrels; the cultivation of sober and profitable conversation; conduct that will enhance one's dignity and prestige.

Ralegh's severest strictures are against oath-breaking, which he condemns as striking at the very roots of social order. His most extended commentary on the subject arises from Joshua's firm observance of faith in his dealings with the Gibeonites, even though his promise had been secured by deception. In this story,

. . . the doctrine of keeping faith is so plainly and excellently taught as it taketh away all evasion, it admitteth no distinction, nor leaveth open any hole or outlet at all to that cunning perfidiousness and horrible deceit of this latter age called "equivocation."

A violated oath is broken not to the man to whom the avowal of truth or the promise was made but to God, in whose name it was made. It is a "God-mocking equivocation" to swear one thing and to "reserve in silence a contrary intent." After drawing in a few examples of God's punishment of oath-breakers,

---

[16] *History*, II, xiii, 7, p. 432. For the brief quotation which follows, see *History*, IV, ii, 11, p. 190.

[17] V, i, 6, p. 349. Revenge: V, ii, 3, p. 389. Envy: II, xiii, 5, p. 426.

158 Of the Architecture of Fortune

even though the promises were made to infidels, Ralegh concludes his discourse, a full two pages long.

> But I will stay my hand; for this first volume will not hold the repetition of God's judgments upon faith-breakers, be it against infidels, Turks or Christians of diverse religions. Lamentable it is that the taking of oaths now-a-days is rather made a matter of custom than of conscience.[18]

As with many of Ralegh's ideas, the topic is a recurrent one in the *History* and may appear in unexpected places. An account of the deceptions practiced upon the Greeks by a Persian commander elicits a special condemnation of lying by men of great authority.

> A lie may find excuse when it grows out of fear, for that passion hath his original from weakness. But when power, which is a character of the Almighty, shall be made the supporter of untruth, the falsehood is most abominable. . . .[19]

In another passage, an instance of deception in the Punic Wars reminds Ralegh of a personal experience: hearing a French commander relate how his army had been attacked and cut to pieces after he had surrendered a town upon promise of safe and honorable departure. Turning back to his ancient example, the historian comments: "It needs not, therefore, seem strange that an heathen

---

[18] II, vi, 8, pp. 327–28. At the time of his execution, when he swore his innocence of some of the charges against him, Ralegh repeated this doctrine of the sanctity of an oath as a promise made to God. See *Works*, VIII, 776; for a more detailed record of his words, see David Jardine, *Criminal Trials*, 2 vols. (London, 1832–35), I, 504.

Following the Gunpowder Plot and the trial of the conspirators, "equivocation" was universally condemned in England as a vice of the Jesuits. In the trial of Garnett, Sir Edward Coke made some gratuitous comparisons of the Gunpowder Treason of 1605 with the alleged offenses of Ralegh in 1603. Handicapped by the fact that Ralegh had been in prison since 1603, Coke had to content himself with a favorite simile: "They all were joined in the ends, like Samson's foxes in the tails, howsoever severed in their heads." See *A True and Perfect Relation* (London, 1606), sig. K1^v. [19] III, x, 7, pp. 118–19.

tyrant should thus break his faith, since kings professing Christianity are bold to do the like or command their captains to do it for them." [20]

A suggested exception in one of these passages—that "a lie may find excuse when it grows out of fear"—is given more explicit statement in a severe paragraph against lying in the *Instructions*. The sharp warning to his son against lying concludes:

> Thus thou mayst see and find in all the books of God how odious and contrary to God a liar is; and for the world, believe it, that it never did any man good (except in the extremity of saving life); for a liar is of a base, unworthy, and cowardly spirit.[21]

Note that the significant parenthesis occurs in relation to the worldly profit of lying, and that neither here nor in the passage about lying out of fear is Ralegh speaking of a formal oath. Again it is tempting to digress into biographical detail, for Ralegh's wiliness in his last captivity, when he was beset by spies and maligned by malcontents of the last voyage to Guiana, seems to fall in this category. But all such detail is encompassed by Ralegh's own ingenuous confession that any of his several careers carried within it the seeds of moral confusion. Ralegh's reputation for veracity was none too good in the days of his greatest political activity, but many who knew him in his last days and who heard him speak from the scaffold were profoundly impressed by his sincerity.

All this staunch praise of honesty does not extend to complete and disarming openness. Ralegh seems to agree with Bacon, who wrote in his essay *Of Simulation and Dissimulation,* "That an habit of secrecy is both politic and moral."

---

[20] V, i, 4, pt. 4, pp. 336–37. A less flagrant instance of deception in war, drawn from personal experience in France, is cited in V, iii, 14, p. 497. Although there are a number of such allusions to bad faith, Ralegh does not mention in the *History* (so far as I know) the disputed circumstances of the surrender and massacre at Smerwick in 1580, when he served under Grey. Probably he shared the opinion of those who regarded the action as covered by the rules of war. [21] *Works,* VIII, 564–65.

160 Of the Architecture of Fortune

But he that makes himself a body of crystal that all men may look through him and discern all the parts of his disposition makes himself (withal) an ass, and thereby teacheth others either how to ride or drive him. Wise men, though they have single hearts in all that is just and virtuous, yet they are like coffers with double bottoms, which when others look into, being opened, they see not all that they hold on the sudden and at once.[22]

This aside is written in commendation of Hannibal, who dissembled his courage to trap a Spanish army. But just as Bacon distinguishes, in diminishing approval, gradations of dissimulation and simulation, so Ralegh has little use for the subtlety of an overreaching cunning.

Now although it were so, that Martius in very few of his actions behaved himself like a man of war, yet in exercise of cunning, which one hath most aptly termed "a crooked or sinister kind of wisdom," he dealt as a craftsmaster, with a restless working diligence. This indeed neither proved his sufficiency nor commended his honesty, since thereby he effected nothing to his own benefit; and, nevertheless, out of envy, vainglory, or such delight as weak and busy-headed men take in creating inexplicable troubles, he directly made opposition to the good of his country.[23]

Such judicious balancing of the virtues of reserve and the perils of dissembling in carrying on negotiations carries us over into the realm of policy as it applies to public as well as to private affairs. Although in these matters Ralegh seems to make broad concessions to the demands of practical politics, the moralist who constructed his *History* on the principle that "the judgments of God are forever unchangeable" and who found examples of "the bitter fruits of irreligious policy" [24] in ancient and modern times alike retains the ascendancy over the politician.

[22] *History*, V, iii, 1, p. 422.
[23] V, vi, 7, p. 749. The definition of cunning apparently is taken from the first sentence of Bacon's essay *Of Cunning*. Ralegh does not name Bacon here, although he quotes him by name with some frequency in the *History*. This reference, almost at the end of the *History*, is to an essay first published in 1612.
[24] Pref., sig. A3ʳ.

II

The principles of statecraft are the subject of a large portion of the posthumous tracts of Ralegh and the occasion of many a digression in the *History*. He was well read in the subject, but far from systematic in his own writings upon it; despite his high reputation as a statesman in the seventeenth century, he never achieved a synthesis of his political learning, let alone a comprehensive philosophy of the state. Historians of political philosophy are inclined to dismiss his writings as unoriginal and disorganized.[25] His eclectic method worked best in the compilation of aphorisms, as in *The Cabinet-Council*; in the illustration of political maxims from personal experience; and in the application of his learning to particular problems, as in the treatises on the marriages proposed for Princess Elizabeth and Prince Henry. The method is neatly epitomized in the title page of a reissue of *The Cabinet-Council*; the new title reads: *Aphorisms of State, Grounded on Authority and Experience and Illustrated with the Choicest Examples and Historical Observations* (1661).[26] But if Ralegh is relatively unimportant in the large perspective of the history of political thought, he is by no means insignificant as a purveyor of that thought, especially in the seventeenth century. His political writings have been well described as serving the function of a "weather-vane." [27]

My concern with these writings is not with their political philosophy in general, but specifically with their ethics and their indebtedness to Machiavelli. "Machiavellianism," for the Eliz-

---

[25] See J. W. Allen, *English Political Thought 1603–1660* (London, 1938), pp. 63–67; Lawrence Stapleton, "Halifax and Raleigh," *Journal of the History of Ideas*, II (1941), 211–24; and N. T. Reed, "The Philosophical Background of Sir Walter Raleigh's *History of the World*," *Summaries of Ph.D. Dissertations, Northwestern University*, II (June–August, 1934), 12–19. Dr. Reed considers the moral intent of the *History* "anachronistic," a judgment warranted perhaps by later developments in historiography but certainly not by the enthusiastic reception of Ralegh's work.

[26] T. N. Brushfield, *A Bibliography of Sir Walter Ralegh* (Exeter, England, 1908), p. 130.   [27] Stapleton, *op. cit.*, p. 211.

abethan a synonym for "atheism," was charged against Ralegh in the libelous days of his trial, and he was credited with the authorship of "certain hellish verses devised by that atheist and traitor Ralegh as it is said":

> Then some sage man among the vulgar,
> Knowing that laws could not in quiet dwell
> Unless they were observed, did first devise
> The name of God, religion, heaven, and hell, . . .
> And those religious observations
> Only bugbears to keep the world in fear.[28]

Although there is nothing in Ralegh's acknowledged writings to justify this ascription, the verses reflect the popular opinion of Machiavellian principles—this one, specifically, that religion was devised to keep men in awe of their governors.

Concerning both Elizabethan knowledge of Machiavelli's writings and Ralegh's use of them we are better informed today than a generation ago, when it was assumed that Elizabethan acquaintance with *The Prince* derived largely from the *Contre-Machiavel* of Innocent Gentillet.[29] Actually, the Florentine's works were available in Italian, Latin, and French editions; there were English translations of *The Art of War* (1560–62) and *The*

[28] Historical MSS Comm., *Calendar of the MSS of the Marquis of Bath*, II (1907), 52–53; quoted by V. T. Harlow (ed.), *The Discovery of Guiana* (London, 1928), p. xxxiv. The entire poem of fifty-nine lines is in this irreligious and seditious vein. This explanation of the origin of religion was, in Elizabethan opinion, one of the most scandalous of the doctrines attributed to Machiavelli; cf. Baines' charges against Marlowe, in C. F. Tucker Brooke, *The Life of Marlowe* (New York, 1930), p. 98.

[29] This systematic confutation of Machiavelli, with some distortion of his meaning, was translated from the French by Simon Paterick with a dedication dated 1577; but the earliest edition extant is *A Discourse upon the Means of Well Governing* (London, 1602). The translation of the *Contre-Machiavel*, as the work was popularly known, may have circulated in manuscript. Edward Meyer, *Machiavelli and the Elizabethan Drama* (Weimar, 1897), quite plausibly argues that Gentillet's book intensified Elizabethan hostility to Machiavelli; but students certainly were not dependent upon it for their knowledge of his works. Meyer has assembled a useful collection of Elizabethan allusions to Machiavelli.

Of the Architecture of Fortune 163

Florentine History (1595); several independent translations of *The Prince* circulated in manuscript;[30] and collections of political aphorisms, some of them in English translations, were drawn in part from Machiavelli. The few doctrines which made his name infamous were condemned; otherwise his works were freely used, at least by the learned. This attitude is nicely phrased by John Levett, in an unpublished translation of two books of Machiavelli's *Discourses;* having defended himself against those who might object to the translating of dangerous works, he refers his critics, in a familiar metaphor, "to the bee, for better answer, who can gather honey out of those plants where poison also is taken."[31] Further complicating any study of the Elizabethan use of Machiavelli's ideas is the recognition, then as now, that Machiavellianism existed long before it was conveniently tagged with a name. In the words of Mario Praz, "Machiavelli was no more the inventor of Machiavellism than Graves is the inventor of Graves's disease. Machiavelli supplied a label, a cliché for describing methods which had been in use since remote antiquity."[32] This point did not escape the Elizabethans; for example, Thomas Milles, who finds precedents for Machiavellianism in the deeds and writings of the ancients.[33] Ralegh

[30] One of the manuscripts has been published by Hardin Craig (Chapel Hill, 1944), with a prefatory note and introduction on the editions of *The Prince* available to Elizabethans. G. T. Buckley, *Atheism in the English Renaissance* (Chicago, 1932), pp. 31–42, traces the early evidences of English knowledge of Machiavelli and the identification of Machiavellianism with atheism.

[31] Napoleone Orsini, *Studii sul rinascimento italiano in Inghilterra* (Florence, 1937), p. 46. Levett is discussed in Professor Orsini's account (chap. i) of unpublished Elizabethan translations of Machiavelli. Levett's two prefaces are printed in full, with one page in facsimile.

[32] "Machiavelli and the Elizabethans," *Proceedings of the British Academy*, XIII [1928], 8–9.

[33] *The Treasury of Ancient and Modern Times* (London, 1613), Bk. IX, chap. x, pp. 915–31. In undertaking to confute Machiavelli's arguments "by reason of state without the consideration of God's justice," Milles cites (p. 917), among other early precedents, Aristotle's *Politics*, V, xi. This is the section of the *Politics* from which part of Ralegh's *Maxims of State* is drawn; see below, footnote 47. *The Treasury* is largely a translation and is so described on its title page.

himself makes a like observation, in ironic comment on a king's treachery to a follower who had executed his bloody commands:

> By this we see that the doctrine which Machiavel taught unto Caesar Borgia, to employ men in mischievous actions and afterwards to destroy them when they have performed the mischief, was not of his own invention. All ages have given us examples of this goodly policy, the latter having been apt scholars in this lesson to the more ancient: as the reign of Henry VIII here in England can bear good witness, and therein especially the Lord Cromwell, who perished by the same unjust law that himself had devised for the taking away of another man's life.[34]

Considered either in terms of the sources or in terms of the works in which citations or quotations appear, Ralegh's use of Machiavelli is extensive. But any study of the methods of his use is greatly complicated by the uncertain chronology and the diversity of his works, problems already explained in Chapter I. *The Cabinet-Council*, the work in which Machiavelli's influence, direct or indirect, is most apparent, was printed in 1658 from a manuscript provided by John Milton, who wrote a brief prefatory note for the publication.

> Having had the manuscript of this treatise, written by Sir Walter Ralegh, many years in my hands, and finding it lately by chance among other books and papers, upon reading thereof I thought it a kind of injury to withhold longer the work of so eminent an author from the public; it being both answerable in style to other works of his already extant, as far as the subject will permit, and given me for a true copy by a learned man at his death, who had collected several such pieces.[35]

That is all we know, from external sources, about the origin and transmission of the work. Although Milton's observation about the style is not amiss, internal evidence shows that *The Cabinet-Council* more nearly approximates a commonplace book than an independent treatise. In method it is somewhere between *The Skeptic*, a direct summarizing translation, and the *Maxims of State*, based upon borrowed materials but better organized than

[34] *History*, V, vi, 1, p. 711.   [35] *Works*, VIII, 36.

Of the Architecture of Fortune 165

The Cabinet-Council. Further, since much of the work is drawn from a collection of political maxims by Francesco Sansovino, some of the borrowings from Machiavelli are at second hand.[36] The term "cabinet" has been interpreted plausibly as indicating a work which could be entrusted only to those who were in the top councils of state, not a treatise for general circulation. But Mario Praz,[37] seizing upon this distinction and emphasizing the contrasts between the private *Cabinet-Council* and the *Maxims of State*, intended for Prince Henry, would date *The Cabinet-Council* in Ralegh's active days (specifically, he conjectures that it may have been written when Ralegh was at Youghal in 1589), and would link the Realpolitik of the work with Ralegh's own political actions. Unfortunately, there is no certain evidence concerning the exact date of composition, and contradictions are found within *The Cabinet-Council* no less than between it and other works in which Machiavelli is cited. For example, as Praz notes, the hateful doctrine that fear is a better ground than love for respect and obedience toward princes is accepted in *The Cabinet-Council* and reproved in the *Maxims of State*; yet the doctrine is rejected, no less than three times, in *The Cabinet-Council* also.[38] Less significantly, because the work is addressed

---

[36] The most complete study of the sources of Ralegh's political writings is that by Nadja Kempner, *Raleghs staatstheoretische Schriften: die Einführung des Machiavellismus in England* (Leipzig, 1928). Her work was anticipated in part by Adolph Buff, "Über drei Ralegh'sche Schriften," *Englische Studien*, II (1879), 392–416; and it has been amended and supplemented by Vincent Luciani, "Ralegh's *Cabinet-Council* and Guicciardini's Aphorisms," *Studies in Philology*, XLVI (1949), 20–30. These studies demonstrate clearly, even in terms of the editions or intermediary works used, the derivation of several of Ralegh's political works. Miss Kempner overestimates the importance of Ralegh (as indicated in her subtitle) in introducing Machiavellianism into England and also, I believe, the extent to which he himself was "Machiavellian" in thought and action. Disagreement in interpretation, however, does not affect the value of her admirable factual study, to which I am greatly indebted.

[37] "Un machiavellico Inglese Sir Walter Raleigh," *La Cultura*, VIII (1929), 16–27; see especially the comment on the Smerwick massacre (p. 18) and the conjecture about the date of composition (p. 24).

[38] *Ibid.*, p. 23. The contradiction which Praz notes is in *Works*, VIII, 14 and 104; for contradictions within *The Cabinet-Council* see *Works*, VIII, 118, 126, 138.

to King James, it is rejected in *The Prerogative of Parliaments*;[39] more significantly, it is rejected in an aside in the *History*, with no suggestion of an ulterior motive. Concerning King Rehoboam's ill-advised and crushing taxation of his people, he writes:

But as it appeared by the success, those young advisors greatly mistook the nature of security, which without the temper of clemency is no other than cruelty itself; they also were ignorant that it ought to be used for the help, and not for the harm, of subjects. For what is the strength of a king left by his people? And what cords or fetters have ever lasted long, but those which have been twisted and forged by love only? [40]

If we turn from these vexatious problems of provenance, chronology, and internal contradictions to a brief summary of the uses to which Ralegh put Machiavelli's writings, we find that they fall into three general patterns: (1) direct borrowing of fairly extensive passages; (2) citation or brief quotation, either for aptness of phrase or for illustration of a point; and (3) citation with sharp reproval. As an example of the first, practically all of Chapter IV of *The Prince*—"Why the Kingdom of Darius, Occupied by Alexander, Did Not Rebel against the Successors of the Latter after His Death"—is incorporated at the appropriate place in the *History*. Likewise a brief portion of *The Prince*, Chapter XII, appears in a discussion of the dangers of using mercenary troops; but here Ralegh extends the illustration to show "the just judgment of God" upon the son of a treacherous mercenary.[41] As already indicated, the borrowing is heavy in *The Cabinet-Council*, though frequently by way of Sansovino's compilation. Chapter XXV of that work, disproportionately long, owes much to Machiavelli; and most of Chapter XXVI is from the *Discourses*.[42]

---

[39] *Works*, VIII, 156, 162.

[40] II, xix, 1, p. 505; cf. also I, ix, 3, p. 183. Neither passage, however, mentions Machiavelli.

[41] *History*, IV, v, 8, pp. 264–65; V, ii, 2, pt. 3, p. 380. Kempner (*op. cit.* p. 26, note 1) cites both these borrowings and a third, "A digression concerning the defense of hard passages," *History*, IV, ii, 3, p. 172.

[42] Kempner, *op. cit.*; much of her study is devoted to these two chapters.

Of the Architecture of Fortune 167

Noncommittal citations or quotations occur in the *History*, in *The Prerogative of Parliaments*, in *A Discourse Touching a Marriage between Prince Henry of England and a Daughter of Savoy*, and in *A Discourse of War*.[43] The last work, however, apart from citations of Machiavelli, contains and ends on a moralizing note [44] in harmony with the *History of the World*.

The most outspoken condemnation of Machiavellian doctrine occurs in the treatise originally entitled *The Prince; or, Maxims of State* (1642). Subsequent editions dropped "The Prince" from the title, and the latest editions, including the commonly used *Works* (1829), omit an interesting section suggesting how the book is to be used.[45] The condemnation is expressed briefly in such phrases as "the false doctrine of Machiavellian policy," "contrary to the rule of Machiavel," and "lewd and impertinent" Machiavellian practice.[46] Comprehensively, ideas popularly associated with Machiavelli (but here taken directly from Aristotle) are condemned in two sections introduced by a warning sentence: "The sophisms of tyrants are rather to be known than practiced . . . by wise and good princes, and are these and such like as follow." [47] Among them is the advice that a prince should (in Ralegh's phrasing) "pretend great care of religion and of serving God." Another is the advice that a Prince who has disgraced a man of prestige and power should not let him escape, since he will seek revenge rather than be thankful for pardon; upon which Ralegh comments that such a response is

---

[43] References, in the order named: *History*, I, i, 15, p. 21; III, vi, 2, p. 62; *Works*, VIII, 198, 207, 247–48, 266, 279, 288, 291–92.

[44] *Works*, VIII, 281–82, 294–97.

[45] Brushfield, *Bibliography*, No. 259. The suggested "Method" of using the book and "in the reading of story" (as published in the 1675 *Remains*) tabulates the details of several events in David's reign and then produces generalizations from these details. The most interesting part of the commentary is on "political nobility." [46] *Works*, VIII, 15, 16, 18.

[47] *Ibid.*, pp. 21–26; the quotations which follow, pp. 25 and 26. Kempner, *op. cit.*, pp. 56–60, prints the parallel passages in the *Maxims of State* and Aristotle's *Politics*, V, xi. The paragraph on pretending religion is correctly traced to Aristotle; but the idea was closely associated in Elizabethan times with the notorious chap. xviii of *The Prince*.

"true in atheists, but not in true Christian nobility." Elizabethan distortion of a few Machiavellian principles made it possible to answer out of Machiavelli himself the popular notion of what he had said—although there is no evidence that such was Ralegh's intent. A paragraph in *The Cabinet-Council* taken from Sansovino goes back to Machiavelli's *Discourses:* "Among men worthy of commendation, those have merited best that first planted true religion; . . . so ought they to be accounted infamous that introduce atheism. . . ."[48]

In brief, Ralegh's attitude toward Machiavelli is like that of other well-read Elizabethans: to use his political wisdom, to decry his immoral or irreligious doctrines. But it is not well to let the matter rest solely in terms of specific indebtedness to, or censure of, Machiavelli. Although that relationship is most pertinent to the discussion of Elizabethan "inward atheism," much of Ralegh's commentary on practical politics is in keeping with the spirit of Machiavelli's realism, just as much of Ralegh's subordination of worldly wisdom to moral law is in opposition to that spirit, without condemnation of Machiavelli by name.

To give but a few examples, Ralegh seemingly approves the use of false propaganda to dispose the people toward war.[49] As an historian he observes that treaties have seldom been kept if it were advantageous to break them. Telling how Quintus Fabius bluntly offered the Roman Senate a choice of peace or war, he comments:

This was plain dealing. To wrangle about pretences when each part had resolved to make war, it was merely frivolous. For all these disputes of breach of peace have ever been maintained by the party unwilling or unable to sustain the war. The rusty sword and the empty purse do always plead performance of covenants. There have been few kings or states in the world that have otherwise understood the obligation of a treaty than with the condition of their own advantage, and commonly (seeing peace between ambitious princes and states is but a kind of

[48] *Works*, VIII, 97; *Discourses*, I, x. See Kempner, *op. cit.*, p. 65.
[49] *History*, V, iv, 8 and 9, pp. 612, 615.

breathing) the best-advised have rather begun with the sword than with the trumpet.⁵⁰

And of this kind of sudden breach of peace he cites examples of recent memory. To the same intent, quoting a phrase from Sir Francis Bacon, he concludes that necessity and the probable loss from breach of a covenant are the surest safeguards for the maintenance of articles of peace.⁵¹ Nor do alliances effected through royal marriages fare better; in a number of instances cited from 1495 to 1558, "the histories of those times tell us that all the bonds, either by the bed or by the book, either by weddings or sacramental oaths, had neither faithful purpose nor performance." ⁵²

Nevertheless, "reason of state" is no excuse for compromising religion. Using as his text the idolatry of Jeroboam, Ralegh quotes a modern historian on the impiety of using the "good of the state" as an adequate excuse for any injustice, dishonesty, or impiety that may serve material ends. The lesson is brought up to date in an example of prime interest to Ralegh's generation.

It was reason of state that persuaded the last famous French King Henry IV to change his religion; yet the Protestants whom he forsook obeyed him, but some of the Papists whom he followed murdered him. So strongly doth the painted visor of wise proceeding delude even those that know the foul face of impiety lurking under it and behold the wretched ends that have ever followed it. . . .⁵³

Even if political wisdom is honestly employed, man's knowledge in the long run is likely to be overridden by his feelings and his appetites.

But unto all dominions God hath set their periods: Who, though he hath given unto man the knowledge of those ways by which kingdoms rise and fall, yet hath left him subject unto the affections which draw on these fatal changes in their times appointed.⁵⁴

⁵⁰ V, iii, 1, p. 426.   ⁵¹ V, iv, 8, p. 613.   ⁵² IV, vi, 5, p. 283.
⁵³ II, xix, 1, pp. 506-7. Kempner, *op. cit.*, p. 41, note 6, identifies the "modern historian" as Giovanni Botero, whose *Della ragion di stato* (1589) Ralegh quotes from a Latin translation.   ⁵⁴ *History*, V, iii, 13, p. 497.

170 Of the Architecture of Fortune

Ralegh has as little admiration for naked force as for political chicanery. He dismisses Alexander, whom he rates as far inferior to Caesar in military prowess, among "other troublers of the world" and approves Seneca's judgment of both Philip and Alexander as "no less plagues to mankind than an overflow of waters" or a great drought.[55] Ralegh's last word on the abuses of all forms of power politics culminates in the best-known paragraph of his *History*.

> For the rest, if we seek a reason of the succession and continuance of this boundless ambition in mortal men, we may add to that which hath been already said: that the kings and princes of the world have always laid before them the actions, but not the ends, of those great ones which preceded them. They are always transported with the glory of the one, but they never mind the misery of the other till they find the experience in themselves. They neglect the advice of God while they enjoy life or hope it, but they follow the counsel of Death upon his first approach. It is he that puts into man all the wisdom of the world, without speaking a word, which God with all the words of his law, promises, or threats, doth not infuse. . . .
>
> O eloquent, just, and mighty Death! Whom none could advise, thou hast persuaded; what none hath dared, thou hast done; and whom all the world hath flattered thou only hast cast out of the world and despised. Thou hast drawn together all the far stretched greatness, all the pride, cruelty, and ambition of man, and covered it all over with these two narrow words, *Hic jacet*.[56]

There is little need to emphasize further the contradictions in Ralegh's writings that deal with man's worldly fortunes. The prevailing philosophy is in accord with the religious doctrine of the *History of the World*; but the courtier and politician intrude upon that philosophy in the exceptional passages cited here by way of illustration. Despite the uncertain dates of composition of some works important for this study, one can see in Ralegh's views on the "architecture of fortune" and on national and international politics, rather than in his religion, something of the change which Bishop Hall described:

[55] IV, ii, 23, pp. 211–12.   [56] V, vi, 12, 775–76.

The Court had his youthful and freer times, the Tower his later age; the Tower reformed the Court in him, and produced those worthy monuments of art and industry which we should have in vain expected from his freedom and jollity. It is observed that shining wood when it is kept within doors loseth its light; it is otherwise with this and many other active wits, which had never shined so much if not for their closeness.[57]

Perhaps Ralegh would have preferred, as the last word on the subject, a significant parenthesis buried in the *History of the World:*

. . . it is the part of an honest and valiant man to do what reason willeth, not what opinion expecteth, and to measure honor or dishonor by the assurance of his well-informed conscience, rather than by the malicious report and censure of others.[58]

[57] Joseph Hall, *The Balm of Gilead* (London, 1646), pp. 216–17, in a section entitled "Comforts against Imprisonment." The passage has been frequently quoted.   [58] III, viii, 8, p. 100.

Chapter 6

Of Miracles; and of Men before Adam

Sure I am, that the discovery of a truth formerly unknown doth rather convince man of ignorance than nature of error

History, I, vii, 2, pp. 100–101

ALTHOUGH Ralegh's activities as a patron of men of science and his own experiments in chemistry and medicine did not occasion many hostile references, he clearly belongs among the "naturalists," whose soundness in religion was suspect. From the time when he became prominent at court, in the early 1580's, through his long imprisonment in the Tower, his interest in natural philosophy seems to have been as continuous as the demands of a busy life and varied intellectual pursuits would permit. He befriended the learned John Dee, whose curiously compounded science and spiritualism brought down the wrath of the multitude, and on one occasion, which Dee gratefully records, reminded Queen Elizabeth to call the philosopher to her side for a few moments' conversation.[1] By engaging Thomas Harriot as his tutor in mathematics, Ralegh earned the praise of Richard

---

[1] *The Private Diary of Dr. John Dee*, ed. J. O. Halliwell, "Publications of the Camden Society," XIX (1842), 20, 21, 54. These references to Ralegh are noted by Charlotte Fell-Smith, *John Dee* (London, 1909), pp. 68, 100, and 261; and in addition she quotes from M. Casaubon, *A True and Faithful Relation* (London, 1659), a passage in which the spirit Madini is pessimistic about the stability of the friendship with Ralegh and other great ones of the court. See also Casaubon, *op. cit.*, pp. 28, 31. For appraisals of Dee's solid accomplishments in science see E. G. R. Taylor, *Tudor Geography, 1485–1583* (London, 1930), pp. 75–139; and F. R. Johnson, *Astronomical Thought in Renaissance England* (Baltimore, Md., 1937), pp. 134–40 and *passim*. I have noted elsewhere (*Huntington Library Quarterly*, X [1947], 365–72) that Dee seems to have regarded himself as the "conjurer" of Parsons' attack on Ralegh.

Of Miracles 173

Hakluyt and the suspicion of those who distrusted mathematician and scientist alike. The association continued even after Harriot entered the service of Northumberland, especially after the Earl joined Ralegh in the Tower.[2] Bacon thought of turning the energies of the three men toward contributions to his *Instauratio Magna,* although nothing seems to have come of the idea. Quite properly, Bacon in the wording of his memorandum places a premium on the services of Harriot when he suggests "the setting on work my lord of Northumberland, and Ralegh, and therefore Harriot, themselves being already incline[d] to experiments."[3] Meanwhile, in a small shed in the Tower yard Ralegh conducted, quite independently of Bacon's design so far as we know, experiments which won him a special notoriety. His famed "elixir," to the modern reader a veritable witches' brew out of the Elizabethan pharmacopoeia, was employed as a last resort in the fatal illness of Prince Henry. The Prince rallied briefly; the same concoction, said the gossips, had poisoned the Countess of Rutland.[4]

Ralegh's laboratory experiments, frequently utilitarian in purpose, were treated with respect in the seventeenth century, and

[2] The apothecary John Hester dedicated to Ralegh *A Hundred and Fourteen Experiments of Paracelsus* (London, 1596), but Hester did not tie himself to one patron. No one of the patrons addressed in the books by Hester which I have seen received a second dedication. The dedication to Ralegh is interesting for its emphasis on independence and originality in natural research, and the book itself concerns one of Ralegh's many interests in the enforced leisure of the Tower. The 1596 edition is probably not the first; see Paul H. Kocher, "John Hester, Paracelsan," *Joseph Quincy Adams Memorial Studies* (Washington, D.C., 1948), p. 628.

[3] Quoted by Geoffrey Bullough, "Bacon and the Defence of Learning," *Seventeenth Century Studies Presented to Sir Herbert Grierson* (Oxford, 1938), p. 16. The original is printed in *Works,* ed. Spedding, Ellis, and Heath, XI (London, 1868), 63.

[4] For the composition of the elixir as described some years after Ralegh's death see John Knott, "Sir Walter Ralegh's 'Royal Cordial,'" *The Dublin Journal of Medical Science,* CXXI (1906), 63–70, 131–43; and the same article, slightly revised and enlarged by the author, in *American Medicine,* New Ser., VI (1911), 157–67, 218–24. John Chamberlain (*Letters,* ed. N. E. McClure, 2 vols. [Philadelphia, 1939], I, 374, 377) records the slander about Ralegh's responsibility for the death of the Countess of Rutland.

manuscript notes concerning them are extant, some of them described as in Ralegh's handwriting.[5] But for his "philosophy of science"—if such a phrase does not dignify his opinions too much—we must look elsewhere. The problems are merely indicated by hostile comments upon his relations with men of science. The "conjurer" of what Parsons called Ralegh's "school of atheism" has been plausibly identified as Thomas Harriot, and in that school, said Parsons, Moses and our Savior were jested at and "the scholars taught among other things to spell God backward." The direct charge of blasphemy implies also the practice of black magic: the spelling of "God" backward may be a crude popularization of the learned conjuring described in the words of Marlowe's Dr. Faustus:

> Within this circle is Jehovah's name,
> Forward and backward anagrammatiz'd.[6]

Harriot is brought into the picture again by Baines, who reported that Marlowe had called Moses a juggler, whose feats were surpassed by "one Heriots being Sir W. Ralegh's man." These hostile comments, brief as they are, point to two of the problems confronting the Elizabethan experimenter who wished to live at peace with his neighbors: first, the still common identification of experimental science with black magic; and second, the suspicion attached to studies which the ungodly might use to undermine the truth of scriptural accounts of miracles. In the *History*, Ralegh addresses himself to both the questions involved in these charges: to what extent is the study of natural magic lawful, and how do conjurers' feats differ from the miracles performed by Moses or Christ?

But the topic is too large to be defined solely by reference to a few hostile allusions, however appropriate. Those of the apologetical writers who regard natural studies as inimical to faith

---

[5] See T. N. Brushfield, *Bibliography of Ralegh* (Exeter, England, 1908), No. 314; and, for the "cordial" and other scientific notes, Nos. 311–13.

[6] The lines in *Dr. Faustus* refer to a recondite form of conjuring with the seventy-two Hebrew names for God; see Paul H. Kocher, *Christopher Marlowe* (Chapel Hill, N.C., 1946), pp. 13, 152, 155.

give us some idea of the negative approach to our subject: the danger of subordinating God to nature, of adopting "philosophical" views of the creation and eternity of the world, of questioning the Bible, especially on the age of the world, the Deluge, and miracles. Ralegh's comprehensive answer to such problems has been presented in his opinions on God and the soul: the supremacy of God over nature; man's inability to penetrate first causes and his limited understanding of second causes; the unquestionable truth of Scripture. But, also in the *History*, he treats these problems in specific as well as general terms; there we may find, sometimes in extended essays, his opinions on the definition and limitations of natural magic, on miracles, on the Flood, on astrology. Akin to these discourses in its implications for the authority of the Bible is his close attention to chronology, in which, of course, science is subordinate to historical records. Here too he seeks the most plausible reckoning consistent with Biblical authority, for Ralegh would have no "men before Adam."

Of Magic

Ralegh devotes to the defense of natural magic an entire chapter, entitled "Of Zoroaster, supposed to have been the chief author of magic arts: and of diverse kinds of magic." [7] He rests his case upon the ancient dignity of magic, both name and thing; the error of confusing natural magic with tricks performed by the aid of the devil; the practical benefits of the study; and its value in refuting slanderers of the Christian religion. After a word about the honorable meaning in ancient times of the name "magus," Ralegh begins his discussion with a threefold classification of magic: divine magic, practiced of old in the service of God,

---

[7] *History of the World* (1614), I, xi, pp. 199–213; the definitions and the principal defense are in sec. 2, pp. 201–5, from which the quotations in this paragraph and the first part of the following paragraph are taken, although not in the order of their occurrence in the section. This account of Ralegh's opinions on magic, miracles, and astrology follows in part my article, "Sir Walter Ralegh on Natural Philosophy," *Modern Language Quarterly*, I (1940), 49–61.

the first and highest kind; that part of astrology which has to do with planting and husbandry (natural astrology); and, his particular interest, natural philosophy in general. This, the third kind of magic, "containeth the whole philosophy of nature; not the brabblings of the Aristotelians, but that which bringeth to light the inmost virtues, and draweth them out of nature's hidden bosom to human use, . . . 'virtues hidden in the center of the center,' according to the chemists." Such was the study of men like Albertus, Arnoldus de Villa Nova, Raymond, Bacon, and others, in these and ancient times and in many lands. "The magic which these men professed is thus defined . . . 'Magic is the connection of natural agents and patients, answerable each to other, wrought by a wise man to the bringing forth of such effects as are wonderful to those that know not their causes.'" In the practical application of this definition, the effects attained solely by natural means may baffle the uninitiated: it is "idle ignorance, the parent of causeless admiration" which brings magic into disrepute. Natural magic is an art, says Mirandola, which "few understand and many reprehend; . . . as dogs bark at those they know not, so they condemn and hate the things they understand not."

To combat this ignorance and prejudice, Ralegh uses the greater part of his chapter to differentiate between lawful magic and the devilish practice of conjuring and witchcraft. Following the classification in the second chapter of Daniel, he lists the synonyms for the various kinds of honest and dishonest magicians, and he glosses further upon the distinctions when he describes the different ranks and orders of the Chaldeans. He invokes the authority of Origen, supported by Jerome, for a partition of magic in two categories: one which works, in fact or pretense, by covenants with the devil, and "the other commended by Origen; which appertaineth to the practic part of natural philosophy, teaching to work admirable things by the mutual application of natural virtues, agent [that is, acting] and suffering reciprocally." Ralegh concludes, therefore, that

Of Miracles

the art of magic is the wisdom of nature; other arts which undergo that title were invented by the falsehood, subtlety, and envy of the Devil. In the latter there is no other doctrine than the use of certain ceremonies, *per malam fidem:* by an evil faith; in the former no other ill, than the investigation of those virtues and hidden properties which God hath given to his creatures, and how fitly to apply things that work to things that suffer.

Since the art of natural magic is no other than "the absolute perfection of natural philosophy," [8] it ill becomes learned men to confuse true and false knowledge and to give them like consideration, "to confound lawful and praiseworthy knowledge with that impious, and (to use St. Paul's words) 'with those beggarly rudiments,' which the Devil hath shuffled in, and by them bewitcheth and befooleth graceless men." If we are to condemn the study of natural philosophy because the Devil, "who knoweth more than any man," is proficient in that knowledge, then we would have to condemn many useful skills, including the medical arts. On these themes—the distinction of true and false magic and the distinction between the use and abuse of a science—Ralegh rings many changes. He devotes a section of his chapter to the argument, popular with the defenders of alchemy, astrology, and other studies with any pretension to usefulness, that "The abuse of things which may be found in all kinds, is not to condemn the right use of them." [9] The honest investigator will not be deterred from using his knowledge for "the help and comfort of mankind" simply because the Devil himself is a skilled teacher of science.

In his discussion of conjuring, Ralegh has one eye on the schoolmaster on the throne of England, who had written with kingly

[8] This and the quotations immediately following are from I, xi, 3, p. 205.

[9] I, xi, 5, p. 207. Thomas Tymme, translator of *The Practice of Chemical and Hermetical Physic* (London, 1605), argues in "The Forespeech to the Reader" that the abuse of alchemy does not "abrogate the right use thereof," and also justifies the interest of a clergyman in science. Christopher Heydon, *A Defence of Judicial Astrology* (Cambridge, England, 1603), applies the argument freely in his treatise; cf. pp. 53, 99, and *passim*. Ralegh himself in this section uses astrology as an example of a useful science abused by the devil's tricks.

authority on demonology. He finds King James agreeing that in the Persian language "magus" had been used to designate a student of divine and heavenly learning, but unjustly so because the Chaldeans knew not the true divinity. King James also says truly, according to Ralegh, that the term magic embraces "all other unlawful arts," and yet James distinguishes magic from necromancy and witchcraft. This interpretation of James's words is misleading, for he distinguishes magic or necromancy on the one hand from witchcraft and sorcery on the other. Ralegh says correctly, however, that James is writing about black magic and that therefore his strictures do not apply to natural philosophy.[10] It should not be inferred from this tenderness about the King's book that Ralegh is merely pretending a politic agreement; despite his gingerly handling of the royal opinions, he quite clearly believes in the possibility of performing feats of magic with the Devil's aid. In this belief, of course, he had distinguished company. But as his descriptions of the kinds of unlawful magic and of certain famous incidents (like the feats of Pharaoh's sorcerers) show, he finds the Devil's power sharply limited to two ways of working: "by knowing the uttermost of nature and by illusion; for there is no incomprehensible or unsearchable power, but of God only." [11] He regards with scorn the hocus-pocus used to confound the simple-minded: if Banks had lived in ancient times he would have surpassed the pretended enchanters of animals by the tricks he had taught his wonderful horse. (Banks and his trained horse were a popular institution in Ralegh's day.) As for such tricks as beguiling serpents out of their holes, "therein I find no other magic or enchantment than to draw out a mouse with a piece of toasted cheese." [12] By these homely comparisons, no less than by his formal limitations upon the Devil's power, Ralegh narrows the field of possible operation of unlawful magic.

[10] I, xi, 2, p. 201. Other references to the *Demonology* occur on pp. 202, 208, 209, and the first page of the preface.
[11] I, xi, 7, p. 211. [12] I, xi, 6, p. 209.

In contrast to these now outdated speculations on the black art, Ralegh strikes a more modern note in his reflections elsewhere in the *History* [13] on the legitimate uses of scientific study. His disdain for the rascal multitude infects his views on the subject to the extent that he doubts, momentarily, the wisdom of publishing scientific discoveries; but a generous policy wins the day, after a brief debate wherein Ralegh reflects upon the inventor's duty to society and the moral responsibility of the scientist in wartime. The occasion of his remarks is the narrative of the Roman siege of Syracuse, during which Archimedes was persuaded to devote his talents to the construction of defensive weapons. He had little liking for the job, for he and his fellows "held it an injury done unto the liberal sciences, to submit learned propositions unto the workmanship and gain of base handicrafts men." Plato, the author of this opinion, likewise "blamed some geometricians that seemed unto him to profane their science by making it vulgar." Nor must we be hasty to condemn Plato's attitude: the ingratitude of the people, who first deride and afterwards depreciate great inventions, is cause enough to make a learned man hesitate to publish his discoveries.[14] Aside from the notorious example of Columbus, even the homely art of brewing, now the trade of ignorant men, had its origin in an "extraordinary knowledge of natural philosophy." Or consider the handicrafts; for example, printing, "which being devised, and bettered, by great scholars and wise men, grew afterward corrupted by those to whom the practise fell; that is, by such as could slubber things easily over and feed their workmen at the

[13] V, iii, 15, pp. 516–17; the quotations in the next two paragraphs are from these pages.
[14] Among Ralegh's contemporaries there was, naturally, a difference of opinion on this problem. Many astronomers realized the value of skilled craftsmen in making instruments and did not neglect the practical ends of their study; for examples, see F. R. Johnson, *op. cit.*, pp. 139, 173, 200, 290. John Dee, on the other hand, complained bitterly throughout his lifetime of the ingratitude of his countrymen and their readiness to slander him as a conjurer. See for example the "Advertisement" prefixed to his *General and Rare Memorials* (London, 1577), which was published in transparent anonymity.

cheapest rate." [15] In the light of this experience, Ralegh thinks the alchemists justified in their secrecy about their discoveries, real or pretended; "for it is a kind of injustice" that the results of laborious research should be wasted on worthless men and that the student or discoverer should derive less benefit from his work than strangers, or even, perhaps, his enemies. Even so, Christian charity requires that we share our knowledge for the good of mankind, especially if a new discovery has in it no potentiality of harmful use.

Nevertheless if we have regard unto common charity, and the great affection that every one ought to bear unto the generality of mankind, after the example of him "that suffereth his sun to shine upon the just and the unjust," it will appear more commendable in wise men to enlarge themselves, and to publish unto the world those good things that lie buried in their own bosoms. This ought specially to be done when a profitable knowledge hath not annexed to it some dangerous cunning, that may be perverted by evil men to a mischievous use. For if the secret of any rare antidote contained in it the skill of giving some deadly and irrecoverable poison, better it were that such a jewel remain close in the hands of a wise and honest man than, being made common, bind all men to use the remedy by teaching the worst men how to do the mischief.

This restriction on the broadcasting of dangerous knowledge Ralegh turns into a special commendation of Archimedes, whose weapons were useful only for defense. The Syracusans could not carry them abroad, "to the hurt and oppression of others." Nor did Archimedes give full information on their construction and use: no more were made after his death, and the Romans did not use those which they captured with the fall of Syracuse. It was enough that Archimedes had given the vulgar a glimpse of the "dignity of his science, and done especial benefit unto his country. For to enrich a mechanical trade, or teach the art of murder-

[15] Ralegh notes elsewhere (V, i, pt. 2, p. 324) that Columbus was little regarded by the English in our grandfathers' times, when he was seeking help in his enterprise. In arguing that the first settlements after the Flood were far to the east of Armenia (I, vii, 10, pt. 4, p. 115), Ralegh cites the use of printing as evidence of the early cultural ascendancy of the East, especially China.

ing men, it was besides his purpose." As Ralegh tells it, the brief story is its own commentary; yet one is tempted to add for the twentieth century a phrase dear to the heart of a seventeenth-century preacher: "De te fabula."

Although Ralegh extols the practical benefits of the study of natural philosophy, his highest admiration is reserved for "pure" science and for mathematics. Telling the story of the death of Archimedes, so absorbed in his studies that he ignored the soldier about to kill him, Ralegh praises his hero's devotion to learning, and in so doing makes a whimsical comment upon the practical father who expects very tangible "results" from a university education.

> Upon his tomb (as he had ordained in his lifetime) was placed a cylinder and a sphere, with an inscription of the proportion between them, which he first found out. An invention of so little use, as this may seem, pleased that great artist better than the devising of all those engines that made him so famous. Such difference is between the judgment of learned men and of the vulgar sort. For many an one would think the money lost that had been spent upon a son whose studies in the university had brought forth such fruit as the proportion between a sphere and a cylinder.[16]

Of Miracles

Properly understood, then, natural philosophy is free from contamination by the black arts, is beneficial to mankind, and

[16] V, iii, 15, p. 521. For illustrations of Ralegh's praise of mathematics, see I, xi, 5, p. 208; II, xxv, 1, p. 592. My distinction between "pure" science and its applications may be misleading in that the Elizabethans extolled mathematics not only as a subject which would elevate the soul above mere sensory apprehension but also as the means of working marvelous mechanical effects. For an exaggerated example, see John Dee's "Mathematical Preface" to Euclid, *Elements of Geometry*, translated by Henry Billingsley (London, 1570). Conversely, there was popular suspicion of the study of mathematics; Francis Osborn (*Advice to a Son* in *Works* [1682], p. 5) notes in his praise of mathematics: ". . . my memory reacheth the time when the generality of people thought her most useful branches, spells, and her professors, limbs of the devil." What was Oxford's praise such people converted to her shame; "not a few of our then foolish gentry refusing to send their sons thither, lest they should be smutted with the black art."

is for its own sake worthy the labors of a choice spirit. But what becomes of our faith in miracles if we pry into the secret properties and operations of the things which God created? For the text of his answer Ralegh quotes at length from the *Apology* of Pico della Mirandola:

> ... for by understanding the uttermost activity of natural agents we are assisted to know the divinity of Christ.... The terms or limits of natural power and virtue not understood, we must needs doubt whether those very works which Christ did, may not be done by natural means.... Therefore I said not heretically, not superstitiously, but most truly and Catholicly, that by such magic we are furthered in knowing the divinity of Christ.[17]

This argument Ralegh heartily endorses. Since the Jews and gentiles have objected that Christ's miracles were not supernatural but were performed by a superfine knowledge of nature, we can see the falseness of their objection when we extend our knowledge of natural magic to the extreme limits of our human capacities. For "the uttermost of nature's works being known, the works which Christ did, and which (as himself witnesseth) no man could do, do manifestly testify of themselves that they were performed by that hand which held nature therein but as a pencil, and by a power infinitely supreme and divine." The argument is like that of Mornay in his defense of the use of reason to support faith; indeed, Mornay made a similar application of the argument when he turned a familiar principle, *ex nihilo nihil fit*, to prove the divinity of Christ.[18] But not everyone

---

[17] This quotation and the next are from I, xi, 2, 204–5.

[18] See above, chap. iii. A similar argument is used to justify the translation of Pliny. In the preface to his translation of Pliny's *History of the World* (London, 1601), Philemon Holland tells how he took counsel with sundry divines on the propriety of publishing an author who "in attributing so much unto nature, ... seemeth to derogate from the Almighty God." Holland ends his preface with a letter from a learned preacher approving the translation and pointing the moral which good Christians should draw from Pliny's errors: "And when they shall perceive that the wisest clerk in natural skill could not learn by the book of heaven and earth to know their maker ... then (I say) they will the more be stirred up by God's grace to make reverent account of

Of Miracles

subscribed to the opinion held by Mirandola, Mornay and Ralegh. Just as some writers doubted the efficacy and pertinence of rational arguments for religious truths, there were critics [19] who remained suspicious of the study of nature as a potential threat to God's omnipotence and providence. This suspicion Parsons turned to account when he accused Ralegh and his circle of jesting at Christ and Moses.

When we turn to Ralegh's explanation of the miracles performed by Moses in Egypt we again find the distinction between feats of conjuring and wonders which either were divinely inspired and directed, or were legitimate works of natural magic. Outwardly, the results obtained by Moses and by Pharaoh's sorcerers appear the same, just "as some virtues and vices are so nicely distinguished, and so resembling each other, as they are often confounded, and the one taken for the other." [20] Even in this context Ralegh would not have the reader assume that a wonderful accomplishment can be explained only as a miracle or as a work performed with the aid of the Devil. "Moses himself,"

---

the Holy Scriptures, which God in rich mercy hath given to them to be a light in all things for to direct them through the errors in nature's blindness."

[19] E.g., Robert Gray, *An Alarum to England* (London, 1609), sig. C1^r, inveighs against those who would account for the destruction of Sodom by natural causes and deplores the current tendency to explain away natural phenomena instead of seeing in them God's warnings: "And amongst us at this day, if any strange accidents do happen either in the air or in the earth or in the waters, we refer them to some natural cause or other, being unwilling (as it were) to acknowledge God to have a hand in them." Thomas Tymme, *A Silver Watch-Bell* (London, 1605), p. 82, comments on the evidence he has presented for the actuality of Hell: "I doubt not, but there are some which ascribe all these things to natural causes and workings, or else will account them no better than fables, as they do all things else which concern religion." Yet Tymme is not hostile to natural philosophy and defends his own interest in medicine (see note 9 above).

[20] The quotations in this paragraph are from II, vi, 7, p. 321. In his chapter on magic (I, xi, 7, p. 210) Ralegh considers various opinions, including those of St. Augustine and St. Thomas Aquinas, on the nature of the tricks worked by Pharaoh's magicians; he concludes, with William of Paris, that the sorcerers' frogs were produced by a deep knowledge of natural processes and not by illusion.

he warns, "doth not charge [the sorcerers] with any familiarity with devils, or ill spirits: words indeed that seldom came out of his mouth"; and he again emphasizes the natural explanation of many seeming wonders:

For the properties and powers which God hath given to natural things are such as, where he also bestoweth the knowledge to understand their hidden and best virtues, many things by them are brought to pass which seem altogether impossible, and above nature or art.

Thus the Cabalists distinguished between the "wisdom of nature," by which Jacob bred the pied lambs in Mesopotamia, and the "wisdom of divinity," by which Moses performed his miracles in Egypt. Moses had from God a double gift: a knowledge of nature "in the highest perfection," and the wisdom of divinity "so far as it pleased God to proportion him." Both gifts, his skill in natural philosophy and his divinely conferred supernatural powers, Moses used for the glory of God who gave them without arrogating to himself the least credit for his achievements. For Ralegh, Moses was not a "juggler," but a man of excellent learning who enjoyed God's special favor, both in his natural human endowments and in the divine aid whereby he worked his miracles.[21] Ralegh would enlarge the field of natural

[21] Pliny, *History of the World*, Bk. XXX, chap. i, gives a disparaging account of the origin of magic (what Ralegh calls "conjuring") and lists Moses among the conjurers. The passage calls for a note (Vol. II, p. 373 in the translation of 1601) lamenting that Pliny's ignorance of the Scriptures led him to range Moses among the sorcerers because the pagans were "not able to distinguish between miracles done by the finger of God or his ministers and the illusions practiced by the Devil and his limbs." Likewise John Dee takes refuge in Pliny's misrepresentation of Moses. Striking back at those who confuse "marvellous acts and feats, naturally, mathematically, and mechanically wrought and contrived" with conjuring, Dee explains Pliny's error and moralizes that if Pliny could be thus mistaken those who are far less learned than he should beware how rashly they abuse honest students. Dee's defense, in the "Digression Apologetical" in his Preface to Euclid's *Elements*, trans. by H. Billingsley (1570), sig. Ai^v–Aiii^r, is like Ralegh's in emphasizing the distinction between natural magic and conjuring. Thomas Nashe (*Works*, ed. McKerrow, II, 116) cites the pagan opinion of Cornelius Tacitus that Moses' discovery of water in the desert was due to natural observations.

philosophy, not by questioning the miracles reported in the divinely inspired Scriptures, but by constricting the area of operations which the popular mind assigned to sorcery.

Of the Deluge

Why a story which has become a nursery symbol should enter into an account of a man's opinions on the scope of scientific study requires a word of explanation. The Elizabethan "atheist" who regarded the story of the Flood and Noah's Ark as a fable had a long ancestry: even the early Christian apologists deemed it necessary to advance arguments for the credibility of the Biblical story. The simple tale in Genesis had been embroidered upon by Jew and Christian, until a seemingly endless commentary on every conceivable detail of the construction, arrangement of quarters, and even the sanitary facilities of the Ark was available to a Renaissance writer. As it was one of the first to be attacked, the story of the Ark was one of the last to give way before the demonstrations of geological and anthropological studies.[22] The answers to the many questions raised about the possibilities of a world-wide deluge and of the preservation of mankind and the animal kingdom in a single vessel reflect the scientific knowledge of a writer and, if the inquiry is extended, of an age. The problems which Ralegh discusses had engaged, and were still to engage for a long time to come, the serious attention of men of great abilities.

Ralegh grapples manfully with the principal doubts raised against the tale: that the Flood described in Genesis was no different from, and may have been identical with, the disasters recorded in pagan legend, like the flood of Oxyges, or of Deucalion; that the Flood was simply a natural disaster, not a divine punishment; and that the story of the Ark is intrinsically impossible

---

For other analogues to Ralegh's opinions on magic see Lynn Thorndike, *A History of Magic and Experimental Science*, VI (New York, 1941), 347-49, 382, 391, 411, 414-15.

[22] A. D. White, *A History of the Warfare of Science with Theology*, 2 vols. (New York, 1896), I, 209-48; a chapter entitled "From Genesis to Geology."

in its details.²³ The first objection he disposes of by arguing, quite consistently with his views on the antiquity and divine authority of the Scriptures, that the floods of pagan story were corrupted versions of the Mosaic account or that they were purely local. By comparative chronology he proves these legendary floods, with their saviors of the human race, to be of later date than Noah's; and to clinch the argument he sees in Noah the prototype of almost every mythological hero with whom the patriarch has anything in common, especially with those who are famed as innovators of human arts and crafts. Ralegh rejects also the purely natural explanations of the universal deluge: although God worked in part through second causes, the catastrophe was too great to proceed from the natural operation of second causes alone. Therefore Ralegh follows Ludovicus Vives in discounting any natural forecast of the Flood by means of an unusual conjunction of the stars; still more emphatically, he denies that such a conjunction could have caused the Flood.²⁴ The simple truth is found in the scriptural account: God warned Noah, who had ample time to build the Ark, and God drowned the world in an unnatural and unparalleled deluge of waters from above and from within the earth.

In his arguments for the plausibility of the story of the Ark, Ralegh brushes aside some, at least, of the minutiae which engaged the commentators: whether the Ark had three decks or four, whether it carried amphibious animals, whether it was lighted by a carbuncle. Although he is duly attentive to such problems as the kind of wood used in building the Ark, he

[23] "Of Noah's Flood," I, vii, pp. 98–128.
[24] I, vii, 5 and 6, pp. 105–7. The conjunction of 1524, which some astrologers held to be like that which preceded Noah's flood and could therefore be expected to produce a like effect, was the subject of extended and bitter controversy. Lynn Thorndike, *op. cit.*, V, 178–233, devotes to the subject an entire chapter, which includes other interesting analogues to Ralegh's discussion. It should be noted that the rational complications of the story of the Flood were increased for Ralegh by the assumption, following a persistent error of his day, that the highest mountain of the world did not stretch "above *thirty* miles" upright (p. 106). See below, chap. vii, note 63.

Of Miracles 187

concentrates on the major issue: that the capacity of the Ark was adequate for its cargo.[25] For his measurements he rejects the "geometrical cubit" (once favored by St. Augustine) because it would result in absurdities if applied to other Biblical stories, and he settles upon a cubit roughly equivalent to two feet. The question of measurement, he concedes, is relative: since the cubit is determined in ratio to a man's forearm, a larger equivalent for the cubit would mean larger men and larger animals, and, in consequence, no enlargement of the vessel's capacity relative to the demands upon it. But like St. Augustine, whom he cites frequently in these passages, Ralegh finds the accommodations of the Ark adequate for man, beast, and fodder. To make his point he first minimizes the number of animals to be carried by lumping together species which in any way resemble each other and by eliminating hybrids, and then, by some rough calculations, he shows that the number of beasts needed to preserve the animal kingdom, with strict observance of the terms of God's command, could be carried in the Ark —with a comfortable margin to take care of any underestimating. Ralegh's chief concern, however, is with the resting place of the Ark, for thereon depends his narrative of the resettlement of the earth and the origins of the nations. Fully half the chapter [26] on the Flood is given over to arguments on this issue. Relying heavily on inferences to be drawn from later events of Biblical story, snatching at the least clue in the story of Noah himself, and applying every scrap of geographical information that will support the theory, Ralegh rejects the belief that the Ark rested on Mount Ararat in Armenia. Ararat is a mountain chain, not a peak, he argues; the resettlement of the earth began

---

[25] I, vii, 9, pp. 110–13. Even on this matter Ralegh's orthodoxy had been challenged. Protesting to the Privy Council concerning the spoils of the Portugal voyage, Sir Roger Williams wrote (July 24, 1589) that Ralegh "belied the Ark of Noah, which was the best ship that ever was." See Oldys, *Life*, in Ralegh, *Works* (1829), I, 119–21. I am indebted to Professor Charles E. Mounts for a complete transcript of Williams' letter, in Harleian MS 6845.

[26] Pp. 113–28. Two double-page maps accompany this discussion and the following chapter on the resettlement of the earth.

not in Armenia but at a point close to India, in the teeming East which surpassed the West in culture and which a few centuries after the Flood poured forth huge armies.

The chapter on the Flood is more interesting for its method than for its obsolete lore. The story is in the Bible and therefore is literally true, even though it "hath not been received by all: for divine testimonies do not persuade all natural men to those things to which their own reason cannot reach." [27] Hence the need for a rational demonstration of its inherent probability. For his argument Ralegh once again pillages the commentaries, though it must be noted that much of the enlargement of this tale was in his time popular knowledge.[28] In his account of the migrations after the Flood he insists upon a respect for geography and therefore decries the extravagances of Josephus, who, he says, "gave all Noah's children feathers, to carry them far away in all haste. For mine own opinion I always keep the rule of neighborhood." [29] What enlivens Ralegh's narrative, however, is not an occasional wryness of phrase but his use of new learning to bolster old beliefs. The process is not peculiar to him, and indeed it was more and more widely employed in later centuries as science and discovery challenged the literal truth of many an Old Testament story. As Ralegh uses it the method is highly personal; he draws his illustrations from activities and experiences which held his keenest interest. Galileo's observations of the planet Venus are called in to provide a natural explanation for phe-

---

[27] I, vii, 1, p. 98.

[28] He gives respectful, but not unquestioning, attention to the opinions of St. Augustine, most of the references being to the *De Civitate Dei* with the commentary of Ludovicus Vives. He quotes and quarrels with Josephus and Pererius; and for the strict reading of critical passages he turns, as elsewhere in the *History*, to the polyglot edition of the Bible by Arias Montanus. He acknowledges Buteo [*De Arca Noe*, of which there is an edition dated Lyons, 1554] as his authority on the number and kinds of animals the Ark carried. D. C. Allen, "The Relation of Drayton's 'Noah's Flood' to the Ordinary Learning of the Early Seventeenth Century," *Modern Language Notes*, LII (1937), 106–11, notes how commonplace the extra-Biblical knowledge of the Flood was and cites a number of commentaries in print. [29] I, viii, 15, pt. 2, p. 172.

nomena associated with the flood of the legendary Oxyges.[30] The waterspouts seen in the West Indies justify the phrasing of Moses, that the "windores" or floodgates of heaven opened.[31] The same process is continued in the following chapter, which deals with the resettlement of the earth. The difficulties of the Spaniards when they attempted to move inland in their unpathed tropical lands make a parallel to the hard conditions of travel immediately after the Flood.[32] The pride and independence of the Spaniards in occupying the New World illustrate the isolationism of the descendants of Noah as they occupied their several provinces.[33] Both the Spaniards in Peru and "the English, which I sent under Sir Richard Grenville to inhabit Virginia" [34] fell into the easy error of mistaking as place names the answers which the natives gave to their questions; the lesson to be derived from their experience is caution in the identification of ancient place names. The griffin of legend guarded gold much as "tigers, lions, and other ravenous and cruel beasts" guard gold in America, or as alligators guard pearls: not that they care for the treasure, but simply that they fight when disturbed by treasure-seekers who come into their country.[35] Even the wicker and leather boats of the ancient Britons are more real to Ralegh because he has seen the like at the Dingle in Ireland.[36] This flair for identifying himself with his subject through his own wealth of experience vivifies many a page of the *History*. Especially in the chapters on the Flood and the resettlement of the earth the personal note lends conviction to his speculations on the fables of antiquity.

Another indication of the seriousness of these discussions may be found in several citations of Ralegh as an authority on the Flood and its consequences. In *Origines sacrae,* a much-commended

---

[30] I, vii, 2, pp. 100–101. This is the context, too, of the quotation at the head of this chapter.   [31] I, vii, 6, p. 107.   [32] I, viii, 3, p. 133.

[33] I, viii, 15, pt. 2, p. 172. Even in this context Ralegh manages to get in a plug for a favorite thesis by pointing out the vulnerability of the Spaniards in America to "invasion, expulsion, and destruction."

[34] I, viii, 15, pt. 5, p. 175.   [35] I, viii, 15, pt. 5, pp. 176–77.

[36] I, viii, 3, pp. 134–35.

Restoration treatise against unbelief, Edward Stillingfleet quotes at length "that judicious historian" on the nature of the Flood: his comparison of the downpour with the West Indian waterspouts, his judgment on how the breaking of the great deep swelled the Flood by releasing the waters beneath the earth, his estimates on the capacity of the Ark.[37] Stillingfleet modifies Ralegh's statements; for example, he corrects the absurd estimate of the height of the highest mountain as thirty miles, and he sees no necessity for enlarging the cubit beyond the common cubit of one and one-half feet. Although he shows a preference for the account by Buteo, from whom Ralegh took the estimates on the number of beasts that would have to be saved, Stillingfleet apparently considered it advantageous to quote the popular historian. A century after the first edition of *Origines sacrae*, Ralegh still rates a footnote, again along with Buteo, in a conservative work entitled *A Treatise on the Deluge* by Alexander Catcott.[38]

But at the end of the eighteenth century a writer who treats the *History* respectfully and even cites it on several points, finds Ralegh's knowledge of science sadly deficient.[39] Just as the works of Stillingfleet and Catcott show the vitality of the lore about the Flood, the comments of this anonymous writer show clearly that opinion has changed, that the natural philosophy and the pseudo-science of Ralegh have become obsolete for the general reader no less than for the specialist:

---

[37] *Origines sacrae; or, A Rational Account of the Grounds of Natural and Revealed Religion*, 8th ed. (London, 1709), pp. 339–45.

[38] (London, 1761), p. 22. A plate facing p. 54 illustrates the theory of the earth's structure by which the waters of the deep contributed to the Flood.

[39] *Literary and Critical Remarks on Sundry Eminent Divines and Philosophers of the Last and Present Age* (London, 1795); cited by J. Beau, "La Religion de Sir Walter Ralegh," *Revue Anglo-Américaine*, XI (1934), 415, who quotes the sentence on Ralegh's rigid orthodoxy. The title page lists a distinguished company of philosophers, divines, and men of letters (Hobbes, Locke, Newton, Dr. Johnson, Hurd, Priestley); and Ralegh's name leads all the rest. But this prominence on the title page is disproportionate to the space allotted to him in the text: the Preface, pp. ii, vii, x–xiii.

Of Miracles

It may be said of Sir Walter Raleigh that his learning was more profound than his sense, he being not a little subject to superstition, and even devoted to magic and astrology, so as almost to speak seriously of the prop of the earth, though it does not appear that he conceived it to be Atlas, an ox, or an elephant: and so ignorant does he seem to have been of astronomy, as not to have known that after the sun's, properly the earth's, standing still in Gilgal, the same impetus was necessary to set it in motion again as at its first creation; and even to give as a reason why the garden of Eden could not be in the moon, that the moon is too near the sun to be habitable. But whatever was his skill in natural philosophy or metaphysics, he was a most learned and valuable historian, excellently acquainted, as appears from his other works, with the human heart and its springs of action. But the reader must regret his rigid orthodoxy, that held him to the literal text of Scripture as if the pens of the writers were always actually guided mechanically by the Holy Ghost, and caused him to deem it entirely free from corruption and sophistication, though he did not deem the translaters infallible.

The writer, be it noted, is not questioning the truth of Scriptures; he is questioning the literalness of Ralegh's interpretation and the accuracy of the science used in explaining the scriptural text. There is a belated and somewhat comic justice in this lament for the "rigid orthodoxy" of the man whom his contemporaries reputed to be an "atheist." Continuing his critique, the writer finds that Ralegh's attribution of every event to particular providence "rendered his work a kind of medley of history and cant, and divests mankind of free agency," and that the author was too restrained in his inquiries.

It is an unhappy thing . . . that so great a man as Sir Walter Raleigh forbore all incursions of speculation, and glided over difficulties lest he should have failed in attempting to penetrate them; and that sacred truths, or any truths should suffer for want of liberal discussion: for certainly where truth lies at the bottom, there is no danger in digging.

The writer lists a number of problems of Old Testament history which Ralegh dodged, among them many details in the account of the Flood: for example, why there were no boats before Noah's

Ark, "though in his discourse of shipping, he gives it as his opinion,[40] that there were ships before the Flood, transporting vessels at least, whereby the world was amply, he thinks, peopled." Thus the critic shrewdly cites Ralegh against himself, and further notes that the "great numbers" of galleys which Semiramis had only four centuries after the Flood indicate the early development of ships. He then mentions a few of the more common doubts about the story and concludes, "About such-like questions Sir Walter seems to have thought it imprudent to stickle; and vain indeed some of them may be."

These few citations of Ralegh in the seventeenth and eighteenth centuries reflect something of the changing emphasis in reading the story of Noah.[41] Not only was Ralegh in harmony with many a godly predecessor who endeavored to rationalize the tale, but his "scientific" comments on the Flood and the Ark continued to be good teaching until the science from which they derived became obsolete for the many as well as for the few.

Of Astrology

When Elizabethans disagreed about the legitimacy of astrology they usually were arguing about one branch of the science, judicial astrology, concerned with foretelling the influence of the stars upon the progress of human affairs. On natural astrology, which was concerned with the influence of the stars upon physical matter and therefore with weather, time of planting, and the like, there is a more general agreement in which Ralegh shares. The numerous attacks on judicial astrology included arguments on rational, ethical, and religious grounds.[42] Rational

---

[40] See *Works* (1829), VIII, 317. But Ralegh contends that all antediluvian boats were too weak to withstand the Flood.

[41] The works cited are merely representative; there is no intent, in my citations, to fix the dates of changing opinions on the Flood. As indicated at the beginning of this section, doubts about the Flood were current centuries before Ralegh wrote the *History*, and, conversely, literal belief in the Flood still persists.

[42] For summaries and descriptions of the principal works see Carroll Camden, Jr., "Astrology in Shakespeare's Day," *Isis*, XIX (1933), 26-73. Moriz Sond-

Of Miracles

arguments involved, among other problems, the difficulty of determining the moment of birth, the problem of the unlike careers of twins, and the overruling of "nativities" by general disasters, which may kill at one stroke many persons who certainly did not have the same birth hour. The ethical arguments pointed to the tendency of evildoers to blame their misdeeds on the stars, and the religious objections were directed against tying God to strict necessity imposed by the stars. Ralegh's position is much like that of sincere defenders of a "science" often discredited by quackery.

In his brief discourse on the subject,[43] Ralegh adheres to the ethical motive which dominates the *History*. He insists that the stars cannot control man's will, which is incorporal, and that man therefore need not be ruled by the stars. Nor does he deviate from the general principle that God is superior to all natural agents and therefore in no way bound by the heavens.

But in this question of fate, the middle course is to be followed, that as with the heathen we do not bind God to his creatures, in this supposed necessity of destiny, so on the contrary we do not rob those beautiful creatures of their powers and offices. For had any of these second causes despoiled God of his prerogative, or had God himself constrained the mind and will of man to impious acts by any celestial enforcements, then sure the impious excuse of some were justifiable; of whom St. Augustine [said] . . . "Where we reprehend them of evil deeds, they again with wicked perverseness urge that rather the Author and Creator of the stars, than the doer of the evil is to be accused."

---

heim, "Shakespeare and the Astrology of His Time," *Journal of the Warburg Institute*, II (1939), 243–59, defines the issues in the controversy. For extended surveys of the conflict of opinion on astrology, see D. C. Allen, *The Star-Crossed Renaissance* (Durham, N.C., 1941), and Thomas Tomkis, *Albumazar: a Comedy*, ed. H. G. Dick, "University of California Publications in English," XIII (1944), Introd., pp. 17–47.

[43] I, i, xi, pp. 14–17. The quotations which follow are from these pages. There are casual references to astrology in the *History*; e.g., I, v, 5, p. 78: three things, "not counting constellations," cause long and healthful life; I, vi, 8, p. 96: "cozening astrologers"; III, viii, 8, p. 100: a condemnation of a general who allowed astrological portents to govern his actions.

But that the stars and other celestial bodies incline the will by mediation of the sensitive appetite, which is also stirred by the constitution and complexion, it cannot be doubted.

The influence, however, is not irresistible if one contends against it; neither sun nor stars have power over the minds of men, except for that which may be exerted through the body.[44] Even such effect as the stars may have upon the corporal part of man and indirectly upon the will may be offset by proper education, "for there are none in the world so wickedly inclined, but that a religious instruction and bringing up may fashion anew, and reform them." Likewise those who are best disposed by nature may be corrupted by the fellowship of evil men. The extreme of virtue is found "where a favorable constellation (allowing that the stars incline the will) and a virtuous education do happily arrive"; and, conversely, the extreme of vice is found when ill nature meets with like nurture.

In these statements Ralegh is not rejecting judicial astrology but is defining the limits of the study in a manner which, the defenders of astrology said, had been followed since the days of Ptolemy. They contended that no reputable astrologer (the terms are not necessarily contradictory at the beginning of the seventeenth century) believed that the stars enforce the will of

---

[44] This is the Christian position, limiting astrology in order to reconcile it with freedom of the will and the omnipotence of God. St. Augustine is a favorite authority with writers on both sides of the question. To more familiar citations of Calvin and William Perkins, among the clergy, may be added Robert Gray's emphatic repudiation of judicial astrology, which is an extension of his judgment on magic already quoted (note 19, above): "The stars do sometimes foreshow such things as happen, but they are not the enforcing causes of such things as happen. Most impious and blasphemous it is, to ascribe these things to the influence and operation of the stars: for it is to rob God of his honor, to derogate from his power, to overthrow his providence, and to tie God to secondary and subordinate causes, and in respect of ourselves, it extinguisheth the fear of God in us, it hinders our repentance and conversion unto God, it draws us to atheism, and to a flat contempt both of God and his judgments. Pharaoh was not moved with all the miracles that Moses and Aaron could do, so long as he saw his sorcerers could do the same; because he attributed whatsoever was in those miracles to art and nature, and not to the power of God." *An Alarum to England* (1609), sigs. C1^v–C2^r.

man or limit the power of God. Christopher Heydon, who wrote a treatise of five hundred and fifty pages in reply to a violent and sometimes scurrilous attack on astrology and astrologers by John Chamber, repudiates again and again any such impious beliefs:

> ... Ptolemy removeth all fatal necessity, other than that which is physical, and supposeth a conveniency of the patient as well as of the agent, leaving nevertheless the liberty of our will unchecked, and the free moderation both of the course and power of the stars unto God.
>
> ... [An infinite number of scholars] all with one consent teach no further, than our schoolmen and divines do second them, namely that the heavens do incline, but not enforce, because they have no direct power over the will of man from whence all human actions, as from their original, do naturally flow.[45]

On these matters the earnest defenders of astrology come close to agreement with their critics. Admitting that man enjoys freedom of the will, that God can overrule the stars, that accidents may intervene, and that the general fate may overtake the particular, they still believe that there remains a wide and legitimate field for their study. Ralegh makes a neat summary of this middle ground:

> But it was well said of Plotinus, that the stars were significant, but not efficient, giving them yet something less than their due: and therefore as I do not consent with those who would make those glorious creatures of God virtueless, so I think that we derogate from his eternal and absolute power and providence to ascribe to them the same dominion over our immortal souls which they have over all bodily substances and perishable natures.

In his chapter on magic Ralegh links astrology with the other arts in his defense that abuse does not invalidate the proper use. Such abuse of astrology did not deter Abraham from his observations of the heavens; "neither can it dehort wise and learned men in these days from attributing those virtues, influences,

---

[45] *A Defence of Judicial Astrology* (Cambridge, 1603), pp. 3, 20–21; cf. pp. 30, 32, 65, 85, 101–2, and *passim*.

and inclinations to the stars and other lights of heaven, which God hath given to those his glorious creatures." [46] The corruption of astrology, like the debasement of magic, is the work of the Devil, who has introduced such superstitious doctrines as the use of incantations, characters, and numbers. He has "taught men to believe in the strength of words and letters (which without faith in God are but ink or common breath). . . ." [47]

Ralegh's comments on natural philosophy and bordering topics chart the course which he and his co-workers in science steered between the authority of Holy Writ and the damnation of the black art. The first was inviolable: Ralegh was indeed, in Hauptmann's phrase, "chained to an ancient book." An inviolable authority, but not encyclopedic in its coverage: where the Scriptures are silent and a matter "is no point of our saving belief, it is lawful for every man to be guided in this and the like questions by the best reason, circumstance, and likelihood." Hence the possibility of thirty-one folio pages on the Flood and fifty on the resettlement of the earth. Throughout the *History* Ralegh's approach to any problem of exegesis is to emphasize by every credible means the reasonableness of scriptural narrative, and, when the limits of credulity are reached, to yield to the divine sanction. But to the Elizabethan who went voyaging on strange seas of thought the winds of popular superstition were no less a hazard than the rock of Biblical authority. By definition, by appeal to godly example and authority, and by persuasion Ralegh tries to free legitimate experiment from the sulfurous taint of black magic. He forms no grandiose Baconian designs for the

---

[46] I, xi, 5, p. 207.

[47] I, xi, 3, p. 206. Ralegh has little to say about astronomy, but in his published opinions he follows the geocentric theory. He marshals against the theory of the crystalline heaven (I, i, 8, pp. 11–12) arguments supported by Biblical authority, but that does not entail a rejection of the Ptolemaic theory.

The distinction in meaning between astrology and astronomy as sciences was clear in the Renaissance; the distinction in *terminology* was less precise. See a note by H. G. Dick (*op. cit.*, p. 32) which concludes: "The free interchange of the words 'astronomy' and 'astrology' does not prove that the concepts were confused."

Of Miracles

government of the province of knowledge; he seems content if his ship has sea room off the shores of that province.

Of Men before Adam

Questions of chronology, both as the science of measuring time and as the record of mankind, absorbed the energies of the most learned men of the Renaissance. The aim of their study was to determine as accurately as possible the date of every important event in human history from the Creation to yesterday's burning of a heretic; their text was the Bible, to which the vast accumulation of Biblical commentary and the pagan histories were appendices; the guide for their investigations was the painstaking computation of time evolved by centuries of astronomical study. It is all too easy to underestimate the quality and value of a scholarly activity of which we are the complacent beneficiaries. In our amusement over research which determined the exact hour, day of the week, and date of the creation, we are likely to forget that the same kind of interest in the problems of time led to the correction of the Julian Calendar and synthesized a large body of historical materials. The details of Biblical chronology, without much question of the abbreviated past which it allotted to the earth and its inhabitants, continued to engage the attention of prominent scholars long after Ralegh's time. Sir Isaac Newton, for example, was quite as interested in the subject as was Sir Walter Ralegh. Indeed, the philosopher and scientist went the Elizabethan amateur one better: Newton labored also over the interpretation of Biblical prophecy, a subject to which Ralegh gave only passing attention.[48]

[48] Newton died before he finished preparing for the press *The Chronology of Ancient Kingdoms Amended* (1728), which had appeared in an unauthorized edition. His tract, *Observations upon the Prophecies of Daniel and the Apocalypse of St. John*, was also published posthumously, in 1733. The *Chronology* contains a short chronicle which was drawn up, Newton says (p. 8) "to make chronology suit with the course of nature, with astronomy, with sacred history, with Herodotus the father of history, and with itself." Both works are cited by Preserved Smith, *A History of Modern Culture*, 2 vols. (New York, 1930–34), II, 267–68; see also the article on Newton in the *Dict. Nat. Biog.* The re-

The questions raised in Renaissance studies of chronology were not simple, nor the answers easy; they touched the intellectual and religious life of the Elizabethan at many points. They were philosophical, in that no less an authority than Aristotle had argued the eternity of the world; religious in that a sacred book was held to be an unimpeachable authority governing all calculations; historical in that pagan records had to be squared with Scripture or explained away; astronomical in that the varieties of calendars used by ancient peoples had to be synchronized.[49] The issues are similar to those encountered in Elizabethan differences about natural philosophy: human testimony, observations, and deductions against a divinely inspired book and an authoritative religion. We have seen how the Christian apologists and Ralegh rejected the Aristotelian concept of the eternity of the world; and it is no matter of surprise that Ralegh should concede to Scripture the same authority in chronology that he accorded to its narratives of the Flood and of miracles. But there remained for his explanation and comment more problems than can be fully discussed within the limits of this chapter. In compiling his *History*, Ralegh apparently subscribed to the thesis of his old friend Hakluyt, who arranged his *Voyages* "by the help of geography and chronology (which I may call the sun and the moon, the right eye and the left of all history)."[50] Ralegh prided himself on his attention to geography, for example in his account of the resettlement of the earth; but he was especially

---

mainder of this chapter follows my article, "Ralegh on the Problems of Chronology," *Huntington Library Quarterly*, XI (1948), 129-48.

[49] Geological evidence on the age of the earth was not unknown or unnoted, but such observations were too limited and too easily explained away in terms of sixteenth-century preconceptions to affect seriously the reading of Genesis; see A. D. White, *The Warfare of Science with Theology*, 2 vols. (New York, 1896), I, 209-14, and *passim*. In Ralegh's *History*, references to geological processes are rare; for example, a brief speculation on the separation of islands like Sicily and Great Britain from the mainland does not imply a time requirement outside the limits of history. The passage (V, i, 4, p. 321) is taken directly from Ortelius; see G. W. Whiting in the *Times Literary Supplement* (July 11, 1936), p. 580.

[50] "Preface to the Reader," *Principal Navigations* (1598).

concerned that his *History* survey the past with a good "left eye." His efforts met with considerable success, for a seventeenth-century biographer and a twentieth-century historian alike praise his "chronological exactness."[51] But the answers he found for various problems in chronology are less important, for this study, than the means by which he arrives at his solutions. Without rebelling against the restrictions which his age and his religion imposed upon him, Ralegh worked thoughtfully to find the skein of truth in the tangled threads of controversy. In the manner of his working much of the quality and temper of his mind is revealed.

The first problem confronting the student of world history was the interpretation of pagan records in the light of Scripture. At worst the ancient histories lent their authority to those who reckoned up "genealogies more ancient than Adam";[52] at best they were sufficiently impressive in extent and authority to require explanation and they constituted a valuable supplement to the Biblical record. The claims of Egypt and other early civilizations to greater antiquity than the Hebrew were by no means

[51] John Shirley, *Life of Ralegh* (London, 1677), pp. 176–77. J. W. Thompson, *A History of Historical Writing*, 2 vols. (New York, 1942), I, 611: "While Ralegh did not approach his sources in a critical spirit, and viewed the past in the light of a moral lesson, he made a step forward in realizing the need of geographical study in connection with history; and chronological exactness is one of his virtues."

[52] John Dove, *A Confutation of Atheism* (1605), p. 5. Earlier and perhaps more pointed is the complaint of Thomas Nashe (*Works*, ed. McKerrow, I, 172): "I hear say there be mathematicians abroad that will prove men before Adam." F. S. Boas, *Christopher Marlowe* (Oxford, 1940), p. 114, takes it for granted that Nashe is referring to Harriot and that the statement which I have quoted "finds support in Harriot's manuscript papers which include calculations about the chronology of Genesis." But as yet no one has shown that Harriot's calculations differ from the hundreds of orthodox attempts to work out the Biblical chronology. Through the courtesy of Dr. John Shirley I have been able to check a few examples of Harriot's figures in microfilms of his papers in the British Museum. Those which I have seen represent attempts to determine, by conventional methods, the Old Testament chronology and to make a theoretical estimate of the rate of population growth. The notes are of a kind which would have been useful to Ralegh, and perhaps were prepared for him.

buried in inaccessible tomes; indeed, convenient summaries of the principal statements concerning a world more ancient than Adam could be found in popular books, sometimes in works which collected such opinions to condemn them. Thus Augustine wrote a brief chapter in *De Civitate Dei* "Of the falseness of that history that saith the world hath continued many thousand years," and another on "The Egyptians' abominable lyings, to claim their wisdom the age of 100,000 years." He rejects such claims to antiquity and explains that the Egyptian year was but four months long. But his commentator, Ludovicus Vives, names his sources more specifically; for persons and events that antedate Adam he cites Pliny, Aristotle, Plato, Cicero, Laertius, Mela, and Diodorus. Montaigne, revising his essays for a sixth edition, probably drew in part on Vives for this information; and his disciple, Pierre Charron, published a similar but shorter list in *Of Wisdom*. Mornay likewise mentions such claims in order to reject them. Thomas Lanquet begins his chronicle with a chapter on the "false opinion of the Ethnic philosopher" concerning the origin of the world and the emergence of man, and dismisses abruptly the rival claims of Ethiopians, Egyptians, and Scythians for the greatest antiquity. For the Elizabethan reader who wished to extend his inquiry there was no dearth of texts of the principal histories from which Vives and other scholars drew their information.[53]

[53] St. Augustine, *Of the City of God* (London, 1610), Bk. XII, chap. x, pp. 449–51, with Vives' commentary; Bk. XVIII, chap. xl, p. 729. The first edition with Vives' commentary appeared in 1522. The passage in Montaigne is a manuscript addition in the Bordeaux copy to the "Apology for Raimond Sebond"; see Montaigne's *Essays*, ed. Jacob Zeitlin, 3 vols. (New York, 1934–36), II, 236, and notes, for parallels to Vives. Charron's list, *Of Wisdom* (London, 1612), Bk. II, chap. ii, p. 258, contains in this edition an obvious error, placing Socrates, instead of Zoroaster, six thousand years before Plato. Philip Mornay, *A Work Concerning the Trueness of the Christian Religion* (London, 1587), chap. viii, p. 115, and chap. ix, p. 136, dismisses the ancient records as based on "month years." Augustine (Bk. XII, chap. xii, p. 452) and Mornay (chap. viii, pp. 126–27) emphasize that any age given to the world, no matter how great, is insignificant in comparison to God's eternity. Lanquet's chapter is the first in his *Epitome of Chronicles* (London, 1559). For additional refer-

Of Miracles

A minor and less easily documented complication in chronology, occasioned by rumors about New World legends of man's antiquity, also calls for a brief word before we turn to Ralegh's *History*. According to Nashe, the atheists "impudently persist in it that the late discovered Indians are able to show antiquities thousands before Adam." [54] Christopher Marlowe was charged by Baines with saying "That the Indians and many authors of antiquity have assuredly written of above sixteen thousand years agone whereas Adam is proved to have lived within six thousand years." [55] The impact of discovery, however, was stronger upon orthodox geographical concepts than upon the orthodox chronology, although European observers, including Thomas Harriot, were quick to note Indian analogues to Christian traditions and beliefs. The "sixteen thousand years" perhaps reflected certain Indian beliefs in successive cycles of creation, destruction and renewal of the earth. Lopez de Gomara in his *Historia de Mexico* reported that the Aztecs believed they were living in the fifth and last "sun" or age, with the year 858 of this last age corresponding to A.D. 1552.[56] A modern scholar has explained that according to this belief the elapsed time from the first creation to the beginning of the present epoch may be variously interpreted as 15,228 or 2,316 or 1,404 solar years.[57] The first figure, especially with the 858 years of the present epoch added, would approximate the 16,000 years of the Baines note. A probable explanation of the references by Nashe and Baines is that they

---

ences see Paul H. Kocher, *Christopher Marlowe* (Chapel Hill, N.C., 1946), pp. 42–45.   [54] *Works*, ed. McKerrow, II, 116.

[55] Kocher, *loc. cit.*, explains briefly the possibility that the reference is to Asiatic Indians. He suggests quite plausibly that the figure "sixteen thousand years" is merely a jingling contrast to the more orthodox six thousand.

[56] In the edition published in Antwerp, "En casa de Iuan Steelsio, 1554," fols. 293b–297b. The *Historia* was translated under the title *The Pleasant History of the Conquest of the West India* (London, 1578), with the account of Aztec numbers, dates, and theory of the creation at pp. 370–78. Following Gomara, Montaigne describes the five ages of the Aztecs in "Of Coaches," in *Essays*, ed. Zeitlin (New York, 1934–36), III, 122; see the notes on the essay.

[57] Daniel G. Brinton, *The Myths of the New World* (Philadelphia, 1896), p. 250.

stem from the oral, rather than the written, reports of voyagers. Ralegh himself makes one brief allusion to traditions of a flood in America, "as I have learned of some ancient soothsayers among them"; [58] but in chronology his attention is fixed upon the Old World, not the New.

Ralegh directs his efforts toward evolving the most reasonable narrative possible within the limits of the Hebrew chronology. The undertaking has a complexity which is a recurrent theme in the *History,* especially in Books I–III; Ralegh develops his views on chronology sometimes in a complete chapter, sometimes in a section, sometimes in connection with the answer to a particular question, and he summarizes the results in an elaborate table at the end of the volume. There is no need to follow the order of his discussion, which is naturally tied to the plan of his work; his problems are more clearly presented in four successive and related parts. What authority is to be allowed the pagan chronicles and how are they to be fitted into the scriptural narrative? In a particular difficulty (for example, the rapid progress of mankind after the Flood), what interpretation of Scripture is most consistent within itself and with human probabilities? On what time scale, or what kind of calendar, are the events of world history to be recorded? And finally, what degree of accuracy can the compiler of chronicles hope to attain?

For the solution of the first of these problems Ralegh undertakes to whittle the heathen narratives down to scriptural size. Conventionally, he dismisses the Egyptian records as based on "lunary years, which made their antiquities seem the more fabulous"; [59] but he extends the familiar explanation: "One great occasion of this obscurity in the Egyptian story was the ambition

---

[58] I, vii, 5, p. 105. Ralegh places these American floods among those attributable to natural causes.

[59] I, viii, 11, pt. 2, p. 155. But Ralegh rejects the idea that the ages of the patriarchs are reckoned in "lunary years, to wit, of a month or thereabouts, or Egyptian years" (I, v, 5, p. 76). Such a mode of computation would make them fathers at six or eight years, and Abraham's "great years" at his death would become a mere seventeen and a half.

of the priests, who to magnify their antiquities filled the records which were in their hands with many leasings." [60] The many dynasties "were not diverse families of kings, but rather successions of regents, ofttimes many under one king"; and again, "the great number of kings which are said to have reigned in Egypt were none other than viceroys or stewards, such as Joseph was, and such as were the soldans in later ages." [61] The heathen records, though they should be compressed in time, represent corrupt and distorted readings of the holy story wherein the devout student may still find "the story of the first age, with all the works and marvels thereof, amply and lively expressed." The Egyptians had some relics of true knowledge of the first age, partly from inscriptions on stone and metal remaining from before the Flood, partly by tradition from Noah to Cham, who was the first king of Egypt after the Flood; "for all that the Egyptians write of their ancient kings and date of times cannot be feigned." Likewise "Homer had read over all the books of Moses, as by places stolen thence, almost word for word, may appear." [62] After the Flood, each of those nations which did not receive the knowledge of divine letters thought itself the most ancient.[63] Of the many passages on this subordinate and auxiliary relationship of heathen letters one which deals with the resettlement of the earth may serve as illustration:

And if any profane author may receive allowance herein, the same must be with this caution, that they take their beginning where the Scriptures end. For so far as the story of the nations is therein handled, we must know that both the truth and antiquity of the books of God find no companions equal, either in age or authority. All record, memory, and testimony of antiquity whatsoever, which hath come to the knowledge of men, the same hath been borrowed thence. . . .[64]

---

[60] II, ii, 1, p. 236.   [61] II, ii, 3, pp. 238–39; II, xxvi, 1, p. 599.
[62] The quotations on the imperfect recollections of Scripture are from I, vi, 1, p. 84; I, vi, 4, p. 86; I, vi, 7, p. 93.   [63] I, vii, 4, pp. 103–4.
[64] I, viii, 2, p. 130; cf. II, i, 1, p. 218. The principle followed by Ralegh and his contemporaries has been almost completely reversed; in a modern commentary on Genesis one is likely to find the non-Hebrew sources given the prime authority in chronology.

Their secondary value, however, does not deprive the pagan records of all authority and dignity, nor are they to be casually dismissed as fictitious. Ralegh maintains his accounting for the Assyrian kings as agreeable to the story of Abraham and therefore most certain, "unless we will either derogate from the truth of Moses his computation, which were impiety; or account the whole history of Ninus and Semiramis to be a fiction, which were to condemn all ancient historians for fablers." [65] He concedes that there might be some propriety in trying to reconcile Scripture to the ancient histories if they were unanimous on a given point. In a passage dealing with the kings who ruled during the Babylonian Captivity he writes:

But indeed I find no other necessity or qualification to be used herein than such as may grow out of men's desire to reconcile the Scriptures unto profane authors. And this desire were not unjust, if the consent of all histories were on the one side, and the letter of the holy text were single on the other side.[66]

But in this instance, he continues, the historians disagree so widely and their evidence is so slender that the scriptural account would be superior even if it were merely of equal authority with the rest. Ralegh's middle-of-the-road attitude toward heathen authorities is apparent in his handling of evidence and is also made explicit.

Therefore, for the antiquity of the Egyptians, as I do not agree with Mercator, nor judge with the vulgar, which give too much credit to the Egyptians' antiquities, so I do not think the report of their antiquities so fabulous as either Pererius or other men conceive it.[67]

---

[65] II, i, 8, p. 229.   [66] III, i, 4, pp. 6–7.

[67] I, viii, 7, p. 160. For a still more liberal attitude than Ralegh's, see Edward Livelie, *A True Chronology of the Times of the Persian Monarchy* (London, 1597). Although not in the least inclined to minimize scriptural authority, Livelie maintains vigorously that neglect of the ancient writers who lived near the times of the Persian monarchy weakens the certainty of Scripture. He begins his book with a number of illustrations of "how great service heathen writers do to the word of God, for opening the true meaning thereof" (p. 22), and he commends "the wisdom of our forefathers, in ordering our universities. Where young scholars are first trained up in the studies of humanity before they enter

Of Miracles

And he repeats his idea that Egyptian traditions reached back to a civilization before the Flood.

In the actual attempt to join in one story pagan history and the narratives of the Old Testament, Ralegh inevitably runs into difficult problems which need not be presented in detail. The earliest histories, including myth and legend, are disposed of by matching a fabulous hero with his most likely Biblical prototype.[68] In later and more certain chronologies the solutions are less fanciful. Ralegh's objectives are limited; he does not aim at a complete synchronization of Hebrew history with all non-Hebrew events:

> The truth is that in fitting those things unto the sacred history which are found in profane authors we should not be too careful of drawing the Hebrews to those works of time which had no reference to their affairs; it is enough that, setting in due order these beginnings of accompts, we join them to matters of Israel and Judah where occasion requires.[69]

He is more confident when pagan records and the Old Testament meet on common ground in Assyria and Persia,[70] and he begins the third book of his *History* with a section entitled, "Of the connection of sacred and profane history." The Biblical references to Nebuchadnezzar provide a key to interrelated events and dates:

> Hence have we the first light whereby to discover the means of connecting the sacred and profane histories. For under Nebuchadnezzar was the beginning of the captivity of Judah, which ended when 70 years were expired; and these 70 years took end at the first of Cyrus,

---

into God his school" (p. 15). Where I have compared them, Ralegh's computation does not differ markedly from Livelie's; the differences which I have noted may be attributed to Livelie's attempts to date events precisely, whereas Ralegh does not regard the exact limits of a regnal year.

[68] E.g., I, vi, pp. 84-97, especially sec. 4: the first Jupiter was Cain, Vulcan was Tubalcain.

[69] II, xxiii, 5, p. 575: "Of the Olympiads, and the time when they began."

[70] II, xxv, 1, p. 591: "These later Assyrian kings and the Persians which followed them are the first of whom we find mention made both in profane and sacred books."

whose time being well known affords us means of looking back into the ages past, and forwards into the race of men succeeding. The first year of Cyrus his reign in Persia, by general consent, is joined with the first year of the 55th Olympiad, where that he reigned three and twenty years before his monarchy, and seven years afterwards, it is apparent and almost out of controversy. Giving therefore four hundred and eight years unto the distance between the fall of Troy and the instauration of the Olympiads by Iphitus, we may easily arrive unto those antiquities of Greece which were not merely fabulous.[71]

To define more precisely this concord of dates Ralegh then turns to establishing the limits of the Babylonian Captivity, the seventy years of which he would have begin with the destruction of the Temple.

Even with the pagan historians accounted for, the Renaissance chronicler still had a rough path to travel. According to the Septuagint the world was twelve or more centuries older than the Hebrew text of the Bible allowed; within any one version of the Bible there were obscurities and seeming contradictions in the references to time; in any one version there was wide latitude for differences of opinion on the translation of critical passages; and certain early chroniclers, like Josephus, had acquired an authority which could not be lightly ignored. The inevitable result was a great diversity not only in the estimates of the age of the world but also in the relative dating of the chief events of history. The contradictions in the evidence are simply and adequately illustrated by the variety of opinions on the date of the Creation, increasing in number as long as the Bible dominated the study of history and geology. Listing only the principal authorities, Meredith Hanmer in 1576 cited seventeen estimates ranging from 3759 B.C. to 5505 B.C. In the eight-

[71] III, i, 1, p. 2. In determining the reigns of the Persian monarchs Ralegh brings in the "astronomical computation of Ptolemy" to confirm his historical demonstration, and favors the Greek account, "which being constant in itself, accordeth also with the computation of other historians and astronomers, and likewise with the Holy Scriptures" (III, iv, 1, pp. 42–44). Less "historical" is the attempt to date the Egyptian dynasties in terms of the chronology required by the story of Babel and the date of Abraham's birth (II, ii, 2, pp. 237–38).

Of Miracles 207

eenth century Alphonse Des Vignoles revised upward a predecessor's statement that there were one hundred and thirty-two opinions on the time from the Creation of the world to the birth of Jesus; Des Vignoles had found over two hundred different calculations, with a range of 3,483 to 6,984 years. In Ralegh's computation the date of the Creation is 4031 B.C., quite close to the 4004 B.C. of Archbishop Ussher, whose chronological outline was to attain a quasi-authoritative status by inclusion in many editions of the Bible.[72]

The principle which Ralegh follows is to seek the longest span of time permitted by the Hebrew text. It has been mistakenly reported that he follows the chronology of the Septuagint;[73] what he actually says is that it would be better to do so than to reduce unnecessarily the time between the Flood and the birth of Abraham. The chapter [74] in which this comment occurs is an excellent illustration of the problems arising from conflicts in interpreting the text of the Bible and of the methods by which Ralegh endeavored to find solutions agreeable alike to Scripture and to human reason. The question is whether Abraham was born when Terah was seventy years old, that is, two hundred and ninety years after the Flood; or sixty years later, when Terah was one hundred and thirty years old. It concerns the Assyrian Empire because Ralegh undertakes to regulate his account of the Assyrian kings by the story of Abraham,

---

[72] The textual evidence was further complicated when the "Samaritan" text of the Bible added still another computation to those derived from the Hebrew text and the Septuagint, but Ralegh did not have to reckon with that problem.

Hanmer's list is in the Preface to *A Chronography Continued from the Birth of Christ* (London, 1576), appended to his translation of Eusebius Pamphilus, *The Ancient Ecclesiastical Histories* (London, 1577). Des Vignoles' statement, from the Preface to his *Chronologie de L'Histoire Sainte*, 2 vols. (Berlin, 1738), has been frequently cited. James Ussher's chronology appeared first in Latin (1650 and 1654) and then in English under the title *The Annals of the World* (London, 1658).

[73] A. D. White, *The Warfare of Science with Theology*, I, 254, thus interprets his remarks.

[74] II, i, pp. 217–35: "Of the time of the birth of Abraham, and of the use of this question for ordering the story of the Assyrian Empire."

since any other course would be "to prove things certain by the uncertain." Emphasizing that he proposes to defend a minority opinion in favoring the later date, Ralegh lists four principal objections to his opinion and proceeds to answer them in a closely reasoned analysis of the life of Abraham. He cites authorities on both sides of the question—the Protestants chiefly for the later date, the Catholics chiefly for the earlier; but he protests that his own judgment is guided by the desire for truth and not by religious prejudice.[75] His final argument, that the later date is conducive to greater reasonableness in the scriptural account, illustrates better than any commentary could the philosophy and method by which Ralegh endeavored to make credible the sudden rise of a vast and populous civilization only a few centuries after the Flood.

And if we look over all and do not hastily satisfy our understanding with the first things offered, and thereby being satiated do slothfully and drowsily sit down, we shall find it more agreeable rather to allow the reckoning of the Septuagint, who, according to some editions, make it above 1072 years between the Flood and Abraham's birth, than to take away any part of those 352 years given. For if we advisedly consider the state and countenance of the world, such as it was in Abraham's time, yea, before Abraham was born, we shall find that it were very ill done of us, by following opinion without the guide of reason, to pare the times over-deeply between Abraham and the Flood; because in cutting them too near the quick the reputation of the whole story might perchance bleed thereby, were not the testimony of the Scriptures supreme, so as no objection can approach it, and that we did not follow withal this precept of St. Augustine: That wheresoever any one place in the Scriptures may be conceived disagreeing to the whole, the same is by ignorance of interpretation misunderstood. For in Abraham's time all the then known parts of the world were peopled; all regions and countries had their kings. Egypt had many magnificent cities, and so had Palestine and all the bordering countries; yea, all that part of the world besides, as far as India, and those not built with

---

[75] II, i, 7, p. 227: "For myself I do neither mislike the contrary opinion because commonly those of the Romish religion labor to uphold it, nor favor this larger account of times because many notable men of the Protestant writers have approved it, but for the truth itself."

Of Miracles

sticks, but of hewen stones and defended with walls and rampiers, which magnificence needed a parent of more antiquity than those other men have supposed. And, therefore, where the Scriptures are plainest and best agreeing with reason and nature, to what end should we labor to beget doubts and scruples or draw all things into wonders and marvels, giving also strength thereby to common cavillers and to those men's apish brains who only bend their wits to find impossibilities and monsters in the story of the world and mankind.[76]

In sum, the Scriptures are consistent, and seeming conflicts are due to our dim-witted interpretations; it is a Christian duty to seek an explanation that will enhance, not diminish, the credibility of the scriptural account; whatever the improbability of an event to human reason, we must rely upon the incontrovertible authority of the Bible.

A like process of textual scrutiny and ratiocination is applied to other chronological difficulties arising from the disproportion between human achievements and the time allotted to them by the Scriptures. Thus Ralegh argues for the development of Egyptian civilization before the Flood on the analogy of the rapid expansion of the kingdoms in the East after the Flood.

And these troops of Semiramis were gathered out of all those eastern kingdoms from Media to the Mediterranean Sea, when there had now passed from the Flood to the time of this her invasion somewhat less or more than 360 years; for much more time the true chronology cannot allow, though I confess that, in respect of the strange greatness of Semiramis' army and the incredible multitudes gathered, this is as short a time as can well be given.

But again the Bible, which tells us that Egypt was "an established kingdom filled with many cities in Abraham's time," is the court of last appeal. The long lives of the patriarchs and the caution which so generous a life span induced also explain reasonably (the premise granted) the speedy repopulation of the earth.[77]

Having settled as best he could the conflicts in sources and

---

[76] II, i, 7, pp. 227–28. Edward Stillingfleet, *Origines sacrae* (1709), pp. 348–49, quotes with approval this entire passage; but, unlike Ralegh, Stillingfleet would follow the longer chronology of the Septuagint.

[77] I, viii, 11, pts. 4 and 5, pp. 157–59.

texts, Ralegh still had to find a common scale on which to record events dated by varied calendars and modes of reckoning time. In the text of the *History* [78] he outlines the principal obstacles in the way of determining a satisfactory calendar—one which records accurately the duration of the solar year and does not result in a progressive derangement of the seasons because of an excess or deficiency of days in the year. He explains the difficulties of the Hebrew lunar year, the devices of intercalation by which the Greeks (notably Harpalus, Meto, and Calippus) endeavored to keep "their year as near as they could unto the highway of the planets," and the great advance made in the calendar ordered by Julius Caesar. This Julian year of three hundred and sixty-five days, with the annual excess of approximately six hours provided for by the intercalation of one day in every fourth year, Ralegh not improperly calls the "last reformation of the calendar," for further change was by way of amendment, not reconstruction.

The correction of the Julian year by Pope Gregory XIII, *Anno Domini* 1582, is not as yet entertained by general consent; it was indeed but as a note added unto the work of Caesar, yet a note of great importance.

England had come close to adopting the Gregorian calendar on the basis of the independent calculation of native mathematicians, including Ralegh's friend John Dee; but the bishops, judging the new calendar by its origin and not by astronomy, decided that they would rather be wrong than be Roman.[79] Ralegh, who

---

[78] II, iii, 6, pp. 255–58: "Of the solary and lunary years, and how they are reconciled with the form of the Hebrew year, and their manner of intercalation." The quotations which follow are from this section. Ralegh may have had help in preparing this brief treatise. The kind of information which it contains was available in books such as those by Joseph J. Scaliger, *De emendatione temporum* (1583) and by Sethus Calvisius, *Opus chronologicum* (1605); but I have not attempted to identify his immediate sources.

[79] John Dee's treatise on the correction of the calendar was checked by other English mathematicians and approved by Sir William Cecil; see the *Dict. Nat. Biog.*, s.v. "Dee." The attempted reform got as far as the preparation of a proclamation by the Queen, "declaring the causes of the reformation of the calendar

Of Miracles 211

obviously approves the correction, makes no comment on his country's failure to adopt it, but turns again to the complexities of the Hebrew year.

This section on the measurement of time, necessary as it is for the interpretation of certain aspects of Old Testament history, is secondary in importance to the practical problem of reducing to terms of the Julian Calendar such systems of dating as from the creation of the world, from the Flood, from the founding of Rome, by Olympiads, or by dynasties and reigns. Ralegh explains both the problem and his solution of it in a note, two pages long, before the "Chronological Table" which concludes the *History*. Not only were the modes of computing time different, Ralegh observes, but the beginning of the year was variously dated, the reigns of kings sometimes overlapped, and the regnal year of a king commonly consisted of parts of two calendar years, as he illustrates by citing the events of the first year of Queen Elizabeth, beginning November 17, 1558. Much of the prefatory note is given over to explaining the mechanics of the table, which aims no higher than approximate accuracy. Ralegh does not attempt to record differences in the beginning of the year, nor does he enter a line for every year only to leave it blank if there is nothing to record therein.[80] As for the slight discrepancies originating in the conflicting dates for the beginning of the year, "the more curious will easily find my meaning; the vulgar will not find the difficulty." The opening sentences of his note to the reader best present his judicious effort to provide a chart for the assistance of the earnest reader seeking a way through what Ralegh elsewhere calls the labyrinth of time:

---

and accompting of the year, hereafter to be observed, to accord with other countries next hereto adjoining" (*Cal. State Papers, Dom., 1581–1590*, p. 107). In "A Short Treatise against Adiaphorists," appended to *A Directory Teaching the Way to the Truth* (1605), p. 550, J. Radford, a Catholic writer, reproaches the bishops for their religious prejudice in rejecting the new calendar. England did not adopt the Gregorian calendar until 1752.

[80] This method is followed in a work which Ralegh cites a number of times: Abraham Bucholcerus (Bucholtzer), *Index chronologicus . . . ad 1580* (1612).

Of Miracles

The use of chronological tables is needful to all histories that reach to any length of time, and most of all to those that are most general, since they cannot, like annals, yearly set down all occurrences not coherent. This here following may serve as an index to the present part of this work, pointing unto the several matters that, having fallen out at one time, are far disjoined in the relation. Certainly it is not perfect; neither do I think that any can be. . . . Neither is it a small part of trouble to choose, out of so many and so utterly disagreeing computations as have already gotten authority, what may probably be held for truth. All this, and a great deal more, is to be alleged in excuse of such error as a more intentive and perfect calculator shall happen to find herein. It may serve to free the book and likewise the reader (if but of mean judgment) from any notorious anachronism, which ought to suffice.

The table is further necessary, Ralegh adds, to correct some printing errors in the text and some "hasty misreckonings of mine own."

Ralegh finds a common denominator for his table in the Julian Period, "devised by that honorable and excellently learned Joseph Scaliger, being accommodated to the Julian years, now in use among us." This Period, as Ralegh explains, consists of 7,980 years, a figure arrived at by multiplying the number of years in the cycle of the moon (19), the number of the years in the cycle of the sun (28), and the number of the years of the cycle of indiction (15). His explanation of the relationship of the greater period to the shorter cycles is too brief for clarity; but Ralegh is less concerned with the convenience of the Julian Period in determining the Golden Number and the Dominical Letter than with its use as a workable yardstick in chronology.

This Julian Period, after the present accompt, always exceeds the years of the world by 682. Besides the former uses, and other thence redounding, it is a better character of a year than any other era (as "from the beginning of the world," "from the Flood," "from Troy taken," or the like) which are of more uncertain position.

What Ralegh neglects to explain is why the Period should "exceed the years of the world." Scaliger had discovered that, when

Of Miracles

he carried back in time the cycles of the moon, the sun, and the indiction, all three had a first year in common in 4713 B.C. January 1 of that year therefore became the starting point for his period of 7980 years, which will run until A.D. 3267. Ralegh is quite right in praising it as a chronological index superior to the popularly used "year of the world," since the latter varied according to which of the diverse estimates of the date of the Creation was used as a starting point. The Julian Period, an "artificial epoch" as Ussher called it, is an oddity in that its beginning antedates most of the popularly accepted estimates of the date of the Creation. Perhaps some confusion about a pre-Adamite year touched off the rumors to which Nashe alluded when he wrote of "mathematicians abroad who would prove men before Adam." Among the learned and godly, however, Scaliger's device was accepted as a convenient scale to which other measurements of time could be readily adapted.[81]

For Ralegh's table itself, the best explanation is to be found in five or ten minutes' study with his own illustrations in mind. Once understood, it is compact and clear. In the first few pages the vertical columns record the years of a patriarch, later of an empire; when the tables are read across the page, the occurrences of diverse reigns and kingdoms are seen in relation to each other. The governing column lists the year of the Julian Period, the year of the world, and the year since one of the critical events which mark

---

[81] For a brief explanation of the Julian Period see Alexander Philip, *The Calendar* (Cambridge, England, 1921), p. 59. James Ussher, *Annals* (1658), Pref., sig. A4ᵛ, gives a more lucid explanation of the Julian Period than Ralegh does, but he assigns the honor of discovery, five hundred years before Scaliger, to an Englishman, Robert Lotharing, Bishop of Hereford. Like Ralegh, Ussher uses the years of the Julian Period as a principal guide in his chronology. In *Tractatus de variis annorum formis* (London, 1605), and in other works growing out of the ensuing controversy, Thomas Lydiat attacked the period devised by Scaliger and proposed one of his own, which failed to win adherents in significant numbers. The Julian Period, despite some dissenters, long continued in high favor with chronologers. Ralegh himself, though he disagrees with Scaliger in some particulars, uniformly speaks of him with respect; e.g., II, xxv, 1, p. 592 (where Ralegh shows awareness of the controversy between Scaliger and Lydiat), and III, i, 5, pp. 8–11.

the periods into which the Hebrew story was conventionally divided: from Adam, from the Flood, from the Promise, and so on. The table is intended for the general reader; Ralegh breaks off his condensed explanation as unnecessary "to such as are conversant in works of this kind: it sufficeth if hereby all be made plain enough to the vulgar." The vulgar, if sufficiently attentive, had no cause to complain.[82]

Many of Ralegh's questions in chronology have long since found more satisfactory answers as historians have won greater freedom of inquiry than he enjoyed. What one remembers of his conscientious efforts to get at the truth is not the factual results but his informed awareness of the complexities of his subject, his pains to keep the record straight, and his rejection of the extreme dogmatism that made the controversial sparks fly but gave little light. Of course he has decided opinions on some topics and is willing to defend them. As he enters upon his argument for a later date for the birth of Abraham he gives the reader fair warning.

Now, since I do here enter into that never resolved question and labyrinth of times, it behoveth me to give reason for my own opinion; and with so much the greater care and circumspection because I walk aside and in a way apart from the multitude; yet not alone and without companions, though fewer in number, with whom I rather choose to endure the wounds of those darts which envy casteth at novelty than to go on safely and sleepily in the easy ways of ancient mistakings; seeing to be learned in many errors or to be ignorant in all things hath little diversity.[83]

Once embarked on the analysis of this problem, he undertakes to supplement the learning of diverse scholars with "somewhat of mine own, according to the small talent which God hath given me."[84] Of another chronological excursion he concedes that

---

[82] A chronological work entitled *Tubus historicus: an Historical Perspective* (London, 1636) was published as "By the late famous and learned Knight Sir Walter Raleigh"; but I find its chronology quite different from that given in the *History of the World*.

[83] II, i, 1, p. 218.   [84] II, i, 3, p. 219.

Of Miracles 215

"more hath been said already than I can stand to, though I hold it no shame to fail in such conjectures." [85] He reminds his readers that in the account of ancient times the best we can hope for is probability, not certainty: "The table and especially the chronology [of early Egyptian kings] is to be confirmed by probabilities and conjectures, because in such obscurity manifest and resistless truth cannot be found." [86] The difficulties of chronology demand of the reader a charitable judgment upon the historian's quest for truth.

The difference of which authors in this point [the time when Homer lived] is not unworthy the reader's consideration, that by this one instance he may guess of the difficulty, and so pardon the errors in the computations of ancient time; seeing in such diversity of opinions a man may hardly find out what to follow.[87]

A similar judgment accompanies the effort to distribute properly the years of the kings who reigned during the Babylonian Captivity.

It now remains that I freely acknowledge my own weakness, who cannot find out how the seventy years of captivity are to be divided among them which reigned in Babylon, though I find that the distribution made of them in such wise as already is rehearsed be ill agreeable to the Holy Scriptures. Wherefore I may truly say with Pererius that we ought liberally to pardon those whose feet have failed them in the slippery ways of chronology, wherein both learning and diligence are subject to take a fall at one time or other, by ignorance, forgetfulness, or heedless reckoning.[88]

These hesitancies and qualifications of course do not touch the Bible itself, for Ralegh can be firm enough when he alleges scriptural authority for his statements. Even so, he stresses not only the conjectural basis of the ancient chronologies but also the uncertainties which attend the interpretation of Biblical references

---

[85] II, xxvi, 1, p. 599.

[86] II, ii, 1, p. 236. In II, xxi, 6, pp. 535–38, Ralegh indulges in "A digression, wherein is maintained the liberty of using conjecture in histories." I discuss this section in my next chapter.

[87] II, xvi, 7, pp. 475–76.   [88] III, i, 6, p. 11.

to time. His attitude is in marked contrast to that of the contentious Hugh Broughton, who begins one work and ends another with the firmness (not the patience) of Job: "And for my resolution touching my adversaries in this case, I will speak from Job: 'All the while breath is in me, God forbid that I should grant your cause to be right.'" [89] Without overstressing a coincidence in phrase which is quite natural in its context, one can turn with relief from such dogmatism to the words of *The Skeptic* with which Ralegh dismisses a vexatious problem in the Hebrew calendar: "Whether this were the practice, I can neither affirm nor deny...." [90]

A brief section devoted in part to "the difficulty in the computation of times" closes with Ralegh's best single comment on the subject. Here in a few lines he rejects the conflicting claims to accuracy made by scholars who enlighten only themselves in their efforts to solve the cruxes of Old Testament history, such as the dates of Abraham, of the Exodus, of the Persian Empire, and (most prolific of controversy) the seventy weeks of Daniel's prophecy.

---

[89] *A Seder Olam* (1594), p. 32; cf. *Texts of Scripture Chaining the Holy Chronicle* (London, 1591), Pref., sig. A3^r. Even in a controversial age Broughton was notorious for his irascibility and may not be fairly representative of the Renaissance chronologers, dogmatic as they often were. I cite him partly because of his personal acquaintance with Ralegh, who on May 3, 1596, wrote to Sir Robert Cecil recommending Broughton for the bishopric of Lismore and Waterford (Edwards, *Life*, II, 124–26). The recommendation was not disinterested: Ralegh wanted to dispossess the Archbishop of Cashel, with whom he was having trouble, and he does not disguise his motive when he places "furtherance of religion" second to "relief of myself." Although he speaks of Broughton as "my very good friend," I find no further evidence of close acquaintance. None of Broughton's books which I have seen are dedicated to Ralegh, who names him in the *History* as one of a list of authorities (II, i, 7, p. 227). Of Broughton's chronological works one of the most interesting, dedicated to Essex, is a table engraved in brass and printed on four large sheets. It begins "Tables of the Fathers' Ages," but in his dedication Broughton calls it "Moses' Sights on Sinai" (*STC* 3873). Ralegh and Broughton are in agreement on the time of Abraham's birth, but they differ in their accounts of the Persian Monarchy. It is a reasonable surmise that, even in the 1590's, Ralegh found Broughton an interesting acquaintance because of his learning in chronology.

[90] II, iii, 6, p. 258. The subhead of Ralegh's *The Skeptic* begins, "The skeptic doth neither affirm, neither deny any position . . ." (*Works*, VIII, 548).

Of Miracles 217

Whether the times of these kings . . . be precisely set down I cannot avow, for the chronologers, both of the former and latter times, differ in many particulars, to examine all which would require the whole time of a long life; and therefore I desire to be excused if in these comparisons I err with others of better judgment. For whether Eusebius and all that follow him, or his opposites (who make themselves so conversant with these ancient kings and with the very year when they began to rule), have hit the mark of time of all other the farthest off and most defaced, I cannot but greatly doubt. First, because the authors themselves from whom the ancientest chronologers have borrowed light had nothing for the warrant of their own works but conjecture; secondly, because their own disagreement and contention in those elder days, with that of our own age among the laborers in times, is such as no man among them hath yet so edified any man's understanding, save his own, but that he is greatly distracted, after what pattern to erect his buildings.

This disagreement is found not only in the reigns of heathen kings and princes, but even in computation of those times which the indisputable authority of Holy Scripture hath summed up, as in that of Abraham's birth, and after in the times of the Judges and the oppressions of Israel, in the times from the egression to the building of Solomon's Temple, in the Persian Empire, the Seventy Weeks, and in what not. Wheresoever the account of times may suffer examination, the arguments are opposite and contentions are such as, for ought that I see, men have sought by so many ways to uncover the sun that the days thereby are made more dark and the clouds more condensed than before. I can therefore give no other warrant than other men have done in these computations; and therefore that such and such kings and kingdoms took beginning in this or that year I avow it no otherwise than as a borrowed knowledge, or at least as a private opinion, which I submit to better judgments. . . . "In ancient things we are not to require an exact narration of the truth," says Diodorus.[91]

With this considered judgment on the uncertain product of the chronicler's painful toil Ralegh may be permitted to rest his case. He has argued it with respect for the integrity and learning of the scholars with whom he disagrees, and he is aware that often the results are tentative at best.

[91] II, xiii, 2, p. 417.

Of Miracles

Our résumé of Ralegh's opinions on chronology brings to a close a survey of his beliefs in terms of the principal Elizabethan meanings of "atheism." On God and the soul, on personal and political ethics, on natural philosophy, and lastly on chronology, where no hint of "men before Adam" prevails against scriptural authority, Ralegh holds staunchly to orthodox positions. Charges of atheism, in any sober Elizabethan sense except perhaps the ethical, cannot be made to stick. There is, of course, ample room for misunderstanding (apart from the inevitable distortions of personal dislike or distrust) in confusion of meanings, as in the debate with the Reverend Ralph Ironside; or in the conflicting attitudes of the age toward scientific studies; or in the independence of judgment which Ralegh reserves to himself in matters where "the Scriptures are silent, and it is no point of our saving belief." [92] But the man revealed in these chapters is obedient to the religious code of his day, yet anxious to define and if possible to enlarge the limits of free intellectual inquiry. His commentary on the problems of chronology, in which so much stress is laid upon the reliability of our information rather than upon the factitious accuracy of the dogmatist, leads us directly to his opinions on the nature of knowledge. Within the topical limitations enjoined by a discussion of Ralegh's religious beliefs, ethical principles, and specialized learning, much has already been said on this subject. We may now turn, without such topical restrictions, to a review of his ideas on authority and method, on the strength and weakness of human reason.

[92] I, viii, 11, pt. 4, p. 157.

Chapter 7

Of Human Knowledge

But for myself, I shall never be persuaded that God hath shut up all light of learning within the lantern of Aristotle's brains

History, Preface, sig. D2ᵛ

STRICT PHILOSOPHICAL SKEPTICISM is far more rare in the history of human thought than is its popular counterpart. The varied manifestations of what is popularly called "skepticism" have in common a tendency to challenge received opinions or the dicta of established authority and to submit them to the tests of reason and experience. Often it is the dogmatism of religion or the weight of social custom that is challenged, and then skepticism in common usage is identified with rebellion against a church or refusal to accept the mores of a time or place as inherently right. It has been necessary to elaborate upon Ralegh's religious beliefs because many of his contemporaries and some of his modern readers and critics have labeled him, wrongly, a religious skeptic. The results are much the same for skepticism directed toward custom: although indifferent to popular opinion during much of his lifetime and not intolerant of divergences from English or European standards, Ralegh is not given in his writings, as Montaigne is, to reflections on the vagaries and conflicts of human conduct.[1] Nevertheless, even putting aside these dominant popular meanings of skepticism as directed against religion and custom, we find in Ralegh's utterances and writings

---

[1] Ralegh is not altogether silent on such matters. For example, he is aware of differences in customs which should be handled tolerantly in law; see *History of the World* (1614), II, iv, 16, p. 293, on the wisdom and propriety of modifying the Mosaic law when applying it to other nations. Perhaps in deference to King James, he opposes dueling and an exaggerated sensitivity to "giving the lie" (V, iii, 17, pt. 2, pp. 544–51). But these and like reflections upon social custom do not affect the overwhelming emphasis, in Ralegh's criticisms of society, upon moral law and an all-ruling Providence.

support for his modest reputation in the seventeenth century as a philosophic skeptic.

Naturally one does not expect to find a systematic philosophy in the work of a man whose studies were, in part, his recreation. Like most men known as skeptics—Montaigne, for example—Ralegh is selective and not always consistent in the application of his doubts. Nevertheless, there is real value in turning first to the relationships between his ideas and the formal skepticism of Greek philosophy. Pyrrhonic skepticism accounts for Ralegh's one direct essay on the subject, *The Skeptic*, in effect an incomplete translation; the ancient skeptical writings, either in originals or more commonly in translations and adaptations, provided the Elizabethan with the tools of skeptical thought; and by Academic skepticism—the formal system which his own loose methodology most closely approximates—one can measure the casual, less consistently skeptical, modes of Ralegh's thought. Usually, however, Ralegh's questioning of authority assumes less technical forms: his distrust of authority stemming from Aristotle or the schoolmen; or his consideration of the problem of historical method. The evidence here is not limited to generalized pronouncements. Both as man of action and as historian Ralegh was frequently confronted with problems which called for decision, and it is therefore possible to check his practice, sometimes credulous, against his skeptical theory.

I

Skepticism of a more thoroughgoing kind than the world has known since was important in Greek and Roman thought for five centuries.[2] During that time it was the philosophy of two schools, one of which was consistently skeptical to the point of rejecting the name of "school" or "sect" as suggestive of dogmatism.

---

[2] In this summary I have followed chiefly Mary P. Patrick, *Sextus Empiricus and Greek Scepticism* (London, 1899), and *The Greek Sceptics* (New York, 1929); and the introduction by R. B. Bury to his translation of Sextus Empiricus, Loeb ed., 3 vols. (London, 1933–36). The works cited above in chap. iii, note 3, have also been helpful.

Of Human Knowledge

Skepticism as a distinct philosophy, not as an element in several early Greek philosophies, began with Pyrrho of Elis in the fourth century B.C., found a home in the New Academy under Arcesilaus, and was invigorated by late disciples of Pyrrho, who regarded Academic skepticism as tending toward dogmatism. Pyrrho himself seems to have been interested chiefly in the ethical aspects of skepticism rather than its application to the problems of knowledge. For studies of the modern period, the most useful distinction of the early skeptical philosophies is between Academic skepticism, which was speculative, and the revived and formalized Pyrrhonism of Alexandria and Rome, which was empiric. This distinction is emphasized in the opening lines of our most comprehensive account of Pyrrhonism (and the source of Ralegh's essay), the *Pyrrhonean Hypotyposes,* or *Outlines of Pyrrhonism,* compiled by Sextus Empiricus about A.D. 200. Sextus begins by classifying three approaches to philosophical problems:

The natural result of any investigation is that the investigators either discover the object of search or deny that it is discoverable and confess it to be inapprehensible or persist in their search. So, too, with regard to the objects investigated by philosophy, this is probably why some have claimed to have discovered the truth, others have asserted that it cannot be apprehended, while others again go on inquiring.[3]

Those who believe they have found the truth are dogmatists (for example, Aristotle, Epicurus, the Stoics); the Academics consider the truth inapprehensible; the Skeptics keep on searching for the truth. Near the end of Book I, Sextus compares skepticism with other philosophies, somewhat at length with the Academic.

Furthermore, as regards the End (or aim of life) we differ from the New Academy; for whereas the men who profess to conform to its doctrine use probability as the guide of life, we live in an undogmatic way by following the laws, customs, and natural affections.[4]

---

[3] *Outlines of Pyrrhonism,* trans. by R. B. Bury, Loeb ed., Vol. I, Bk. I, chap. i. Hereafter references to the *Outlines* will be to this edition and, unless otherwise indicated, to Book I, by chapter and section.

[4] Chap. xxxiii, sec. 231; cf. sec. 226.

Herein lies an important difference between the two main skeptical philosophies, recognized also by later historians, who do not, however, follow Sextus in his identification of skepticism with Pyrrhonism alone. The Pyrrhonists, says Sextus, regard sense impressions as equally probable or improbable; the Academics find some impressions probable and others improbable. The distinction which he makes is an important one. Arcesilaus had based his theory of ethics on what appears reasonable, and the Academy under Carneades developed a theory of probabilities which classified sense impressions in such a way as to make possible a relative assent, even though objective knowledge was deemed impossible.[5] The Pyrrhonists did not deny that the truth could be known; their argument was that it was not yet known, that they suspended judgment and continued the search. Both philosophies were based upon the inability of the senses alone to inform us of the true nature of what is perceived, and both evolved, with the differences indicated, into logical complexities which do not bear upon Ralegh's less subtle reflections.

So many connotations have clustered about the term "skepticism" in modern times that it is desirable, before turning to *The Skeptic*, to note some of the principal tenets and characteristics of the Pyrrhonism from which it derives. As the system evolved, it was defined in a number of tropes ("a manner of thought, or form of argument, or standpoint of judgment"): first ten, then five, and finally two.[6] The purpose of the tropes is to demonstrate that phenomena, or appearances, are so involved in relativity and change that they offer no satisfactory foundation for knowledge. The ten tropes from which Ralegh takes his essay are, except for the tenth, concerned with the unreliability of sense perception, either because of physical differences in the observers or because of external differences. The Pyrrhonists did not doubt the appearances, but whether the reality corresponds to the appearance; indeed, their criterion *is* the appearance:

[5] Bury, Introd., p. xxxvi.
[6] Patrick, *Sextus Empiricus and Greek Scepticism*, pp. 31, 36.

For since this lies in feeling and involuntary affection, it is not open to question. Consequently, no one, I suppose, disputes that the underlying object has this or that appearance; the point in dispute is whether the object is in reality such as it appears to be.[7]

Contrary to the jeers of scoffers, these skeptics did not deny sensation, did not pretend that in freezing weather they felt no cold, although Pyrrho himself was credited with indifference to extreme discomfort. They argued not that they were immune to feelings but that their refusal to consider one state better than another made suffering more easily endured. Their aim was peace of mind (*ataraxia*), which they thought could be best attained by suspending judgment in investigations and ceasing to fret over the difficulty of knowing, "for the man who opines that anything is by nature good or bad is for ever being disquieted."[8] Unlike later and less formal skepticism, Pyrrhonism was conservative in its tendencies. Since we do not know what is true, or which of two things is better, we must accept the reports of our senses as a practical guide in life and we must conform to the religion and morality of the society in which we live. "Adhering, then, to appearances we live in accordance with the normal rules of life, undogmatically, seeing that we cannot remain wholly inactive."[9] The method by which the Pyrrhonists arrived at this *modus vivendi* was by opposing the testimony of one sense to that of another sense, or the testimony of one sense under certain conditions to the testimony of the same sense under other conditions, or one argument to another argument. (As we shall see, this method of opposing arguments to each other is one element in Pyrrhonism which left a durable impress upon Ralegh's thought.) In time the skeptical attitude came to be summarized in certain phrases: "I know nothing"; and "no more" (that is, no more one thing than another).

This limited summary, largely of the first book of the *Outlines of Pyrrhonism*, may give some idea of the context of Ralegh's skeptical essay and, in general, may provide the background

[7] Chap. xi, sec. 22. [8] Chap. xii, sec. 27. [9] Chap. xi, sec. 23.

needed to interpret his less formal adaptations of skeptical thought and method. *The Skeptic* is a translation,[10] with some condensations, omissions, and a few changes, of the first three Pyrrhonic tropes and part of the seventh. Its heading—"The skeptic doth neither affirm, neither deny any position; but doubteth of it, and opposeth his reasons against that which is affirmed or denied, to justify his not consenting"—is adequately explained as a brief statement of the skeptic position; the phrasing, however, has parallels in the *Outlines*, Book I, Chapter XXIII: "Of the Expression 'I Determine Nothing.' " In the present state of our bibliographical information, all that we know about the essay is that it was first published in 1651 under the title *Sir Walter Ralegh's Skeptic; or, Speculations*. Following it in the same volume are two other works which also have proved to be in large part translations: *Causes of the Magnificency and Opulency of Cities*, and the *Seat of Government*. A few letters, poems, and Ralegh's speech on the scaffold complete the book. After this first edition *The Skeptic* was frequently reprinted as part of the volume entitled *Remains*, and Brushfield reports a copy of the essay, with the position of some paragraphs altered, in the Lansdowne Manuscripts.[11]

In his short treatise, which occupies only eight and one half pages in the *Works*,[12] Ralegh gives a fairly complete version of

[10] G. T. Buckley, *Atheism in the English Renaissance* (Chicago, 1932), pp. 146–49.

[11] T. N. Brushfield, *A Bibliography of Sir Walter Ralegh* (Exeter, England, 1908), Nos. 219-a and 278. See also above, chap. i, note 15. I have checked the first edition of *The Skeptic*, and other early editions; but I have not seen the copy in the Lansdowne MSS.

[12] (1829), VIII, 548–56. The First Mode takes up fully two-thirds of *The Skeptic* (pp. 548–53), but even so it is greatly condensed. The Loeb edition of the *Outlines of Pyrrhonism*, Book I, is a convenient standard for comparison of content, although of course it could not serve for a detailed study of Ralegh's phrasing. The sources of *The Skeptic* are the First Mode, secs. 40–78; Second Mode, secs. 78–89; Third Mode, secs. 90–99; Seventh Mode, secs. 129–33, only represented in the last paragraph of *The Skeptic*, which ends abruptly, without application or comment. Of secs. 40–99, Ralegh omits 45, 46, and 72; 85 and 86 (which extend to the soul the contrasts among men); 90. Other changes:

the First Mode, but as he progresses his cuts and changes become more drastic. The skeptic's "first reason ariseth from the consideration of the great difference amongst living creatures, both in the matter and manner of their generation, and the several constitutions of their bodies." If the instruments of sense are changed, their perceptions change: things appear pale to a man with jaundice, distorted to one who rubs his eyes. Everyone knows what oddities appear in convex or concave mirrors. Why, then, is it not reasonable to assume that diverse animals, with eyes shaped quite differently, see objects in a variety of ways? The same argument applies to the other senses. One can report the appearance of things, but not "what they are in their own nature." Nor is it just for man to prefer his judgment of things perceived to that of other animals.

They are living creatures as well as I: why then should I condemn their conceit and phantasy concerning any thing, more than they may mine? They may be in the truth and I in error, as well as I in truth and they err.

The argument that man's imagination is superior is rejected by citing instances of the intelligence of dogs; and if speech (a dubious accomplishment at best) is to be considered, animals too can communicate with each other.

Moving on to the Second Mode, even if we concede the superiority of man's judgment over that of animals, men differ greatly among themselves in their faculties. One man's meat is another man's poison. Nor can we find a guide to the true nature of things in opinion:

. . . for either we must believe what all men say of it, or what some men only say of it. To believe what all men say of one and the same thing is not possible; for then we shall believe contrarieties; for some men say that the very thing is pleasant which others say is displeasant.

---

sec. 76 may be represented by a single sentence; a summary after what corresponds in *The Skeptic* (p. 550) to sec. 58 has no exact counterpart in the Loeb ed., but there is something like it in secs. 126–27; the name of Pythagoras is added (p. 554) to the list of philosophers cited in sec. 88; a sentence, enlarged from sec. 54, is added to a paragraph derived from secs. 94–95.

If we are to believe only some men, which of the philosophers, each praised by his own school, shall we follow? The Third Mode concerns the contradictory reports of the several senses upon the same objects; as, "Honey seemeth to the tongue sweet, but unpleasant to the eye; so ointment doth recreate the smell, but it offendeth the taste." When we see how the perceptions of a man who is born blind and deaf are limited, so that he will conclude that an object has only those qualities which are apparent to his other senses, how can we be sure that objects under our observation do not have more qualities than we can perceive with our own five senses? Shifting abruptly to the Seventh Mode, Ralegh concludes the summary (in the form in which it has come down to us) with a short paragraph on the differences in the appearances of things under different circumstances; for example, "Sands being separated appear rough to the touch, but in a great heap soft."

When we go outside the Ralegh bibliography for information on the translations of Sextus Empiricus the results are tantalizing and inconclusive. Thomas Nashe, in his Preface to Sidney's *Astrophel and Stella* (1591), refers to the works of Sextus Empiricus as "lately translated into English, for the benefit of unlearned writers." Then, in *Summer's Last Will and Testament* (probably performed in 1592; published 1600), Nashe versified an extended borrowing from Sextus which makes up seventy lines of a long speech by Orion. This is one of the better-known passages from the *Outlines of Pyrrhonism,* describing the reasoning powers and special abilities of dogs. Further, a very similar version of the praise of dogs occurs ten years after the first appearance of *Summer's Last Will* in a work attributed to Samuel Rowlands, *Greene's Ghost Haunting Conycatchers* (1602). The late R. B. McKerrow made a comparative study of the passages in Nashe and Rowlands and of the corresponding Latin version in the edition by Henri Étienne in 1562, but without reference to Ralegh's *The Skeptic.* Dr. McKerrow considered it unlikely that Nashe followed either the original Greek or the Latin of Étienne; he found that Rowlands' version was more complete than that of Nashe and that he kept the order of Sextus; and he noted that Nashe and Rowlands have one passage (*Summer's Last Will*, lines 692–97) which is not in Sextus. He considered several possible explanations of the relationships between the versions by Nashe and Rowlands, and inclined to the belief that both were using an English translation. However, he left the question open because the translation, which should be dated about 1590, is not known today.[13]

Does Ralegh's *The Skeptic* derive from the lost translation? Is it possible that Ralegh himself was the translator of 1590? Dr. McKerrow cites two "errors," in other references to Sextus by Nashe, which may serve as clues. Nashe's version reads "ashes" where the original calls for "asses," and so does Ralegh's; but, unfortunately for a suggestive lead, so does the first full-length English translation of the *Outlines of Pyrrhonism* known to me: that by Thomas Stanley in *The History of Philosophy* (1659).[14] The second error by Nashe (a reading of "bones" for "beans") occurs in a passage which is omitted entirely from Ralegh's *The Skeptic* and which Stanley translates correctly. The fact that Nashe, Ralegh, and Stanley agree on the first error suggests that it originates in the sixteenth-century Greek or Latin text, neither of which have I seen. The passage on the intelligence of dogs is greatly condensed in *The Skeptic*, so that comparison with the extended versions by Nashe and Rowlands is of little avail. In short, the relationship of *The Skeptic* to the English translation of 1590 cannot be determined on the basis of the meagre evidence now available; for Ralegh's essay, as for the immediate origin of

[13] *The Works of Thomas Nashe*, ed. R. B. McKerrow, 5 vols. (London, 1904–10), IV, 428–31. For the preface to *Astrophel and Stella* see III, 332; and for the passage in *Summer's Last Will* see III, 254–56.

[14] In five parts, each with separate title page. The title page of the first part is dated 1660, all others 1659. Stanley's translation is *The Fourth Part: Containing the Sceptic Sect* (1659). I find no evidence of a connection between Stanley's work and Ralegh's *The Skeptic*. The possible errors in translation cited by Dr. McKerrow occur in Nashe's *Works* at I, 174 (line 4) and I, 185 (line 8).

the passages used by Nashe and Rowlands, the question is still open.

The passages used by Nashe and Rowlands, the reference to a translation extant in 1591, and miscellaneous allusions and borrowings show that the Pyrrhonic philosophy was not unfamiliar to the Elizabethans. Two editions of the Latin translation of Sextus Empiricus by Henri Étienne [15] were available; and the convenient summaries and anecdotes by Diogenes Laertius were somewhat more detailed for Pyrrhonism than for other philosophies. The skeptical point of view was presented also in works which, although less systematic than the *Outlines of Pyrrhonism*, show their indebtedness to Sextus Empiricus. Such a book is Henry Cornelius Agrippa's *Of the Vanity and Uncertainty of Arts and Sciences*,[16] which falls short of "pure" skepticism in method but nevertheless is a compendium of skeptical arguments, sometimes stated in the phrasing of the *Outlines of Pyrrhonism*. Agrippa's book is uncertain in intent, and there is some justification for the translator's assertion, in his preface to the reader, that Agrippa attacks not learning and reason but their abuses. He protests the tyranny of authority, and exalts ignorant piety over the false learning of men. By way of incidental comment, Nashe makes references to skeptical philosophy other than those already noted, and blames the "pyrrhonics" for the atheist position that there is no hell or misery but opinion.[17] One chapter of a book maintaining that specters exist and do appear to men is devoted to a refutation of the "opinions of the followers of Pyrrho, the skeptics" on the untrustworthiness of the senses.[18] In his defense of astrology, Sir Christopher Heydon charges his opponent, John

---

[15] The British Museum *Catalogue* lists editions published at Paris, 1562, and Antwerp, 1569. An even more accessible discussion of skepticism, chiefly of the *Academy*, was Cicero's *Academica*.

[16] Trans. by James Sanford (London, 1569). For an example of direct borrowing from Sextus Empiricus, see chap. l, "Of the Principles of Natural Things," which follows the *Outlines of Pyrrhonism*, Bk. III, chap. vi.

[17] *Works*, ed. McKerrow, II, 116. See also I, 173, 188–89, and McKerrow's notes.

[18] Pierre Le Loyer, *A Treatise of Specters* (London, 1605), chap. vi.

Chamber, with unacknowledged, as well as acknowledged, borrowing from Sextus Empiricus. That philosopher, says Heydon, tried by wit to prove all arts false; since he held nothing to be certain, his arguments have little value in this dispute, especially when we consider the superiority of our instruments to those of the ancients.[19] Best known today of all sixteenth-century Pyrrhonists, of course, is Montaigne, who at one stage of his reading was so powerfully impressed by the skeptical tropes that he had some of them inscribed on the beams of his study. Indeed, Montaigne's indebtedness to Sextus Empiricus has misled one scholar into finding in the *Essais* the source of Ralegh's *The Skeptic*.[20]

Before we turn to more general evidences of Ralegh's skepticism, it would be well to draw together a few conclusions about *The Skeptic*, warranted by this survey of its background and of the content of the document itself. Clearly, in this brief exercise Ralegh is not an innovator; he is exercising his intellectual curiosity in a field which in the sixteenth century had already aroused a speculative interest. His essay is limited to those parts of the *Outlines of Pyrrhonism* concerned with the unreliability of sensory knowledge; if, as seems probable, he read further in that work, he could have found in a later chapter [21] ammunition for his own attack on the "principles." One point about the essay that cannot be overstressed is its isolation. There is no comment, such as enlivens some of the borrowed passages in the *History*; most significantly, there is no relationship whatever between this exercise—well described in the first edition as "speculations"— and Ralegh's discourses on religion. When skeptical arguments are applied to religion, as they are occasionally in the Preface to

[19] *A Defence of Judicial Astrology* (Cambridge, England, 1603), pp. 127–28, 134–35, and *passim*.

[20] See A. H. Upham, *The French Influence in English Literature* (New York, 1908), pp. 289–93. In an appendix, pp. 540–44, are listed parallels between *The Skeptic* and Montaigne's *Essais*. But the content of Ralegh's essay, as we have seen, is taken directly from Sextus Empiricus.

[21] *Outlines of Pyrrhonism*, Bk. III, chap. vi. As I point out below, the direct source is Charron.

the *History*, they are used in defense of faith, in the manner of the Christian apologists, not to discredit it. Finally, as we have seen many times over in quotations from the *History*, Ralegh subordinates reason to faith and to scriptural authority; but in that he considers reason a dependable guide to trustworthy conclusions he is not a good Pyrrhonist. There are exceptions, it is true, in notable passages in the *History* which exalt experience over reason; but the evidence of the *History* is overwhelmingly on the side of a method which argues from reason and probability. In that, and in his most definite statement of method, Ralegh inclines toward the skepticism of the Academy rather than that of Pyrrho.

II

A bridge between Ralegh's brief exercise in formal skepticism and his less systematic challenges of intellectual authority is found in a strongly worded passage in the Preface of the *History*. The context is an attack upon Aristotle's denial of the Creation in time, a doctrine of faith which is "too weighty a work for Aristotle's rotten ground to bear up." Despite its length, the passage merits quotation in full, for it offers the best single explanation of Ralegh's philosophy and also suggests, in the context of Elizabethan scholarship, the reasons for the easy misinterpretation of his position.

And it is no less strange that those men which are desirous of knowledge (seeing Aristotle hath failed in this main point [that is, in denying the creation] and taught little other than terms in the rest) have so retrenched their minds from the following and overtaking of truth, and so absolutely subjected themselves to the law of those philosophical principles, as all contrary kind of teaching, in the search of causes, they have condemned either for fantastical or curious. But doth it follow that the positions of heathen philosophers are undoubted grounds and principles indeed, because so called? Or that *ipsi dixerunt* doth make them to be such? Certainly no. But this is true: That where natural reason hath built anything so strong against itself as the same reason can hardly assail it, much less batter it down, the same in every question of nature and finite power may be approved for a fundamental law of human knowledge. For, saith Charron in his book *Of Wisdom*, "Tout proposition humaine a autant d'authorité que l'autre, si la raison n'on fait la différence; Every human proposition hath equal authority, if reason make not the difference," the rest being but the fables of principles. But hereof how shall the upright and unpartial judgment of man give a sentence, where opposition and examination are not admitted to give in evidence? And to this purpose it was well said of Lactantius, ... "They neglect their own wisdom, who without any judgment approve the invention of those that forewent them, and suffer themselves, after the manner of beasts, to be led by them." By the advantage of which sloth and dullness, ignorance is now become so powerful a tyrant as it hath set true philosophy, physic, and divinity in a pillory, and written over the first, *Contra negantem principia;* over the second, *Vertus specifica;* and over the third, *Ecclesia Romana.*

But for myself, I shall never be persuaded that God hath shut up all light of learning within the lantern of Aristotle's brains; or that it was ever said unto him, as unto Esdras, "Ascendam in corde tuo lucernam intellectus"; that God hath given invention but to the heathen; and that they only have invaded nature, and found the strength and bottom thereof; the same nature having consumed all her store and left nothing of price to after-ages. That these and these be the causes of these and these effects, time hath taught us, and not reason; and so hath experience, without art. The cheese-wife knoweth it as well as the philosopher that sour rennet doth coagulate her milk into a curd. But if we ask a reason of this cause, why the sourness doth it? whereby it doth it? and the manner how? I think that there is nothing to be found in vulgar philosophy to satisfy this and many other like vulgar questions.[22]

The passage concludes with remarks, already quoted, on the presumption of many, who, while ignorant of very simple things in nature, will attempt to "examine the art of God in creating the world."

This key statement illustrates the application of some traditional skeptical arguments to two major obstacles to independent investigation: the domination of the "principles" and the author-

[22] Pref., sig. D2^v.

ity of Aristotle. Both problems have appeared with some frequency in discussions reported in earlier chapters; the "principles" figured especially in Christian arguments that divinity, like other sciences, was entitled to proceed from accepted premises, and it was on the issue of "principles" that Ralegh and Ironside disagreed. A third idea in the passage, the occasional defeats of reason by experience, is here secondary to the central issue of freedom of investigation. Although Ralegh's statement is marked by the characteristic vigor of his style, the ideas are not novel; indeed, the interest of the quotation lies partly in the evidence it offers on the transmission of skeptical ideas.

Take, for example, Ralegh's approving quotation from Charron, which reads in its context:

> There have been some in our time [marginal note: Copernicus, Paracelsus] that have changed and quite altered the principles and rules of our ancients and best professors in astronomy, physic, geometry, in nature, and the motion of the winds. Every human proposition hath as much authority as another, if reason make not the difference. Truth dependeth not upon the authority and testimony of man: there are no principles in man if Divinity have not revealed them; all the rest is but a dream and smoke.[23]

Charron's book *Of Wisdom* is largely a systematization of Montaigne's "essais," and the lines which Ralegh approved come from the famous *Apology for Raimond Sebond:*

> For every science has its presupposed principles by which human judgment is hemmed in on all sides. If you happen to drive against this barrier where the principal error lies, they have instantly this saying in their mouths: that there is no disputing with persons who deny first principles.
>
> Now, there can be no first principles for men, if they are not revealed to them by Divinity; of all the rest—the beginning, the middle, and the end—there is nothing but dream and vapor. Against those who argue by presupposition we must presuppose the opposite of the

[23] Peter Charron, *Of Wisdom*, trans. by Samson Lennard (London [1612]), p. 168. Ralegh quotes Charron elsewhere in the *History;* e.g., in the section on nobility (I, ix, 4, p. 184) and in V, ii, 4, p. 384.

Of Human Knowledge

very axiom which is in dispute. For every human presupposition and every enunciation has as much authority as any other, if the reason does not distinguish between them. Therefore they are all to be put into the balance, and first the general axioms and those which tyrannize over us.[24]

The ultimate source of this denial of the authoritative principle is the *Outlines of Pyrrhonism*, a work which made a far more profound impression upon Montaigne than it ever did upon Ralegh. There is no record that Ralegh scratched the skeptical tropes on the beams of *his* Tower. According to Sextus Empiricus, "The main basic principle of the Skeptic system is that of opposing to every proposition an equal proposition; for we believe that as a consequence of this we end by ceasing to dogmatize."[25] And most pertinent is the chapter entitled "Of the Phrase 'To Every Argument an Equal Argument is Opposed'":

So whenever I say "To every argument an equal argument is opposed," what I am virtually saying is "To every argument investigated by me which establishes a point dogmatically, it seems to me there is opposed another argument, establishing a point dogmatically, which is equal to the first in respect of credibility and incredibility"; so that the utterance of the phrase is not a piece of dogmatism, but the announcement of a human state of mind which is apparent to the person experiencing it.[26]

In such a roundabout fashion, although he knew the *Outlines*

---

[24] *Essays*, tr. and ed. Jacob Zeitlin, 3 vols. (New York, Knopf, 1934–36), II, 202. The essay "That Our Desires Are Augmented by Difficulty" (Zeitlin, II, 277) begins: "There is no reason that has not its opposite, says the wisest school of philosophers." Pierre Bayle, in his *Dictionary* (London, 1710), IV, p. lii, remarks (not with complete accuracy) upon the different receptions accorded to the casual reflections of Montaigne upon religion and morality and the systematic presentation of the same ideas by Charron. The Faculty of Divinity of France, writes Bayle, left untouched all of Montaigne's maxims, "who, without following any system, method, or order, heaped together and spun out whatever his memory presented to him. But when Peter Charron, a priest and theological, came to vent some of Montaigne's sentiments methodically in a systematical treatise of morality, the divines were no longer silent."

[25] *Outlines of Pyrrhonism*, Bk. I, chap. vi, sec. 12; cf. chap. ix, sec. 18.

[26] *Ibid.*, Bk. I, chap. xxvii, sec. 203.

Of Human Knowledge

of Pyrrhonism, did Ralegh sometimes derive his skeptical arguments. Likewise some phrases and the point of view of the extended quotation from his Preface are in harmony with the opening pages of Agrippa's *Of the Vanity and Uncertainty of Arts and Sciences:*

> For every science hath in it some certain principles, which must be believed and cannot by any means be declared: which if any will obstinately deny, the philosophers have not wherewith to dispute against him, and immediately they will say, that there is no disputation against him which denieth the principles. . . .[27]

In the same context, Agrippa quotes as an example of slavish obedience to intellectual authority the Pythagoreans' "Ipse Dixit," spoken of their master. Since Ralegh makes no reference in this passage to Agrippa—as he does to Charron—these particular verbal similarities are interesting chiefly as showing how early in the Elizabethan period skeptical ideas found popular expression.

Turning from questions of the derivation and currency of these ideas to an analysis of Ralegh's meaning, we find his first proposition—that philosophical principles are not exempt from liberty of examination—limited to matters which can be encompassed by the legitimate activity of the human intellect: ". . . where natural reason hath built anything so strong against itself as the same reason can hardly assail it, much less batter it down, the same *in every question of nature and finite power* may be approved for a fundamental law of human knowledge." The exception, here italicized, is of the utmost importance, for it concedes to the supernatural and to Infinite Power an area of operation in which "natural reason" must yield to revelation. Over and over again, in *The History of the World*, Ralegh has deferred first to Scripture, and then to reason and probability. But "in every question of nature and finite power" the reason is helpless if it is to be held spellbound by the "fables of principles." Ignorance, too dull and slothful to reexamine his inherited knowledge, has become a

[27] (1569), fols. 4ᵇ–5ᵃ.

Of Human Knowledge

tyrant who pillories true philosophy, physic, and divinity: true philosophy, with the common retort of the schools, "contra negantem principia"; true physic, by labeling it "vertus specifica"; and true divinity, by calling it the Roman Church.[28]

This attack upon the tyranny of the "principles," even though it has a counterpart in Pyrrhonic arguments, differs in language and objectives from that negative system. At this point, as commonly in the *History*, Ralegh appeals to reason, which the true Skeptic distrusts. As for objectives, he clearly believes in the possibility of extending the bounds of knowledge, once so-called laws are submitted to "opposition and examination." This applies especially to his emphasis on the need for independent research in natural philosophy, related in Chapter VI. But apart from science, Ralegh's point of view inclines to the Academic skeptical position, which sees as possible at least a relative truth. When he relies upon "reason and the most probable circumstances thereon depending," or "nature, reason, policy, and necessity," or "reason and probable conjecture," [29] he is using neither the language nor the method of a Pyrrhonist. For Ralegh, as for many another "skeptic," skepticism is not a system, not a philosophy of life, but a weapon for an attack upon dogmatism.

One possible inconsistency in Ralegh's attitude toward the "principles" must be noted. In a discussion of the extent to which the laws of Moses are authoritative for other peoples, he draws an analogy between the debt of political institutions to Moses, the

---

[28] The "vertus specifica" is probably in allusion to the Galenists' hostility to the claims of the Paracelsians and other innovators in the medical arts. The remark about divinity is apparently aimed at the sects. In a passage commending Moses' reverent care of the tabernacle when the army of Israel was on the march, Ralegh laments that this ceremonial observance "is now so forgotten and cast away in this superfine age, by those of the Family, by the Anabaptist, Brownist, and other sectaries, as all cost and care bestowed and had of the Church, wherein God is to be served and worshipped, is accounted a kind of Popery, and as proceeding from an idolatrous disposition. . . ." II, v, 1, pp. 296-97.

[29] These phrases, illustrative of many, may be found in I, vii, 10, pt. 2, p. 114; I, viii, 3, p. 135; I, viii, 15, pt. 6, p. 177.

lawgiver appointed by God, and the debts of the "sciences" to metaphysics:

> Wherefore that acknowledgment which other sciences yield unto the metaphysics, that from thence are drawn propositions able to prove the principles of sciences which out of the sciences themselves cannot be proved, may justly be granted by all other politic institutions to that of Moses; and so much the more justly by how much the subject of the metaphysics, which is *Ens quatenus Ens*, being as it is being, is infinitely inferior to the *Ens Entium*, the being of beings, the only good, the fountain of truth, whose fear is the beginning of wisdom.[30]

Although Ralegh is here citing the principles merely for a rhetorical comparison and is not passing judgment upon them, the figure of speech is in an entirely different vein from the forthright approval of the skeptical pronouncement out of Charron.

The rejection of the principles as eternally valid led naturally to the denial of the authority of Aristotle, the second major point in the quotation from Ralegh's preface. The declaration of intellectual independence quoted at the head of this chapter is comparable to Bacon's "knowledge derived from Aristotle, and exempted from liberty of examination, will not rise again higher than the knowledge of Aristotle."[31] But neither Bacon in 1605 nor Ralegh in 1614 was an innovator in this particular phase of intellectual history; it is especially true of Ralegh that his share in the overthrow of Aristotle's authority lies largely in the authority of his own name and the magic of his pen. For Bacon, of course, the story is different and of greater significance in the history of thought; but he, too, is a late recruit in the attack upon Aristotle, however sweeping and influential his plans for the advancement of learning.[32]

---

[30] II, iv, 16, p. 294.

[31] *The Advancement of Learning*, ed. W. A. Wright (Oxford, 1869), p. 37.

[32] There is no intent in this comparison to equate Ralegh's observations with Bacon's elaborate and systematic plans for the advancement of science, even though their names have sometimes been bracketed as leaders in this movement. According to F. R. Johnson and S. V. Larkey, "Robert Recorde's Mathematical Teaching and the Anti-Aristotelian Movement," *Huntington Library Bulletin*, No. 7 (April, 1935), pp. 59–87, Aristotelianism was largely discredited when

Aristotle enjoyed a paradoxical reputation in the sixteenth century. On the one hand he was considered the apostle of the atheistic doctrine that the world was eternal (the context, be it remembered, of the extract from the *History* now under discussion); on the other hand, much of his philosophy had become identified with Catholic teaching to the point that, in some quarters, an attack on Aristotle was itself construed as irreligious. A striking example of such an attitude is found in the scene in Marlowe's *Massacre at Paris*,[33] wherein Ramus, a victim of the St. Bartholomew's slaughter, is taunted by the Duke of Guise for challenging the logic of Aristotle. Opposition to the authority of Aristotle took many forms, ranging from the deferential attitude of critics who respected his great learning, but insisted on recognition of the advancement of knowledge through discoveries in astronomy, geography, and natural philosophy, to impatient denunciations of the tortuous methods of the Aristotelians. Aristotle's system of logic had been criticized with such effect by Ramus that the "new" logic was widely accepted among Protestants; and in the experimental sciences there had been, throughout the sixteenth century and especially in the latter half, a firm insistence on the need for testing old "facts" and on the possibility of new knowledge.[34]

Bacon made his attack, save in academic strongholds. They suggest that Bacon was exposed to Ramist philosophy at Cambridge, then lost touch with scientific thought, and therefore, when he made his attack, reverted to a full-scale onslaught in the manner of Ramus, which he had observed in his youth.

[33] Scene vi, in the edition by H. S. Bennett (New York, 1931). The incident in Marlowe's play is cited by Roy W. Battenhouse, *Marlowe's "Tamburlaine"* (Nashville, Tenn., 1941), p. 27, note.

[34] Numerous instances of this attitude, often accompanied by disagreement with Aristotle and the ancients, are cited by F. R. Johnson, *Astronomical Thought in Renaissance England* (Baltimore, Md., 1937). See also Lynn Thorndike, *A History of Magic and Experimental Science*, VI (New York, 1941), 565, 570–71, and *passim*. For a brief account of the influence of Ramist philosophy on Protestant thought see *The Puritans*, ed. Perry Miller and Thomas H. Johnson (New York, 1938), pp. 27–41; and F. P. Graves, *Peter Ramus and The Educational Reformation of the Sixteenth Century* (New York, 1912), chap. ii, "The Breach with Aristotle." F. R. Johnson, *op. cit.*, p. 191, notes briefly the intrusion of the dispute over Ramus into the Nashe-Harvey quarrel.

Consequently, when Ralegh denies to the ancients the exclusive possession of nature's secrets he is joining a progressive party, not founding one. Nevertheless, academic devotion to Aristotle continued strong, and the encounter with Ironside, who argued from logical principles and the authority of Aristotle, is an example of it from Ralegh's own experience. He had no reason to assume that the spirit of free inquiry, even in the restricted area which he assigned to it, had won the day. It must be remembered, too, that in scientific studies academic conservatism was only one obstacle, no longer as formidable as it had once been; in his discussion of natural magic and miracles, described above in Chapter VI, Ralegh is more concerned with superstitious prejudice than with the barriers raised by a system of logic and by ancient authority. His own attitude toward Aristotle is usually denunciatory, especially where his opposition has religious support. Thus he adds a skeptical judgment to a statement from Aristotle on the soul, and dismisses certain opinions of the Aristotelians on natural magic as "brabblings." [35] He finds most of the Schoolmen

> ... rather curious in the nature of terms, and more subtle in distinguishing upon the parts of doctrine already laid down, than discoverers of anything hidden, either in philosophy or divinity; of whom it may be truly said ... "Nothing is more odious to true wisdom than too acute sharpness." [36]

And in the same vein,

> But this I dare avow of those Schoolmen, that though they were exceeding witty, yet they better teach all their followers to shift than to resolve by their distinctions.[37]

If we bring to the support of this brief summary of Renaissance opinion on Aristotle a few specific references we may perhaps see

---

[35] Aristotle on the soul, I, ii, 1, p. 23; see above, chap. iv, notes 41 and 50. "Brabblings": I, xi, 2, p. 202. Like his contemporaries, Ralegh is selective in his condemnation. He cites Aristotle respectfully on politics; e.g., V, ii, 2, pt. 4, p. 385.

[36] I, i, 7, p. 9. Cf. his condemnation of the subtlety of the schoolmen in distinguishing the "image and similitude of God," I, ii, 1, pp. 22–23.

[37] I, iii, 7, p. 45.

Ralegh's position in better perspective. In his notes on Augustine's *City of God*[38] Ludovicus Vives comments that Plato was long preeminent over Aristotle until mercenary ends brought about the decline of learning; then Aristotle's logic and physics drove out not only Plato but better works of Aristotle. Because they do not understand Plato and because he teaches no tricks of disputation, the Schoolmen have nothing to do with him. A marginal note, presumably by the translator or a late editor, enforces the point: "This is no good doctrine in the Louvainists' opinion, for it is left out as distasteful to the schoolmen, though not to direct truth." Again, Vives reproves Aquinas and others for defining matters of divine nature "according to Aristotle's positions, drawing themselves into such labyrinths of natural questions that you would rather say they were Athenian sophisters than Christian divines." A marginal note adds: "No word of this in the Louvain copy." Here we have the mark of a broad, but of course not always consistent, division: the Protestants leaning upon the teachings of Plato and Augustine, the Catholics following Aristotle and Aquinas.

Skepticism in general about the authority of Aristotle, without immediate religious bias though concerned with the relationship of reason and faith, is found in Montaigne's *Apology for Raimond Sebond*. In a passage immediately preceding the comment on the principles, quoted above as Charron's source, Montaigne observes that

> ... the opinions of men are adopted in conformity with ancient beliefs, upon authority and trust, as if they were religion and law. What

---

[38] The comments and marginal notes cited in this paragraph are, in the English translation (London, 1610), on Bk. VIII, chap. x, p. 315, and Bk. XXI, chap. vii, p. 847. In the Preface to *De disciplinis*, Vives balances the respect due the ancients and the freedom of inquiry to be allowed the moderns. He extols Aristotle, "for whose mind, for whose industry, carefulness, judgment in human arts, I have an admiration and respect, unique above all others." But, he continues, "Nature is not yet so effete and exhausted as to be unable to bring forth, in our times, results comparable to those of earlier ages. . . . Truth stands open to all. It is not yet taken possession of." See Foster Watson, *Vives: On Education* (Cambridge, England, 1913), pp. 8–9.

is commonly believed about it is accepted as if by rote. This truth, with its whole structure and equipment of arguments and proofs, is received as though it were a firm and solid body which is not to be shaken, not to be subjected to judgment. On the contrary, everyone, as best he may, cements and fortifies this belief with the utmost power of his reason, which is a supple and pliable instrument, and adaptable to every shape. And thus the world comes to be filled and stuffed with inanities and falsehoods.

The reason why men raise so few doubts is that they never put common impressions to the test. . . . The god of scholastic learning is Aristotle; it is an impiety to dispute his decrees, as it was to dispute those of Lycurgus at Sparta. His doctrine, which is perhaps as false as any other, is by us treated as magisterial law. I do not know why I should not as readily accept either the Ideas of Plato, or the Atoms of Epicurus [Montaigne continues with a list of major philosophies]. . . . And yet all this [the opinion of Aristotle on the principles of natural things] no man must dare to disturb except for an exercise in logic. Nothing therein is discussed with a view to raising doubts, but only to defend the founder of the school against objections from without. His authority is the mark beyond which it is not permitted to inquire.[39]

Even apart from the similarity due to Ralegh's borrowing from the disciple of Montaigne, the historian and the essayist are on common ground in their scorn of the blind acceptance of authority. Montaigne is far more vigorous than Ralegh in his denunciation of the pretensions of reason, but neither man holds consistently to that skeptical position.

These illustrations, which could be extended indefinitely, may be brought to a close by two quotations so dated that the publication of the *History* falls midway between them. Addressing Ralegh as a patron in 1596, John Hester makes a plea for free-

---

[39] *Essays*, tr. and ed. Zeitlin, II, 200–201. Professor Zeitlin (II, 542) comments on this passage: "The questioning of Aristotle's authority was no novelty in the sixteenth century." He cites the activities of the Paduan school of philosophers, and the belief that Ramus was killed because of his opposition to Aristotelianism. (The quotations from this work are made by permission of the publishers, Alfred A. Knopf., Inc.)

dom of research outside the province of divinity, which rightly requires obedience and belief.

[All other faculties] tending to government or ornament of a life natural so carry a privilege of more liberty in search, and large scope in practise, that to rest content with the inventions of other is as odious to the learned as it is for frank hearts to feed on other men's trenchers, or fine wits to be set to tell the clock while grosser heads are better employed.[40]

Although he does not name Aristotle, Hester's plea clearly merits a place among the many statements challenging the prerogatives of authority. More explicit is a statement published almost twenty years after the *History* by a clergyman who admires the great learning of Aristotle but emphasizes the limits imposed upon his observations, for example by his restricted knowledge of geography. In an essay addressed "To the venerable artists and younger students in divinity in the famous University of Cambridge,"[41] William Watts discusses the problem of harmonizing the remarkable discoveries in North America with Aristotle's rules. "Of this one thing am I confident," he tells the students, "that you are all so rational and ingenuous as to prefer truth before authority: *amicus Plato, amicus Aristoteles,* but *magis amica veritas.*" The same God who gave Aristotle his good parts has also raised up many other excellent spirits, and it would be a discouragement of invention and observation to submit all their work to Aristotle's authority. "Let it not then be thought unequal to examine the first cogitations of the old philosophy by the second thoughts of our more modern artists." In that way we may expect the same improvement in "physics" that we have already made in geography, mathematics, and mechanics. Watts names and praises famous scholars who have already stood against the authority of Aristotle. The date of Watts's essay indicates that if Ralegh were

---

[40] *A Hundred and Fourteen Experiments* of *Paracelsus* (London, 1596), dedication, sig. A2^r. See above, chap. vi, note 2.

[41] Appended to Thomas James, *The Strange and Dangerous Voyage* (London, 1633); my quotations are from sigs. R4^v and S4^r. Watts's essay is cited by Johnson, *Astronomical Thought,* p. 331.

not the first to assail the dragon Error neither, in the first years of the seventeenth century, was he tilting at windmills.

The third point in Ralegh's skeptical pronouncement is the praise of experience over reason—as he puts it, "time hath taught us, and not reason; and so hath experience, without art." At first glance this disparagement of reason and learning has the appearance of true skepticism; but in its full context the few sentences on this theme are a transition to the main point of a very long paragraph: the presumption of man, helpless to explain some of the simplest phenomena of nature but confident in determining the secrets of God. Here again skepticism is enlisted in the cause of religion. But the disparagement of reason is not wholly inconsistent with setting up natural reason, a few sentences earlier, as a better guide to knowledge than docile acceptance of the principles. The praise of reason emphasizes man's powers; the disparagement of reason emphasizes the limitations upon those powers. The first passage concerns the exercise of "natural reason," assisted by "opposition and examination"; reason in the second passage seems to be akin to ratiocination. Elsewhere in the *History* Ralegh illustrates, from one of the great lessons of geographical discovery, the value of experience over "contemplation." While agreeing that the terrestrial paradise was not located "under the equinoctial," Ralegh dismisses the ancient argument, in its day a "reasonable conjecture," against such a location: that the extreme heat of the tropics would be unbearable.

... yet now we find that, if there be any place upon the earth of that nature, beauty, and delight that Paradise had, the same must be found within that supposed uninhabitable burnt zone, or within the tropics and nearest to the line itself. For hereof experience hath informed reason, and Time hath made those things apparent which were hidden and could not by any contemplation be discovered.[42]

[42] I, iii, 8, p. 45. In the Preface (sig. E1r), this same ancient error about the tropics becomes, with less credit to Ralegh, a logical flourish against the idea that the incorruptibility of the heavens proves the eternity of the world: either the ancients were wrong about the destructive heat of the tropics or the world has changed since their day. There seems to be little doubt about Ralegh's own choice of these alternatives.

Of Human Knowledge

Thus the errors in the maps of geographers, who mark the unknown regions of the earth according to hearsay, are "many times controlled by following experience and found contrary to truth."[43]

Ralegh's concise statement of his skeptical position in the Preface to the *History* is not isolated like *The Skeptic*, but incorporated in his major work. The value of this passage lies in its concentration on a few major issues, by which we may define Ralegh's place among his contemporaries. We find him an advocate of ideas neither entirely new nor yet firmly established. The "principles" were still valid in argument; the authority of Aristotle still weighty; reason still the acknowledged means for determining truth on the basis of facts already known.[44] Ralegh's skeptical opinions on such matters were understood and shared by many men of letters and of science in his day, but they were open to misunderstanding in the confusion of an age which sometimes identified the teachings of Aristotle with Christianity. To understand the operative limits of Ralegh's skepticism, however, we must turn from the compact selection from the Preface to a sampling of his working methods in handling the varied problems which attracted his interest.

III

Something of the temper of Ralegh's mind has already been disclosed in a review of his opinions on religion, ethics, and science; for example, in his efforts to find the most probable and reasonable explanations of Scriptural problems, his avoidance of dogmatism in painstaking attempts to solve problems of chronology, and his defense of natural magic and of freedom in experimentation. There remains the broad question to which suggestive but partial answers have been given in earlier chapters: to what extent is Ralegh the historian, or Ralegh the empire-builder,

---

[43] II, xxiii, 4, p. 573. The context of this passage is discussed below, in sec. iii of this chapter. Ralegh would allow both geographer and historian considerable latitude in dealing with a scarcity of factual information.

[44] See Hardin Craig, *The Enchanted Glass* (New York, 1936), pp. 156–59.

governed by the skeptical attitude displayed in the Preface? The question may be answered, apart from what has already been said about his practices and beliefs, by a specific consideration of his historical method and of some of his credulities.

The dominant idea of *The History of the World* is that all human affairs are under God's providence, sometimes inscrutable but always operative. The purpose of the historian is didactic, but he is free to explain, if he can, the agency of second causes in performing God's will. In the exposition of second causes, Ralegh's virtue lies less in careful sifting of evidence than in fair warning to the reader of the uncertain state of the question in hand. His method varies: where he is greatly interested, as in problems of chronology and geography, he proceeds carefully and judiciously; where he is not interested, or where he finds the evidence scanty and entangled in conjecture, he is likely to become impatient and hack at knots indiscriminately.

A good starting point for a review of Ralegh's method is a section entitled "A digression wherein is maintained the liberty of using conjecture in histories." [45] After some highly speculative discourse on the parentage of Joash and his relationship to Athaliah, Ralegh observes:

In handling of which matter, the more I consider the nature of this history and the diversity between it and others, the less, methinks, I need to suspect mine own presumption, as deserving blame for curiosity in matter of doubt or boldness in liberty of conjecture. For all histories do give us information of human counsels and events, as far forth as the knowledge and faith of the writers can afford; but of God's will, by which all things are ordered, they speak only at random and many times falsely.

[45] See II, xxi, 6, pp. 535–38, for all quotations in this paragraph. Ralegh likewise approves the liberty taken by Xenophon (and others) in writing dialogue and interpreting events: "Neither can it indeed be affirmed of any the like writer, that in every speech and circumstance he hath precisely tied himself to the phrase of the speaker or nature of the occasion, but borrowed in each out of his own invention, appropriating the same to the times and persons of whom he treated." III, ii, 3, p. 28.

The merit of the history of the kings of Israel and Judah is that it refers

all unto the will of God, I mean to his revealed will; from which, that his hidden purposes do not vary, this story by many great examples gives most notable proof. True it is that the concurrence of second causes with their effects is in these books nothing largely described, nor perhaps exactly in any of those histories that are in these points most copious. For it was well noted by that worthy gentleman, Sir Philip Sidney, that historians do borrow of poets not only much of their ornament but somewhat of their substance. Informations are often false, records not always true, and notorious actions commonly insufficient to discover the passions which did set them first on foot.

Although the historian may be excused "when finding apparent cause enough of things done [he] forbeareth to make further search," nevertheless the motivation of great events is often to be found in seeming trifles. "For the wisest of men are not without their vanities which, requiring and finding mutual toleration, work more closely and earnestly than right reason either needs or can." Since it is the "end and scope of all history to teach by example of times past such wisdom as may guide our desires and actions," it is no wonder that the chronicles of the kings of Judah and Israel, written by men divinely inspired, should be concerned with teaching us the way to true felicity rather than with elaborating upon second causes. Yet one may lawfully gather such information from pagan histories or other circumstances as long as he does not "derogate from the first causes by ascribing to the second more than was due."

Such, or little different, is the business which I have now in hand, wherein I cannot believe that any man of judgment will tax me as either fabulous or presumptuous. For he doth not fain that rehearseth probabilities as bare conjectures; neither doth he deprave the text that seeketh to illustrate and make good in human reason those things which authority alone, without further circumstance, ought to have confirmed in every man's belief. And this may suffice in defense of the liberty which I have used in conjectures, and may hereafter use, when occasion shall require, as neither unlawful nor misbeseeming an historian.

A like tolerance toward historical invention is shown in dealing with periods barren of records. If the stories of Annius are to be regarded as always untrustworthy, how is it that information not available in any other source turns up in histories by "painful and judicious writers"? [46] Concurrent history supports the particular fact in question, the duration of the reign of Phul, an Assyrian king; "yet all of them took it from Annius." It is a just punishment for his falsehoods that Annius is doubted when he speaks truth; although, Ralegh notes slily,

> for our own sakes we make use of his boldness, taking his words for good, whereas (nothing else being offered) we are unwilling ourselves to be authors of new, though not unprobable, conjectures. Herein we shall have this commodity, that we may without blushing alter a little to help our own opinions and lay the blame upon Annius, against whom we shall be sure to find friends that will take our part.

To enforce his argument in support of the historian's liberty to construct the most plausible story he can out of meagre resources, Ralegh turns to analogy and anecdote.

> I neither do reprehend the boldness of Torniellus in conjecturing, nor the modesty of Scaliger and Sethus Calvisius in forbearing to set down as warrantable, such things as depend only upon likelihood. For things whereof the perfect knowledge is taken away from us by antiquity must be described in history as geographers in their maps describe those countries whereof as yet there is made no true discovery; that is, either by leaving some part blank or by inserting the land of pigmies, rocks of loadstone, with headlands, bays, great rivers, and other particularities agreeable to common report, though many times controlled by following experience and found contrary to truth. Yet indeed the ignorance growing from distance of place allows not such liberty to a describer as that which ariseth from the remediless oblivion of consuming time.

The errors in geography can be corrected. Neither climate nor danger will restrain the daring seaman; he will go where he will,

---

[46] See II, xxiii, 4, pp. 573–74, for all quotations in this paragraph.

Of Human Knowledge 247

and return to damn the fictions of the cartographer. Ralegh recalls that he once asked a distinguished prisoner, Don Pedro de Sarmiento, whether an island in the Straits of Magellan had not hindered his attempts to plant a Spanish colony there.

> . . . he told me merrily that it was to be called the Painter's Wife's Island; saying that, whilst the fellow drew that map, his wife, sitting by, desired him to put in one country for her, that she in imagination might have an island of her own. But in filling up the blanks of old histories we need not be so scrupulous. For it is not to be feared that time should run backward and, by restoring the things themselves to knowledge, make our conjectures appear ridiculous. What if some good copy of an ancient author could be found, showing (if we have it not already) the perfect truth of these uncertainties? Would it be more shame to have believed, in the meanwhile, Annius or Torniellus than to have believed nothing? . . . Let it suffice that, in regard of authority, I had rather trust Scaliger or Torniellus than Annius; yet him than them, if his assertion be more probable and more agreeable to approved histories than their conjecture. . . .

Thus Ralegh, content to discriminate for his readers fact and conjecture, regards a plausible story as better than none.

An attitude so tolerant of speculation hardly qualifies as "skeptical"; but many of his other comments on historical guesswork are more in the vein of the Preface. In the very chapter which contains the digression on liberty of conjecture, he declines to extend the discussion of the alternate names of Joash:

> . . . yet because I find no other warrant hereof than a bare possibility, I will not presume to build an opinion upon the weak foundation of mine own conjecture, but leave all to the consideration of such as have more ability to judge and leisure to consider of this point.[47]

The heading of another section carries the warning, "A private conjecture of the author." [48] Concerning the Roman wars in Spain he concludes, "I am weary of rehearsing so many particularities whereof I can believe so few. But since we can find no better certainties, we must content ourselves with these." [49] The *History*

---

[47] II, xxi, 5, pt. 3, p. 534. [48] III, i, 13, p. 23. [49] V, iii, 11, p. 474.

abounds in "asides" such as these, some of the best in the comments on chronology already quoted.[50]

The questioning of Aristotle and the Schoolmen extends to other forms of intellectual authority outside the requirements of religious faith. These challenges in the *History* read like variations on a theme. Disagreement may be respectful, as toward the church fathers:

And it is true that many of the Fathers were far wide from the understanding of this place. I speak it not that I myself dare presume to censure them, for I reverence both their learning and their piety, and yet not bound to follow them any further than they are guided by truth; for they were men, *Et humanum est errare*.[51]

On the other hand, Annius, who is accepted in the absence of other authority when his yarns are plausible, receives a wry dismissal when they are not: "The obscurity of the history gives leave to Annius of saying what he list. I, that love not to use such liberty, will forbear to determine anything herein." [52] Even more tart is the comment on the learned Goropius Becanus: "But as he had an inventive brain, so there never lived any man that believed better thereof and of himself." [53] Perhaps the best single pronouncement on the proper attitude toward authority is what Ralegh says of his own opinions on the location of the terrestrial paradise: ". . . this is the reward that I look for, that my labors may but receive an allowance suspended, until such time as this description of mine be reproved by a better." [54]

Naturally, Ralegh encountered in the course of his historical work many problems not reduced to such simple terms as the acceptance or rejection of authority. Novelty for its own sake does not interest him; he is inclined to suspect the motives of too eager a pursuit of originality.

As for those that with so much cunning forsake the general opinion when it favoreth not such exposition as they bring out of a good mind

[50] See above, pp. 214–17.   [51] I, iii, 1, pp. 33–34.   [52] II, xiv, 1, p. 448.
[53] I, iv, 2, p. 67.   [54] I, iii, 15, p. 65.

to help where the need is not over-great, I had rather commend their diligence than follow their example.[55]

Such wrongheaded independence may serve to introduce and propagate error.

There is no error which hath not some slippery and bad foundation, or some appearance of probability resembling truth, which, when men who study to be singular find out (straining reason according to their fancies), they then publish to the world matter of contention and jangling; not doubting but in the variable deformity of men's minds to find some partakers or sectators, the better by their help to nurse and cherish such weak babes as their own inventions have begotten.[56]

Ralegh is critical of those who "prefer the commentator before the author; and to uphold a sentence giving testimony to one clause do carelessly overthrow the history itself, which thereby they sought to have maintained." [57] Sometimes he records the process of change in his own opinions. For example, "following the common belief and good authority," he had once thought reverently of the Sibylline oracles; but he was well on the way to abandoning that credulity "when that learned and excellent work of Master Casaubon upon the *Annals* of Cardinal Baronius did altogether free me from mine error." In like fashion, the legend of Simon Magus probably originated in a false conjecture.

Such conjectures, being entertained without examination, find credit by tradition, whereby also, many times, their fashion is amended and made more historical than was conceived by the author.[58]

In actual practice, when he is weighing the truth or falsehood

---

[55] II, xiii, 8, p. 444.   [56] I, iii, 13, p. 57.

[57] III, i, 8, p. 15. Ralegh himself shows little regard for consistency in his citations of authority. In the skeptical passage analyzed in sec. ii of this chapter, he uses a sentence from Lactantius against a docile acceptance of inherited knowledge; in the first pages of the *History* (I, i, 10, p. 13) he quotes Lactantius on the futility of man's efforts to learn how God works through nature, "seeing it is not yet comprehended after so much time and so many wits have been worn out in the inquiry of it."

[58] This and the quotations immediately preceding are part of the same discussion: V, v, 9, pp. 705–6.

in the many stories which crowd the pages of the *History*, Ralegh shows the same mixture of hardheaded practicality and easy gullibility which contribute to the fascination of the Elizabethan Period. He records omens seriously, yet he can remark ironically, concerning a Roman disaster at sea, that the Romans "knew better how to fight than how to navigate, and never found any foul weather in the entrails of their beasts, their soothsayers being all land prophets." [59] Heathen oracles and prophecies he distrusts as devised after the event; but, in keeping with his reverence for Holy Writ, he denounces Porphyry bitterly for applying the same argument to the prophecies of Daniel.[60] Spanish stories of help in battle from the Virgin and angels he dismisses as "Romish miracles"; but he accepts as "certainly true" that the mass desertion of the dogs belonging to a French army clearly presaged its ensuing defeat.[61] Reports of unusual natural phenomena he is usually inclined to accept; in one instance he calls upon hearsay, authority, and a none too closely reasoned personal experience to support a reference to a fountain.

> that at midnight is as hot as boiling water and at noon as cold as any ice, to which I cannot but give credit, because I have heard of some other wells of like nature, and because it is reported by Saint Augustine, by Diodore, Herodotus, Pliny, Mela, Solinus, Arianus, Curtius, and others; and indeed our Baths in England are much warmer in the night than in the day.[62]

Like his contemporaries, he has exaggerated ideas of the height of mountains, the highest of which, he affirms, does not rise above thirty miles.[63] The vitality of the men of old is attested by the

---

[59] V, i, 10, p. 367. For a sober compilation of historical omens, see V, vi, 11, pp. 767–68.

[60] E.g., on heathen oracles, IV, i, 1, p. 158; V, v, 1, p. 640; and on the rejection of "that wretched man Porphyry," III, i, 2, p. 3.

[61] IV, ii, 7, p. 183.   [62] IV, ii, 7, p. 184.

[63] I, vii, 6, p. 106; cf. I, vii, 10, pt. 11, p. 124. For Ralegh, Tenerife is the world's highest peak. Pliny, in his *History* (1601), Bk. I, chap. lxv, p. 31, rejects a low estimate of the height of Pelion and asserts that the Alps "for a long tract together arise not under fifty miles in height." Estimates of the height of Tenerife went as high as seventy-two miles, although experienced sailors re-

Of Human Knowledge 251

fact that "Galen did ordinarily let blood six pound weight, whereas we (for the most part) stop at six ounces." [64]

The most notorious of the credulities charged against Ralegh is found in *The Discovery of Guiana*. Trusting to hearsay, Ralegh avows his belief in the existence of a race of monstrous men.

... on that branch [of the river] which is called Caora are a nation of people whose heads appear not above their shoulders, which, though it may be thought a mere fable, yet for mine own part I am resolved it is true, because every child in the provinces of Arromaia and Canuri affirm the same. They are called Ewaipanoma; they are reported to have their eyes in their shoulders and their mouths in the middle of their breasts, and that a long train of hair groweth backward between their shoulders. [Ralegh cites confirmations by the son of the chieftain, Topiawari, and continues] ... but it was not my chance to hear of them till I was come away, and if I had but spoken one word of it while I was there I might have brought one of them with me to put the matter out of doubt. Such a nation was written of by Mandeville, whose reports were held for fables many years, and yet since the East Indies were discovered we find his relations true of such things as heretofore were held incredible. Whether it be true or no the matter is not great, neither can there be any profit in the imagination; for mine own part I saw them not, but I am resolved that so many people did not all combine or forethink to make the report.[65]

As Mr. Harlow notes, the legend was persistent among the Indians, and this loose-jointed passage is not quite as droll as it appears to a better-informed posterity. In a sense, this is a premature application of Ralegh's faith in the correction of reason by experience, decidedly faulty because "for mine own part I saw them not" and neither the affirmations of "every child" nor the assurances of a chieftain's son are impressive evidence. Also, the story appears in a propagandist work in which Ralegh is throwing together every possible argument to enlist official support for occupying Guiana. He dangles the lures of gold, of other

---

jected such figures; see Lynn Thorndike, *A History of Magic and Experimental Science*, VI, 380; also V, 27; VI, 50, 366.
[64] I, v, 5, p. 78. [65] Ed. V. T. Harlow (London, 1928), pp. 56–57.

rich resources, and of advantage against Spain. If the marvelous will help, in it goes; though he is careful to note that the accuracy of the tale does not affect his main purpose.

In the *History* Ralegh disavows such a reliance on hearsay, as of "no authority or credit." [66] And for a marvel similar to that which entertained the readers of *The Discovery of Guiana* he has rational explanations to offer. The legendary Arimaspi who fought the griffins for their gold were called one-eyed "by reason that they used to wear a vizard of defense with one sight in the middle to serve both eyes, and not that they had by nature any such defect." [67] The fable, he explains, can be moralized to mean:

> That if those men which fight against so many dangerous passages for gold or other riches of this world had their perfect senses and were not deprived of half their eyesight (at least of the eye of right reason and understanding) they would content themselves with a quiet and moderate estate, and not subject themselves to famine, corrupt air, violent heat, and cold, and to all sorts of miserable diseases.

Thirdly, although the griffins are feigned, it might in a sense be truly said that in America wild animals defend the mines of gold and alligators guard precious pearls—simply because gold and pearls are found in dangerous places, not because they are valued by the denizens of those regions. "And though the alegartos know not the pearl, yet they find savor in the flesh and blood of the Indians whom they devour." All this rationalizing is preceded

---

[66] He continues, in the sentence quoted at the head of my first chapter: "For common bruit is so infamous a historian as wise men neither report after it nor give credit to anything they receive from it" (I, vii, 10, pt. 10, p. 123). In the quite different context of a speech in Parliament concerning legislation to repress the Brownists, Ralegh called for a clear distinction between the legal "fact," for which one could be properly tried, and the mere judgment of "men's intentions" by a jury. He opposed the legislation because he considered it unenforceable and in violation of the basic principles of law, not because he was partial to the sect, whom he considered "worthy to be voted out of a commonwealth." See Edwards, *Life*, I, 271; W. K. Jordan, *The Development of Religious Toleration in England . . . to the Death of Queen Elizabeth* (London, 1932), pp. 214–15.

[67] For this quotation and those which follow in the paragraph, see I, viii, 15, pt. 5, pp. 176–77.

by a blunt rejection of fables about the Arimaspi and the Cyclops: "But (for mine own opinion) I believe none of them."

Ralegh does not link his discussion of the Arimaspi with his own tale about the "Ewaipanoma"; but in another, and not dissimilar, instance, he does use the *History* to support a story in the *Discovery*. He devotes an entire section, two pages in length, to what the historians, including Spaniards and Portuguese reporting on discoveries in South America and Africa, have had to say about the Amazons; and concludes:

> I have produced these authorities in part to justify mine own relation of these Amazons, because that which was delivered me for truth by an ancient Casique of Guiana, how upon the river of Papamena (since the Spanish discoveries called Amazons) that these women still live and govern, was held for a vain and unprobable report.[68]

On this story, of course, Ralegh finds himself in better company than in his account of the telescoped Ewaipanoma. The measure of his success or failure in judging such tales is not simply by his belief or disbelief, nor according to later verification or exposure; but by his adherence to his own standards of evidence. He can thrust aside the Arimaspi; he can muster help against the Amazons; but when he encounters the marvelous Ewaipanoma he falls victim to his own propaganda.

[68] IV, ii, 15, pp. 195–96; for "mine own relation" see *The Discovery of Guiana*, ed. Harlow, pp. 26–27.

Chapter 8

The Judicious Historian

Informations are often false, records not always true, and notorious actions commonly insufficient to discover the passions which did set them first on foot

History, II, xxi, 6, p. 536

THE CHRONICLE of Ralegh's fame and disrepute, in Chapter II, stops with his imprisonment for treason in 1603, although a number of later allusions have been cited for their bearing upon specific problems in the interpretation of his writings. Some further samplings of opinion about him, especially in the century after his death, will be helpful both in concluding this survey of his thought and influence and in evaluating recent theories about his association with a "School of Night." After 1603 popular feeling against him subsided, or perhaps it would be more accurate to say that his unpopularity waned into neglect; and after his death admiration for his achievements outran memories of partisan strife.

I

The change in Ralegh's reputation is epitomized in the contrast between the harsh accusations of the judge who sentenced him in 1603 and the temperate words of his judge in 1618: "Your faith hath heretofore been questioned, but I am satisfied you are a good Christian, for your book, which is an admirable work, doth testify as much."[1] The "damnable fiend of hell,/Mischievous Machiavel" of the early libels is permitted to say, balladwise:

A Christian true I die:
Papistry I defy,

[1] David Jardine, *Criminal Trials*, 2 vols. (London, 1832–35), I, 501.

> Nor never atheist I
> as is reported.[2]

The unfair trial in 1603; the loss of oppressive powers which, in their exercise, had made Ralegh hated; his *History*; his speech upon the scaffold; the course of events which raised him, the anti-Spanish victim of a Stuart king, to a kind of martyrdom: all tended to soften gossip into legend, bitter conflicts into conflicting evidence. Not that imprisonment and execution killed all enmities: to the day of his death he suffered an opposition ranging from the indifference of a changed Court to active hostility; after his death, his integrity was challenged in the pamphlets of Stukeley and Bacon;[3] and in the next generation his son, Carew, sought to retrieve his losses in name and property.

The importance of the *History* in offsetting the old charges of atheism derives from the high esteem in which that work was held in the seventeenth century, when it went through twice as many editions as the collected works of either Spenser or Shakespeare. Naturally enough, Ralegh's exploits at Court and in the field figure prominently in histories and memoirs, sometimes with unfriendly comment; but his fame in the century following his death encompasses all his varied interests and activities without disproportionate emphasis upon his political career. He was credited with a statesman's wisdom; his miscellaneous writings were sought after and frequently published; his name was often invoked in opposition to Spain; even his experiments, and most notably his "cordial," were held in respect for a generation or two. But dominating all, and in a sense including all, was *The History of the World*, with its religious orthodoxy, its moral philosophy, and its frequent digression into commentary on affairs of state. In a book on history which served as a text at Cambridge until the beginning of the eighteenth century, the scholar Dig-

---

[2] "Sir Walter Ralegh His Lamentation," from a Huntington Library photostat of the unique original copy in the Pepysian Collection, Magdalene College, Cambridge. In 1918 the ballad was twice reprinted (once with an accompanying reproduction) in connection with the Ralegh Tercentenary Commemoration.

[3] Quoted above, chap. iv.

gory Whear [4] praised Ralegh for his "universal history"; the soldier Oliver Cromwell [5] commended the *History* to his son; the churchman Edward Stillingfleet [6] quoted it on the Flood; the antiquary Sir William Dugdale [7] could not "better express or account for" the origin of government "than in the words of Sir Walter Ralegh"; and the philosopher John Locke [8] recommended the work for "general history."

These representative judgments in the seventeenth century are not without parallels in the eighteenth, perhaps with greater emphasis on the style of the *History*. One of the most extravagant encomiums is from the pen of Henry Felton:

Sir Walter Ralegh's *History of the World* is a work of so vast a compass, such endless variety, that no genius but one adventurous as his own durst have undertaken that great design. I do not apprehend any great difficulty in collecting and commonplacing an universal history from the whole body of historians; that is nothing but mechanic labor. But to digest the several authors in his mind, to take in all their majesty, strength, and beauty, to raise the spirit of meaner historians, and to equal all the excellencies of the best, is Sir Walter's peculiar praise. His style is the most perfect, the happiest, and most beautiful of the age he wrote in; majestic, clear, and manly; and he appears everywhere so superior, rather than unequal, to his subject that the spirit of Rome and Athens seems to be breathed into his work. . . . If he had attempted the history of his own country, or his own times, he would have excelled even Livy and Thucydides; and the annals of Queen Elizabeth by his pen, without diminishing from the serious, judicious Camden, had been the brightest glory of her reign, and would

---

[4] *De ratione et methodo legendi historias dissertatio* (Oxford, 1625); 1st ed., 1623. In the 1625 edition the praise of Ralegh's *History* is in a marginal note (sig. F3^r). In the expanded 1637 edition, the comment is incorporated in the text (p. 45) and includes praise of Ralegh as well as of his book.

[5] Charles H. Firth, "Sir Walter Raleigh's *History of the World*," *Proceedings of the British Academy*, VIII (1918), 15.

[6] See above, chap. vi.

[7] *Origines juridiciales*, 3d ed. (1680); quoted by William Oldys, *The British Librarian* (1738), p. 169.

[8] "Some Thoughts Concerning Reading and Study for a Gentleman," *Works*, 9 vols. (London, 1824), II, 409.

The Judicious Historian   257

have transmitted his history as the standard of our language even to the present age.[9]

Of the writers before 1650, only King Charles I, in Felton's judgment, is comparable in his style to Sidney, Bilson, Hooker, or Ralegh. Tempering this fulsome praise, Samuel Johnson considers Ralegh's *History* "deservedly celebrated for the labor of his researches and the elegance of his style," but concludes that "he has produced an historical dissertation, but seldom risen to the majesty of history."[10] The opinions of Felton and Johnson must stand here for many. In the course of the eighteenth century, Ralegh's *History* lost the immediacy in content and method that it had for the preceding age, and some pertinent comments reflecting the change have already been cited.[11]

Not even the *History*, thus commended and read, cut off entirely the memory of his reputation as a freethinker. When the provincial inquiry at Cerne Abbas had been long forgotten in the scandals of the court of James I, when even Father Parsons' widely published *Responsio* had been buried under an avalanche of new controversial pamphlets, the tradition of Ralegh's "atheism" remained alive. References to it in the seventeenth century illustrate further the three principal definitions of "atheism" by which I have examined Ralegh's works in Chapters IV to VI. Thus Ralegh's alleged denial of God becomes an instrument to puff a translation of a book written by Leonard Lessius "against atheists and politicians of these days."[12] The translator, A. B., entitles his work *Ralegh His Ghost*, and in prefatory remarks by "The Apparition to His Friend" allows the ghost of Ralegh

[9] *A Dissertation on Reading the Classics and Forming a Just Style*, 2d ed. (London, 1715), pp. 245–48.
[10] *The Rambler*, No. 122, Saturday, May 18, 1751; in *Works*, 16 vols. (New York, 1903), III, 66. Johnson's subject is the difficulty of writing narrative prose and the deficiencies of the British as historians.
[11] See above, chap. vi, "Of the Deluge."
[12] *Ralegh His Ghost. Or a Feigned Apparition of Sir Walter Ralegh to a Friend of His, for the Translating into English the Book of Leonard Lessius (That Most Learned Man) Entitled "De Providentia Numinis et Animi Immortalitate"* . . . Translated by A. B. ([St. Omer], 1631).

to reject "a foul and most unjust aspersion upon me for my presumed denial of a Deity," to appeal to his "friend's" recollection of his praise of Lessius, and to call for a translation of this "proof of the being of a Deity." With an unghostly concern for the book trade, the prefatory spirit further charges, "Let the title bear my name, that so the readers may acknowledge it as done by my solicitation." The translator, in his preface to the reader, blandly acknowledges his fiction as a device to attract readers:

> I have feigned the occasion hereof to be an apparition of Sir Walter Ralegh's ghost to a living friend of his, entreating him to translate the same. My reason of using this fiction is because it is well known that Sir Walter was a man of great natural parts, and yet was suspected of the most foul and execrable crime of atheism. How truly, God and himself only know; though I must think the best of him, and the rather in regard of that most excellent and learned description of God which himself setteth down in the first lines of his history or chronicle.
>
> Now, in regard of his eminency in the world when he was alive, I am the more easily persuaded that the very name of him (by way of this feigned apparition, and the like answerable title of the translation) may beget in many an earnest desire of perusing this book. . . .

The device, says A. B., wrongs no one, not Sir Walter "since I do vindicate and free him from the former blot as presuming him to be innocent of the suspected crime." The Preface, of course, has no independent value, either as a "vindication" of Ralegh or as a confirmation of the old charges. The clumsy trick is worth citing only as an indication of the drawing power of Ralegh's name, of the lingering record of his "atheism," and of the influence of the *History* in countering that tradition.

An association between "atheism" and misconduct is made by an early biographer, John Shirley. Aware of the charges against Ralegh but ignorant of any formal record of them, Shirley seeks an explanation in his hero's misdeeds.

> [Ralegh] was seized with the idle court-disease of love, the unfortunate occasion of the worst action of his whole life. For in the year

1595, I find him under a cloud, banished the court, and his mistress' favor withdrawn, for devirginating a maid of honor. But why for this one action he should lie under the imputation of an atheist, and from a single crime get the denomination of a debauch, is the logic of none but the vulgar.[13]

By this logic, writes Shirley, other favorites—Leicester, Cecil, and Essex—merit the same titles; "neither ever was it accounted any great crime in the orb of courts." A direct connection between Ralegh's alleged offense and his reputation as an atheist is pure guesswork on Shirley's part. What is interesting about his explanation is that he is living in a religious and moral climate enough like that of the Elizabethans to accept wrongdoing as a possible definition of "atheism."

A third allusion to Ralegh's atheism links it with his independence in philosophy. This one, from the pen of Francis Osborne, is also muddled in its facts but clear in intent.

Sir Walter Ralegh was the first (as I have heard) that ventured to tack about, and sail aloof from the beaten tract of the Schools: who upon the discovery of so apparent an error as a torrid zone intended to proceed in an inquisition after more solid truths, till the mediation of some whose livelihood lay in hammering shrines for this superannuated study possessed Queen Elizabeth that such doctrine was against God no less than her father's honor, whose faith (if he owed any) was grounded upon school-divinity. Whereupon she chid him, who was (by his own confession) ever after branded with the title of an atheist, though a known asserter of God and providence.[14]

Bacon and Selden, Osborne continues, suffered a like imputation. With all its distortions and ambiguities, Osborne's statement contains one significant idea: that Ralegh's "atheism" was some-

---

[13] *Life*, 8vo. ed. (London, 1677), pp. 36–37. See above, chap. i, note 1.

[14] *A Miscellany of Sundry Essays, Paradoxes, and Problematical Discourses* (London, 1659), Preface, sig. (a)2. Quoted in part by J. Beau, "La Religion de Sir Walter Ralegh," *Revue Anglo-Americaine*, XI (1934), 410–22. Ralegh appears as a skeptic in an anecdote (too late in origin to have any value) which illustrates the untrustworthiness of eyewitness accounts. See T. N. Brushfield, *Bibliography of Sir Walter Ralegh* (Exeter, England, 1908), No. 171 and the references there cited.

how associated with his hostility to scholasticism, a hostility which we have seen in action in the debate with Ironside.

There is little profit in following through the eighteenth and nineteenth centuries the commentary upon Ralegh as a "free-thinker." Two of these later comments, however, are noteworthy as showing how the passage of time had obscured certain Elizabethan concepts. The first, by the philosopher Dugald Stewart writing "Of the Fundamental Laws of Human Belief," concerns the skeptical passage from Ralegh's Preface which I have discussed at length in Chapter VII. The significant point about Stewart's remark is a slip in quotation which transforms Ralegh into a thoroughgoing rationalist.

It has been observed to me very lately by a learned and ingenious friend, that in one of the phrases which I have proposed to substitute for the *common sense* of Buffier and Reid, I have been anticipated, two hundred years ago, by Sir Walter Ralegh. "Where natural reason hath built anything so strong against itself, as the same reason can hardly assail it, much less batter it down; the same, in every question of nature and infinite [*sic*] power, may be approved for a *fundamental law of human knowledge*." (Preface to Ralegh's *History of the World*.) The coincidence, in point of *expression*, is not a little curious, but is much less wonderful than the coincidence of the *thought* with the soundest logical conclusions of the eighteenth century. The very eloquent and philosophical passage which immediately follows the above sentence is not less worthy of attention.[15]

Had Ralegh actually written "in every question of nature and *in*finite power" he would have contradicted himself on almost every page of his *History*. For Stewart, of course, this is merely an aside of small consequence to his own work, and he may have taken his quotation at second hand; but the unconscious reversal of Ralegh's meaning highlights the difference in philosophy between the sixteenth century and the Age of Reason. Elsewhere,

---

[15] *Collected Works*, ed. Sir William Hamilton, 11 vols. (Edinburgh, 1854-60), III, 376. Stewart's references to Ralegh have been quoted in part by Macvey Napier, "The Life and Writings of Sir Walter Raleigh," *Edinburgh Review*, CXLIII (1840), 67, 96.

The Judicious Historian

Stewart approves the linking of the names of Bacon and Ralegh, in terms that are flattering but free from gross error.

Both of them owed to the force of their own minds their emancipation from the fetters of the school; both were eminently distinguished above their contemporaries by the originality and enlargement of their philosophical views; and both divide, with the venerable Hooker, the glory of exemplifying to their yet unpolished countrymen the richness, variety, and grace which might be lent to the English idiom by the hand of a master.[16]

The second comment, by Matthew Arnold, also bears upon the quality of Ralegh's thought, with no advantage to the Elizabethan. Where Henry Felton had detected the "spirit of Rome and Athens" in the *History* and considered Ralegh, had he but written of his own times, capable of excelling even Livy and Thucydides, Arnold uses the *History* to demonstrate why Thucydides is more "modern" than Ralegh. He compares the two on "the manifestation of a critical spirit, the endeavor after a rational arrangement and appreciation of the facts." Thucydides chooses his subject for its meaningfulness and undertakes to present it in perspective. Here Arnold quotes a few lines from the opening of Ralegh's discussion of the terrestrial paradise, as an example of woolgathering in content and method.

Which is the ancient here, and which is the modern? Which uses the language of an intelligent man of our own days? which a language wholly obsolete and unfamiliar to us? Which has rational appreciation and control of his facts? which wanders among them helplessly and without a clue? Is it our countryman, or is it the Greek? And the language of Ralegh affords a fair sample of the critical power, of the point of view, possessed by the majority of intelligent men of his day; as the language of Thucydides affords us a fair sample of the critical power of the majority of intelligent men in the age of Pericles.[17]

---

[16] "Dissertation Exhibiting the Progress of Metaphysical, Ethical, and Political Philosophy, Part I," *Works*, ed. Hamilton, I, 78.

[17] "On the Modern Element in Literature," *The New Eclectic Magazine*, V (July, 1869), 54–55. Arnold's comment on Ralegh has been quoted in part by Charles H. Firth, *op. cit.*

The passage which Arnold quotes from the *History* serves his purpose well. That it does not represent fully either Ralegh or his book, or that Arnold could have found passages comparable to what he admires in Thucydides, is beside the point. Even allowing for Arnold's strict doctrine on what is "classic," we have here a clear indication that the part of the *History* which was once much admired has become obsolete, something to be dismissed by others than David Hume as "rabbinical learning."

This selection of widely dispersed comments on Ralegh and the quality and independence of his thinking emphasizes the need, if we would understand him, of reading his works in their Elizabethan setting. The judgments of his seventeenth-century readers, even when marked by errors in fact or bias in politics, show at least an understanding of his "language." Later changes in philosophy, religion, and language carry with them inevitable changes in emphasis and construction; in time the reputation for freethought and independence that was once a liability to Ralegh becomes his praise—but with equal dangers of distortion. In most of the biographies down to the late nineteenth century, references to Ralegh's "atheism" are brushed aside, sometimes lightly (as belied by the evidence) and sometimes indignantly. In the studies of the past half century there has been a tendency to accept the Elizabethan charges against him as evidence, at the least, of broad views in religion. The discovery and publication of the testimony at Cerne Abbas accelerated this trend and led to the elaboration of theories about a "School of Night," to which we must now turn.

II

Arguments for the existence in the sixteenth century of a "School of Night," a coterie interested in esoteric studies, begin with the topical possibilities of Shakespeare's play, *Love's Labour's Lost*. A prime target for banter in that play is the ease with which nobles sworn to intellectual pursuits are distracted by an embassy of fair ladies. To Berowne's description of his lady, "No face is fair that is not full so black," the King replies:

> O paradox, Blacke is the badge of Hell,
> The hue of dungions, and the Schoole of night:
> And beauties crest becomes the heauens well.[18]

About the time of the first performance of *Love's Labour's Lost* appeared George Chapman's *The Shadow of Night* (1594), two abstract and obscure poems exalting the studious, careful approach to learning:

> No pen can anything eternal write
> That is not steeped in humour of the Night.[19]

In a dedication to Matthew Royden, Chapman laments the neglect of learning, with one note of optimism:

> But I stay this spleen when I remember, my good Matthew, how joyfully oftentimes you reported unto me that most ingenious Derby, deep-searching Northumberland, and skill-embracing heir of Hunsdon had most profitably entertained learning in themselves, to the vital warmth of freezing science and to the admirable luster of their true nobility. . . .

Comparing these lines and their contexts, Mr. Arthur Acheson,[20] early in the present century, developed the thesis that *Love's Labour's Lost* and *The Shadow of Night* are antagonistic. Later elaborations of this theory, notably by the editors of the "New Cambridge Shakespeare," make Matthew Royden, the three noblemen praised by Chapman, and Chapman himself the nucleus of the "School of Night," devoted to the serious study of the arts and sciences.[21] The next step is to unite with them

---

[18] Quoted with the spelling and punctuation of the 1598 Quarto, sig. F2ʳ; IV, iii, 254–56, in the conventional numbering of the lines.

[19] "Hymnus in Noctem," lines 376–77.

[20] *Shakespeare and the Rival Poet* (New York, 1902).

[21] *Love's Labour's Lost*, ed. Sir Arthur Quiller-Couch and John Dover Wilson (Cambridge, 1923), pp. xviii–xxxiv, 97–130, and notes on IV, iii, 250–52. Cf. *Willobie His Avisa*, ed. G. B. Harrison (London, 1926), pp. 181–231; and G. B. Harrison, *An Elizabethan Journal, 1591–1594* (New York, 1929), Appendix I (b), "Topical Allusions."

the "School of Atheism," charged to Ralegh's leadership by the Jesuit Parsons. Northumberland, mentioned by Chapman, was Ralegh's friend, and, as we have already seen, Harriot and Marlowe have been brought, the latter by inference, into Ralegh's group.[22] The study of astronomy, the philosophical doubt, the air of aloofness and superiority attributed to these men have led to the identification of Ralegh's "School of Atheism" with the "School of Night" to which Shakespeare presumably refers. Other tenets ascribed to the group are a devotion to art for art's sake, a conviction of the need for deep study to accomplish anything worth while, and an affectation of the vague symbolism of Night and the presiding deity Cynthia. The Elizabethan charge of atheism against them has been variously construed—rarely in its strict modern meaning, more commonly as implying unorthodox opinions and religious liberalism.

Opposed to the "School of Night," according to the theory, is another coterie, in which the chief figures are Shakespeare, his patron Southampton, and his patron's friend, Essex. These gentlemen profess to scorn the laborious nocturnal way of study, and their philosophy is summed up in Berowne's excuses for the sudden renunciation of academic retirement by the King and his three courtiers:

> Never durst poet touch a pen to write,
> Until his ink were temp'red with Love's sighs; . . .
> From women's eyes this doctrine I derive:
> They sparkle still the right Promethean fire;
> They are the books, the arts, the academes,
> That show, contain, and nourish all the world. . . .[23]

Earlier Berowne had objected to the studious retirement in these words:

> Small have continual plodders ever won,
> Save base authority from others' books.[24]

---

[22] See above, chap. ii.
[23] IV, iii, 346–53. In this quotation and the next I follow the text of *The Complete Plays and Poems of William Shakespeare*, ed. W. A. Neilson and C. J. Hill (Cambridge, Mass., 1942). [24] I, i, 86–87.

The Judicious Historian 265

In the opposition of the two groups, say those who argue for the existence of the "School of Night," lies part of the meaning of *Love's Labour's Lost*.

This theorizing has done much to color Ralegh studies, simply by postulating for him an intellectual and temperamental outlook that derives more from his assumed associations than from anything he said or wrote. Some writers have accepted these postulates as established and have based their interpretations upon them. Miss M. C. Bradbrook [25] has used the theory as a convenient point of reference for the discussion of Ralegh, Marlowe, Chapman, and, finally, Shakespeare's satirical allusions. Miss Frances A. Yates,[26] however, broadens the field to find in *Love's Labour's Lost* references to a number of literary rivalries (for example, John Florio and John Eliot, Gabriel Harvey and Thomas Nashe, Shakespeare and Chapman), allusions to the marital difficulties of Ralegh's friend, Northumberland, and even a defense of Sidney's "Stella." A critique of these conjectures, which show how involved the ramifications of the "School of Night" theory have become, lies outside the province of this study. For the understanding of Ralegh, we must reexamine the foundation upon which this theory has been built, and not the superstructure of conjectural identifications of characters in Shakespeare's play.

In printing the King's speech, quoted above from the 1598 quarto of *Love's Labour's Lost*, the New Cambridge editors retain the wording of the original text, but eliminate a comma after "dungions" and capitalize "night," so that the lines read:

> O paradox! Black is the badge of hell,
> The hue of dungeons and the School of Night;
> And beauty's crest becomes the heavens well! [27]

The change in punctuation alters the reading from "Blacke is . . . the Schoole of night" (an awkward reading if "Schoole"

[25] *The School of Night* (Cambridge, England, 1936).
[26] *A Study of "Love's Labour's Lost"* (Cambridge, England, 1936).
[27] IV, iii, 250–52, in the New Cambridge edition. For the quoted comment which follows, see the note on this passage.

is taken to mean a group of men) to "Black is . . . The hue of . . . the School of Night"; and the capitalization of "Night" emphasizes the phrase. These changes are justified by Mr. Acheson's contention that Shakespeare here intended an allusion "to an actual coterie, for which presumably Chapman composed his *Shadow of Night*, 1594, and upon which the 'academe' of Navarre is itself a satire." But this comes perilously close to explaining the King's speech by the theory and then using the speech to support the theory. If we examine the lines as one problem in establishing a text, without a predisposition in favor of Mr. Acheson's interpretation, what reading of the passage can be justified?

This rather specialized question may be answered here in a summary of arguments which I have elsewhere presented in detail.[28] The New Cambridge editors regard the spelling of the 1598 quarto as a laborious reproduction of the copy, but they consider the punctuation bad. Therefore they reject customary emendations of "Schoole," and to bring out the possible allusion they alter the punctuation, although it is defensible as it stands. The lines in question are not without analogues in other works by Shakespeare; indeed, he is fond of variations on the theme of night, especially in terms of garments, as "cloak of night," or "night's black mantle." Hence the readiness of those who preceded the New Cambridge editors to emend "Schoole" to read "suit" (a change supported by early pronunciation of "suit" as "shoot," evidence for which is found in this very play), or "shade," or "stole." Such emendations, based upon analogues in figurative language and upon paleographic clues, are rejected by the New Cambridge editors as "rank guesses"—although, using the same kind of evidence elsewhere, they are willing to

[28] "The Textual Evidence for 'The School of Night,' " *Modern Language Notes*, LVI (1941), 176–86. For an explanation of the system of punctuation used in the New Cambridge edition, see *The Tempest* (Cambridge, 1921), pp. lvii–lx. For emendations of the disputed passage, and for analogies in language, see my note on "The Textual Evidence" and the notes in the Furness *Variorum* edition of *Love's Labour's Lost* (1904), IV, iii, 272.

The Judicious Historian 267

credit the compositor of *Love's Labour's Lost* with an error two stages removed from his copy.[29]

Another difficulty is that, if a reference to a coterie is intended in the phrase "Schoole of night," the method of introducing it is quite different from that used by Shakespeare in his known topical allusions. Those concerning which there is any unanimity of opinion are recognizable, in the context, as allusions: for example, the reference to Essex in *Henry V*, or to Elizabeth in *A Midsummer Night's Dream*. In *Love's Labour's Lost* Mr. Acheson and the New Cambridge editors find an allusion in a single phrase, one of three symbols for blackness, introduced into a passage of sixty lines devoted to sophistry and banter on the familiar "black is fair" theme. By this construction of Shakespeare's lines, we are asked to believe that one phrase picked from its context by an alert and informed audience or pointed by the actor, would convey a specific secondary meaning. It is presumed that "Schoole of night," meaning Ralegh and his associates, would suggest blackness as readily as do hell and dungeons. I have brought together in this study numerous hostile references to Ralegh or members of his retinue, but I do not know of a single unmistakable instance in which his group was called the "School of Night." What we have to justify such a precious reading of the lines is not textual evidence, but, to borrow a phrase from the New Cambridge editors, "nothing more secure than internal evidence interpreted through a critic's own proclivities of belief." [30]

Questions of membership in the "School" are scarcely less tortuous than the problems of text. Charter members, if we so read Chapman's dedicatory letter to Royden, were the Earl of Derby, who died in 1594; Henry Percy, the ninth Earl of Northumberland, long a friend of Sir Walter Ralegh and later his fellow prisoner; and Sir George Carey, later the second Baron Hunsdon. Northumberland, the "Wizard Earl," would be an ideal candidate for the "School," as postulated; but what of Sir

[29] V, ii, 123 and note. Cf. Introd., p. xxix.   [30] *The Tempest*, p. xix.

George Carey, "the skill-embracing heir of Hunsdon" in Chapman's phrase? Once Chapman's lines are before the reader, Sir George usually disappears from the discussions of the "School." He simply does not fit into the picture. From 1594 until 1603 Shakespeare's dramatic company was under the patronage of a Carey: under Henry, first Baron Hunsdon and Lord Chamberlain, until his death in 1596; then, as "Hunsdon's Men," under Sir George Carey, the second Baron Hunsdon; and when Sir George succeeded to his father's office the company again was known as the "Lord Chamberlain's Men." And before the Carey's patronage in 1594, Shakespeare's company was most probably under the protection of the same Earl of Derby named by Chapman. Any date for the performance of *Love's Labour's Lost* that would satisfy the requirements of the "School of Night" theory would fall in the period when either actors' patron, or their patron's son, was a member of the group at whom the satire is aimed! [31] The difficulties multiply if we pursue the problem into the complexities suggested by Miss Yates. To give but one example: Nashe and Shakespeare, in Miss Yates's account, belong with the "villanists," those who learn by life rather than by academic study; the "School of Night" holds with the "artists," who value laborious and obscure study. But Carey is Nashe's patron, as well as Shakespeare's; for a time Nashe lived with Sir George, praised him extravagantly in *The Terrors of Night*, dedicated that work to Sir George's daughter, and dedicated another to his wife.[32] In short, if the evidence alleged for the

---

[31] This paradox has been noted by Sir Edmund K. Chambers, *William Shakespeare*, 2 vols. (Oxford, 1930), I, 337. A kindred difficulty, that the indictment of the supposed "School" is made by the King, who is a member of the group, has led Janet Spens to regard the play as a "quite friendly burlesque"; see her "Notes on *Love's Labour's Lost*," *Review of English Studies*, VII (1931), 333. To remove this difficulty, Miss Yates, *op. cit.*, p. 9, suggests alternate identifications: the studious young men in the play may be either the Ralegh group or the Essex group who laugh at their studious pretentions!

[32] *The Works of Thomas Nashe*, ed. R. B. McKerrow (London, 1904-10), I, 341-42, 374-75; II, 9-11. Aside from his patronage of Nashe, Sir George Carey's intellectual interests, so far as I have been able to follow them, do not suggest the one-sidedness attributed to the "School."

The Judicious Historian 269

"School of Night" means anything, Carey should be included; but the facts about his literary and personal relationships run directly counter to his association with the group as it is usually described.

The personal relations of other supposed members of the "School" are, in terms of the theory, clouded by contradictions, even by conflicts. Although there is practically no evidence for the close association of Marlowe and Ralegh, their friendship is taken for granted. Chapman sought his patrons among men presumably in the hostile camp. Even the closest of friends are not always as harmonious as this theory presupposes. The friendship of Ralegh and Northumberland was of long standing, and the recorded instances of their meetings are numerous; yet Northumberland once remarked that Ralegh has not trusted him completely, and the Earl's description of his friend in a letter to James is not altogether flattering.[33] Aside from occasional disagreements in personal affairs, it is extremely unlikely that acquaintance or friendship can be taken as a certain indication of harmony of opinions and beliefs. The associations of the supposed coterie were certainly of short memory. In *The History of the World*, a reference to the telescope suggests to Ralegh praise of Galileo,[34] not of Harriot, whose observations in astronomy were contemporaneous with those of Galileo and must have been known to his patrons, Ralegh and Northumberland, both in the Tower. The mention of Tamerlane evokes no reference to Marlowe; yet, just a few pages before one such allusion, an account of the death of Philotas [35] contains fourteen lines of

---

[33] *Cal. State Papers, Dom.*, 1603–1610, p. 23; *Correspondence of King James VI of Scotland with Sir Robert Cecil and Others*, ed. John Bruce, "Camden Soc. Publications," LXXVIII (1861), 66–67. Similar difficulties in establishing the fact of friendly relations among alleged members of the "School," and in deducing from friendship a harmony of belief, have been discussed by Paul H. Kocher, *Christopher Marlowe* (Chapel Hill, N.C., 1946), pp. 7–18.

[34] I, vii, 2, p. 100.

[35] Tamerlane: Pref., sig. D2^r; IV, ii, 18, p. 202. Philotas: IV, ii, 17, p. 199. Ralegh quotes the opening lines of the Chorus at the end of Act III of *The Tragedy of Philotas*. He does not mention Daniel by name.

verse by "a poet of our own"—Samuel Daniel, who is not included in the "School of Night." English verse is seldom quoted in the *History*, and it is possible that the lines from Daniel's *Philotas* were read by Ralegh as a reflection of the circumstances of his own trial. Nevertheless, it is remarkable that the many digressions of the leisurely *History* contain no hint of associations that are presumed to have been intimate.

Finally—and briefly, since this entire study is pertinent to the question—I find little agreement between the doctrines credited to the "School of Night" and the opinions of Ralegh that can be derived from his own speeches or writings. The doctrines of the "School," as variously described by proponents of the theory, imply more radical departures from orthodox religious thought than I have been able to find in Ralegh. He had a driving curiosity, abetted by an impulsiveness of temperament, which led him to seek knowledge where he could find it; but these very qualities make him a poor candidate for a coterie. In his studies he commonly sought practical ends: improved navigation; better ships; a more effective cure-all in physic; success in politics; a stronger empire—and personal power. When he is meditative and speculative, as he often is and in the grand manner, he keeps within the limits of a serious, even somber, ethic and an orthodox religion.

The fundamental difficulty of the "School of Night" theory, of course, goes back to Shakespeare's text. Those who propound the theory find an allusion in *Love's Labour's Lost* and develop to the utmost the topical possibilities of that play, with the result that, as in most studies of Elizabethan topical allusions, identifications abound and conflict. I find no personal allusion in the King's scoffing rejection of Berowne's praise of his "black" lady, and I believe that other evidence for a "School" has been applied too selectively to be convincing. The great value of studies of the "School of Night" has been the light they have thrown upon some literary relationships and theories in the flourishing last decade of the sixteenth century. That value remains even when we abandon attempts to organize these impermanent and often casual associations into formally opposed coteries, and to discover in Shakespeare's play topical allusions of a subtlety one would be surprised to meet in Elizabethan literature.

III

Clearly, three and a half centuries have witnessed wide fluctuations in opinion about Ralegh. He has appeared posthumously in even more roles than he attempted in his tempestuous lifetime, and his reputation has changed as near-contemporaries who shared his intellectual background yielded to writers who judged him by different standards. With such diverse and even flatly contradictory estimates before us, simple caution enjoins a recollection of the premises and major themes of this study before we attempt to draw from it any general conclusions. The most severe limitation upon the available evidence is that we know so little about Ralegh's youth, and the little we know about his early years concerns almost entirely his active, not his contemplative, life. Keeping in mind the problems of evidence set forth in Chapter I, we must be content to base our conclusions on our knowledge of Ralegh in his thirties and of his life thereafter.

In brief, Ralegh's reputation as an "atheist" is traceable in large part to the Catholic polemics against him, especially Parsons' widely circulated attack, and to the casual usage of "atheist" in moral censure. Whatever the cause of the reputation, Ralegh's arrogance and unpopularity did nothing to abate it, although his trial and imprisonment paradoxically won him a reprieve in the court of public opinion. Yet sober accounts of his table talk, by such competent reporters as the Reverend Ralph Ironside and Sir John Harington, in no wise support the charge of "atheism" against him; and his conversations on religious topics, as reported, are consistent with the orthodoxy of his published writings. Only by reading his remarks or his writings out of their Elizabethan setting, or by underestimating the place of natural theology in Elizabethan religious thought, is it possible to discern in Ralegh, so far as we know him, any signs of radical departure from the dominant religious beliefs of his time and country. By finding in his works sober answers to Elizabethan questions designed to ferret out dangerous opinions, and by matching with his statements passages from works of known orthodoxy, I have attempted to restore Raleigh's opinions on religion to their sixteenth-century context. In ethics, as we have seen, it is another story: in action, and to some extent in thought, Ralegh perhaps earned the epithet "Machiavellian," one of the many Elizabethan synonyms for "atheist." Although his excursions in natural philosophy may have deepened popular distrust of his orthodoxy, where science conflicted with religion Ralegh chose religion, notably in his painstaking attempts to harmonize chronology and Scripture.

The key to Ralegh's skepticism and to its utility is his exception from dogmatic principles of "every question of nature and finite power." If skepticism about the powers of human reason is invoked at all in religious discussion, it is in defense of faith. Ralegh's attack on Aristotelian principles could be construed as heretical only if those principles were wrongly identified (as they were in some minds) with the essentials of Christian belief —what Ralegh sometimes called our "saving faith." As I have suggested, some such misunderstanding may have arisen from the debate with Ironside. But in the realm of second causes Ralegh is indeed a "free" thinker. Once we rid ourselves of the notion that his philosophical skepticism applies to religion, or that his theology is in advance of his time, we can see Ralegh more clearly as an influential worker in a transitional period.

Ralegh's boldest statement of the skeptical position, his attack on the "principles" in the Preface to the *History*, is of ancient lineage. It is possible to trace his ideas, both directly and indirectly, to the skeptics of Greece and Rome, and to distinguish in them a partiality for the Academics, who were willing to reason from probabilities, rather than for the uncompromising

The Judicious Historian   273

position of the Pyrrhonists. Thoroughgoing Pyrrhonism is found only in his fragmentary translation from Sextus Empiricus and in some sentences of the Preface, there worked into the framework of a philosophy intended to produce results by investigation of second causes. The distinction is significant in its effects: as one historian of philosophy has pointed out, Pyrrhonism strictly and consistently followed was sterile, though it could be the prelude to "freedom of conscience and rational criticism and the absolute right of scientific thought."

The Skeptics, however, reaped none of the benefits of their own system. They remained, as it were, always on the threshold of possible progress. With the keys to great discoveries in their hands, the doors of philosophical and scientific advancement were for ever closed to them by limitations of their own system. The inherent weakness of Pyrrhonism lay in its psychological inconsistency and its negative character. I think that we may safely say that Pyrrhonism was the most consistent system of Skepticism ever offered to the world, and yet it proves most decidedly that complete Skepticism is psychologically impossible.[36]

From such frustration Ralegh was happily free, both by temperament and by philosophy. It would be an exaggeration to trace his respect for reason and his acceptance of probability directly to the formal philosophy of the Academy; the connection is interesting largely because it places his thought in historical perspective. In practice Ralegh belongs with those men, conspicuous in times of transition, for whom skepticism is a highway, not a dwelling place. Skepticism serves chiefly for the criticism of dogma, and if the criticism is effective the discredited ideas are superseded by new beliefs.[37] In this practical function the popular forms of skepticism are akin to the more strictly defined modes of philosophical criticism.

Hence the importance of such amateurs as Ralegh in the history of ideas. Sir Francis Bacon wrote to his uncle Lord Burghley, in the famous letter of 1592 which takes all knowledge as his

---

[36] Mary Mills Patrick, *Sextus Empiricus and Greek Scepticism* (Cambridge, England, 1899), pp. 96–97.   [37] *Ibid.*

province for reform, that he sought a "place of any reasonable countenance" because it "doth bring commandment of more wits than a man's own." By his own high place in the last decades of the sixteenth century, Ralegh secured just this command of other "wits" and exercised the command by patronage of men of science—or worked as a partner through his own studies in natural philosophy and navigation. The universal appeal of his *History* extended his "command" posthumously and won for Ralegh a respectful hearing in the seventeenth century.

As I indicated at the beginning of my study, it would be misleading to generalize about an age from the intensive study of one man, however representative he may have been. Professor Lynn Thorndike's observations concerning the careers of Lucilio Vanini and Francesco Sanchez rightly emphasize the subtle gradations of belief and disbelief which may be found in individuals.

These two cases lend support to the point which we have made more than once: that there is no regular correlation or variation in inverse ratio between theology and science, skepticism and the occult, or science and superstition. In one's man's mind they made one combination: in another, another.[88]

Keeping in mind this salutary caution, we may yet find in the varied passages from other writers cited by way of parallel to Ralegh's remarks some indication of the extent to which his thought is in harmony with that of his contemporaries. He is throughout more a spokesman than an innovator. His moral philosophy and his religion are deeply rooted in the past, and he shows no inclination to uproot the ancient growth, although he is willing to prune some superfluous branches of Biblical exegesis. He shares some of the superstitions and credulities of his age. But in the new world opening before him, literally in the lands across the sea and figuratively in the science of his day, he seeks, with his fellows, the opportunity for free exploration, unhampered by the "fables of principles." Certain beliefs remain inviolate: the truth of Scripture, the primacy of wisdom

[88] *A History of Magic and Experimental Science*, VI (New York, 1941), 572.

The Judicious Historian

over knowledge, of goodness over intellect. Ralegh is neither the Elizabethan "atheist" (save perhaps in the broad implications of ethical criticism) nor the freethinker of twentieth-century fame, but a leader in that energetic company who did not find religious faith a barrier to philosophical and scientific speculations. There are many echelons in the progress of human thought: Ralegh's company was not the vanguard, though some seventeenth-century writers assigned him that post; yet it constituted a body of support without which a vanguard is lost in premature action.

Index

A. B., tr. of Lessius, 257, 258
Abbot, George, abp., 136
Abernethy, John, 79
Academic skepticism, 221 f., 230, 235, 272
Acheson, Arthur, 263, 266, 267
Acton, Lord, 10
Adam, men before time of, 175, 197-218; *see also* Chronology
Advertisement, An (Parsons), 25, 28, 30
Agrippa, Henry Cornelius, 228, 234
Aldrich, Simon, 17
Alexander, William, 91
Allen, Thomas, 50
Allen, William, Cardinal, 27
Amazons, 253
Ambition, 156
Anatomy of Melancholy, The (Burton), 79*n*, 84*n*
Animals, senses, 225; intelligence, 225, 227
Annius, reliability of, 246, 247, 248
Aphorisms of State . . . , new title of *The Cabinet-Council* (*q.v.*), 161
Apology for Raimond Sebond (Montaigne), 232, 239
Apologia Pro Rege Catholico Philippo II (Stapleton), 28, 34
Apology (Mirandola), 182
Appio, 71
Arcesilaus, 221, 222
Archimedes, 179, 180, 181
Architecture of fortune, 148-71; *see* entries under Worldly aims and success
"Arian" document among Kyd's papers, 94
Aristotle, 69, 74, 76, 78, 92, 95, 103*n*, 123, 126, 142, 167, 200; re argument about creation of the world, 105, 106, 107; doctrine of the soul, 116, 126 f., 128, 140; Oxford dominated by Aristotelianism, 141; Ralegh no respecter of, 145, 147, 219, 220; denial of the authority of, 219, 236-41 *passim*, 272; attack upon his doctrine of Creation in time, 198, 230 ff.; paradoxical reputation in sixteenth century, 236 ff., 243
Arnold, Matthew, 261
Arnold, William, 101
Art of War, The (Machiavelli), 162
Arundel, Charles, 19
Arundel, Dorothy, 38
Arundel, Sir John, 36
Ascham, Roger, 85, 92
Ashmole, Elias, 115
Assyrian kings, 204, 205, 207
Astrology, natural, 176, 177*n*, 192; two kinds defined, 192; judicial, 192 ff.; bibliography re conflict of opinion on, 193*n*; defining the limits of the study, 194; the Christian position: Augustine and other authorities, 194*n*; abuse vs. use of, 195; distinction between astronomy and, 196*n*
Astronomy, 196*n*, 197
Astrophel and Stella (Sidney), 226, 265
"Atheism, School of," *see* "School of Atheism"
Atheism and atheists, Elizabethan meanings of, 6 f., 61-97, 148; usage as "snarl words": personages accused of, 61; many contexts in which found, 62; treatises against, 63-82; force of reason vs. appeals to revela-

278 Index

Atheism and atheists, (*Continued*) tion, as means of convincing the atheist, 72 ff.; principles which led to variety of meanings, 82 ff.; treatises with motive of persuasion, 84 ff.; kinds of atheists, 84, 87; causes, 89 ff.; reasons for omission of charges against named persons, 93; accessibility of works in print, 93 f.; particular aspects symbolized by ancient writers, 95 f.; terms used by later generations, 96; omnibus charge of "inward atheism," 148 ff.; Machiavellianism a synonym for, 161 f., 272; charges against Ralegh not substantiated, 218, 271 f.

Atheist's Tragedy, The (Tourneur), 87, 88, 92

Atheomastix (Fotherby), 81

Aubrey, John, 44, 46, 99, 132, 134, 137, 146; statement re Harriot, 105

Augustine, St., 69, 99, 114, 124, 126, 183n, 187, 239; on the soul, 118, 120; an authority on astrology, 194n; claims to antiquity of the world rejected by, 200

Authority, acceptance or rejection of, 220, 230-53 *passim*

Bacon, Anthony, 35

Bacon, Sir Francis, 90n, 91, 159, 160; Ralegh compared to, 131, 259, 261, 273 f.; condemnation of Ralegh by, 136, 255; quoted by Ralegh, 160n, 169; denial of authority of Aristotle, 236

Bacon, Sir Nicholas, 30

Badger, Sir Thomas, 135

Baines, Richard, 40n, 41, 42, 72, 131, 201

Baker, Thomas, 49n

Banks and his trained horse, 178

Barlow, William, 52

Baronius, Cardinal, 249

Basanier, Martin, 20

Battenhouse, R. W., 120n, 129n

Bayle, Pierre, 233n

Beau, J., 14

Berrio, Antonio de, 146

Bible, *see* Scriptures

Bilson, Thomas, 123

Black art, *see* Demonology

Book of Christian Exercise, A ... (Bunny's adaptation of Parsons), 66

"Books of Resolution, The" (Parsons), 63-72; bibliographical information about, 65 ff.; purpose: arguments, 68 ff.

Borrowings, literary, 12, 13

Botero, Giovanni, 12n, 169n

Bowes, T., 93

Bradbrook, M. C., 131, 265

Brief and True Report of ... *Virginia, A* (Harriot), 44, 45

Brief Answer unto Those ... *Quarrels of R. P.* ... (Bunny), 66n

Broughton, Hugh, 216

Browne, Sir Thomas, 134

Brownists, sect, 252n

Brushfield, T. N., 224

Bucholcerus, Abraham, 211n

Buckley, George T., 18

Bullinger, Henry, 125

Bunny, Edmund, 65 ff.

Burghley, Lord (William Cecil), 6, 19, 259, 273; Catholic writers attacks on, 28-39 *passim*

Burton, Robert, 79, 84, 87

Buteo, John, 190

Cabinet-Council, The (Ralegh), 12, 137; new title, 161; origin, transmission, and character of; influence of Machiavelli, 164 ff.; first printed: Milton's preface, 164

Cabot, Sebastian, 21

Caesar, Julius, 210

Caius, John, 61

Calendars, Julian, 197, 210, 212; va-

rieties of, by ancient peoples, 198;
Gregorian: Greek: obstacles in way
of determining, 210; *see also* Chronology
Calvin, John, 114, 194*n*
Cambrensis, Giraldus, 23
Carey, Sir George (Baron Hunsdon),
263, 267, 268
Carey, Henry (Baron Hunsdon), 268
Carleton, Sir Dudley, 59*n*, 146
Carneades, 222
Carr, Sir Robert, 156
Casaubon, Isaac, 249
Catcott, Alexander, 190
Catholics, archpriest controversy, 31;
see also Jesuits
*Causes of the Magnificency and
Opulency of Cities* (Botero, tr. by
Ralegh), 12, 224
Cecil, Sir Robert, 9, 36, 52, 138, 149;
letters to discredit Ralegh, 53
Cecil, Sir William, *see* Burghley,
(William Cecil), Lord
Celsus, 95, 96
Cerne Abbas investigation, 15, 37, 43,
44, 46-52, 101, 132, 134; beginning of story at Trenchard's supper
party, 47; bibliographical sources,
46*n*, 98*n*, 139*n*; names and function
of investigating committee, 49; no
formal charges or action, 51; effects
of discovery and publication of testimony at, 262; *see also the Ironside-
Ralegh debate under* Ironside, Ralph
Chamber, John, 195, 229
Chamberlain, John, 134
Chapman, George, 263, 265 266, 268
Charles I, King, 257
Charron, Peter, (Pierre), 200, 232,
233*n*, 236
Cholmeley, Richard, 40, 42, 148
Christ, 95; miracles, 72, 74, 87,
182 f.; Ralegh's profession of faith
in, from scaffold, 134, 135; allusions to, in the *History,* 137

Christian and Heavenly Treatise, A
(Abernethy), 79*n*
Christian Directory, A . . . (Parsons), 66
Chronology, 175, 197-218; Julian
Calendar, 197, 210, 212; Renaissance scholars absorbed by questions
of: aim of their study, 197; authority conceded to Scriptures, 198,
209, 215, 218; interpretation of
pagan records in their light, 199,
202, 205; Egyptian antiquity and
records, 199 f., 202 ff., 209, 215;
sources for persons and events that
antedate Adam, 200; solar years
from time of first creation to beginning of modern epoch, 201; New
World legends of man's antiquity,
201; Ralegh's efforts to evolve a
reasonable narrative within limits of
Hebrew chronology: four major
problems, 202 ff.; biblical obscurities and seeming contradictions: resulting problems, 206 ff.; great
number of authorities and opinions
on date of creation, 206; varied
calendars and modes of reckoning
time: finding of a common scale,
210; problem of reducing to terms
of Julian Calendar the varied systems of dating, 211 ff.; Ralegh's
"Chronological Table," 211, 213;
his conscientious efforts to get at the
truth, 214 ff.; conflicting claims to
accuracy rejected, 216
Church doctrine and creed, faith in,
134
Cicero, 24, 90*n*, 95, 110, 200
Cobham, Henry Brooke, Lord, 53,
57
Coke, Sir Edward, 57, 158*n*
Colonization in the New World, religious propaganda for, 20-25; *see
also* Guiana; Virginia
Columbus, Christopher, 179, 180*n*

Commission for Causes Ecclesiastical, 50
Confutation of Atheism (Dove), 78, 83*n*, 90*n*, 116, 199*n*
Conjecture, use in history, 242, 244; in geography, 246
Conjuring and witchcraft, 176, 178
Contre-Machiavel (Gentillet), 162
Corbet, Richard, 45
Corderoy, Jeremy, 79, 83, 90*n*, 92*n*, 127
Cornelius, John (alias Mohun, or John Mooney), 36 ff., 49, 146
Creation, Mornay's theories about eternity and, 76; linked with God's providence, 104-15; attack upon Aristotle's doctrine of, 106-8, 230 ff.; variety of authorities and estimates on date of, 206; variety in dating events by, 213
Creswell, Joseph ("John Pernius," pseud.), 28, 29, 33
Cromwell, Oliver, 5, 164, 256
Cubit, geometrical, 187, 190
Cunning, 160

Danchin, F. C., 46*n*, 139*n*
Daneau, Lambert, 92*n*
Daniel, Samuel, 270
Davies, Sir John, 85, 125, 144
Davis, John, 48, 143
Decades (Bullinger), 125
Deception, 158 ff., 168 f.
De Civitate Dei (Augustine), 188, 200, 239
Declaration of the True Causes of the Great Troubles, A (Verstegen?), 28
Dee, John, 43*n*, 179*n*, 184*n*, 210
Degree, doctrine of, 153, 154
Deluge, Noah's Ark, resettlement of the earth, and origins of the nations, 175, 185-92, 196, 198, 203, 209; pagan legends, 185, 189; extra-Biblical knowledge, 188*n*; changing emphasis in reading of, 192; method of argument: use of new learning to bolster old beliefs, 188; number of pages on, 196; allusion to a flood in America, 202
Demonology, debasement of magic as work of the Devil, 176 ff.; corruption of astrology, 196
Demonstration of God in His Works, A (More), 78
Derby, Earl of, 263, 267, 268
Desire, three sorts, 121
Des Vignoles, Alphonse, 207
Deucalion, flood of, 185
Dialogue between a Jesuit and a Recusant, A, 37*n*
Diogenes Laertius, 228
Discourse of War, A (Ralegh), 167
Discourses (Machiavelli), 163, 166, 168
Discourse Touching a Marriage between Prince Henry ... and a Daughter of Savoy, A (Ralegh), 167
Discovery of Guiana, The (Ralegh), 11, 14, 22 f., 162*n*; credulities found in, 251 ff.
Dissembling, 158 ff., 168 f.
Dogmatism, skepticism a weapon of attack upon, 220, 235
Dogmatists, 221
Dogs, intelligence, 225, 227
Donne, John, 93
Dove, John, 88, 93; confutation of atheism, 78 f., 83*n*, 90*n*, 116, 199*n*
Drake, Sir Francis, 34*n*
Du Bartas, 85, 102*n*
Dugdale, Sir William, 256

Egyptian antiquity and chronology, 199 f., 202 ff., 209
Eliot, John, 265
Elizabeth, Queen, 3*n*, 11, 19, 61, 256, 259, 267; proclamation of 1591, against Jesuits: response from the Catholic press, 27-40 *passim*;

Index

charged with atheistic religious policy and knighting of pirates, 34; Ralegh a favorite, 39; proclamation re calendar, 210*n*
Elizabethae . . . (Parsons), *see Responsio*
Ellis-Fermor, U. M., 130, 131
Englefield, Sir Francis, 28
Epicurus, 86, 91, 95
Essais (Montaigne), 200*n*, 201*n*, 229, 232, 240
Essex, Robert Devereux, 2d Earl of, 3, 5, 9, 10, 36, 52, 259, 264, 267; Ralegh's opposition to, 54, 57; verses by partisans of, 54 ff.
Étienne, Henri, 226, 228
Eusebius, 217
Exemplar Literarum . . . (Creswell), 27, 29
Exercise of a Christian Life, The (Loarte), 65
Experience exalted over reason, 230, 242

Fall of the Late Arian, The (Proctor), 41
Felltham, Owen, 144
Felton, Henry, 256 f., 261
Ficino, Marsilio, 108
First Book of the Christian Exercise, The . . . (Loarte, enlarged by Parsons), 65
Fitzjames, John, 47, 142
Flood, *see* Deluge
Florentine History, The (Machiavelli), 163
Florio, John, 265
Foley, Henry, 38
Fortune, architecture of, 114, 148-71; *see entries under* Worldly aims and success
Fotherby, Martin, 79, 81 f., 90

Galen, 69, 78, 251
Galileo, 188, 269

Gascoigne, George, 4, 18
Gentillet, Innocent, 162
Geography, 198, 199*n*; fact and conjecture, 246
Geological evidence of age of earth, 198*n*
Gibbon, Edward, 8
God, Parsons' argument for, 68 ff., Mornay's, 75; Ralegh's beliefs about God, the soul, the Scriptures and salvation, 98-147; the being of God, 99-104; anagram of Dog, 99, 132; His providence and the creation of the world, 104-15, 244; debate between Ironside and the Raleghs on the soul and, 139 ff.; *see also* Ironside, Ralph
Golding, Arthur, 63
Gomara, Lopez de, 201
Goropius, Joannes Becanus, 248
Gray, Robert, 194*n*
Greeks, calendar, 210; skepticism (*q.v.*), 220 ff.
Greene, Robert, 63, 67, 85, 92, 94
Greene's Ghost . . . (Rowlands), 226
Gregorian calendar, 210
Gregory XIII, Pope, 210
Grenville, Sir Richard, 189
Guiana, voyage to, 3; missionary purposes of colonization, 22; arguments for occupying, 251; *see also Discovery of Guiana, The*
Gunpowder Plot, 158*n*

Hakluyt, Richard, 4, 45, 52, 198; propaganda in behalf of colonization and missionary work, 20-25 *passim*
Hall, Joseph, 170
Hampden, John, 5
Hanmer, Meredith, 206, 207*n*
Harington, Sir John, 59, 146, 271
Harlow, V. T., 129, 130, 131, 251
Harriot, Thomas, 4, 21, 58, 59, 201,

282　Index

Harriot, Thomas (*Continued*) 264, 269; called Ralegh's man, 41; their association, 42 ff., 46; question of his orthodoxy, 44 ff., 50, 132; death, 44, 105, 106; said to doubt story of the creation, 104; chronological calculations, 199n
Harrison, G. B., 46n, 139n
Harvey, Gabriel, 94, 265
Hatton, Sir Christopher, 30
Hawley, Francis, 49
Henry IV of France, 169
Henry VIII of England, 111, 164
Henry, Prince, 161, 165, 167
Hester, John, 240
Heydon, Sir Christopher, 195, 228
Histoire notable de la Floride, L' (Laudonnière), 20, 21
Historia de Mexico (de Gomara), 201
History of Philosophy, The (Stanley), 227
History of the World (Pliny), 182n, 184n
History of the World, The (Ralegh), 11, 37n, 42, 58, 61, 72, 97, 219n; book and chapter references, 4n; for two centuries read as a guide to life and model of prose, 5; why the greatest authority as a guide to Ralegh's thought, 12, 14; problems of authenticity and originality, 13; digression and personal comment in, 14, 270; pictorial il. in frontispiece, 24, 109; statements on God and the soul, with excerpts, 98-147 *passim*; extensive commentary on the problems of religion, 98, 229; comparisons between Chap. II of, and *A Treatise of the Soul*, 116, 123 ff.; treatment in Preface, of moral basis of worldly aims and success, 150 ff.; principles of statecraft, 161; indebtedness to Machiavelli, 166-71 *passim;* best-known paragraph, 170; problems of philosophy of science (natural philosophy) treated in, 175, 179, 193, 196, 198, 202 ff.; sections in which definitions and principal defense occur, 175n ff.; vivified by identification of subject with author's wealth of experience, 189; chronological questions and computation, with excerpts, 198, 202-17; passage in Preface a key statement of skeptical philosophy, text, 230 f.; appeals to reason, 235; value of experience over reason illustrated, 242; method and credulities considered, 244 ff.; the dominant idea in, 244; acceptance or rejection of authority, 247 ff.; held in high esteem: its many editions, 255; representative judgments about, with excerpts, 255 ff.; style, 256; effect of its universal appeal in seventeenth century, 274
Holland, Philemon, 182n
Hooker, John, 23, 25
Hooker, Richard, 85, 92n
Horsey, Sir Ralph, 36, 37, 47, 49, 51
Howard, Henry, accusations against Ralegh, 53
Howard, Thomas, Viscount, of Bindon, 49
Hues, Robert, 59
Hull, John, 85
Hume, David, 10, 262
Hunsdon, Barons, *see under* Carey

Image, term, 123
Immortality, 77, 122, 127
Indians, American, 45, 201, 251
Instructions to His Son and to Posterity (Ralegh), 138, 154-60 *passim*
Intellectual authority, *see* Authority
Inventions, wisdom of making public, 179
Irish History, The (Hooker), 23
Ironside, Ralph, debate with Carew and Sir Walter Ralegh, at Tren-

Index

chard's supper party, 37, 47, 72, 75, 80, 97, 139-47 *passim*, 238; sworn statement about it, 48, 49; nature of his record of debate: resulting variety of interpretations, 142; disagreement on the issue of "principles," 232; *see also* Cerne Abbas investigation

Jackson, Thomas, 79 f., 82 *n*, 84, 92, 97, 105
James I, of England, 53, 78, 111, 136, 166, 219*n*, 269; on magic, 178
James VI, of Scotland, *see* James I, of England
James, Francis, 49
Jefferys (Jeffries), Nicholas, 48
Jerome, 119, 176
Jesuits, Queen's proclamation against: response from Catholic press, 27-40 *passim*; breach between lay Catholics and, 31; reasons for abuse of Ralegh, 34 ff.; Ralegh's attitude toward, 36 ff., 52; after-effects of edict against, 50
Jesus, attacks by anti-Christian writers, 95; *see also* Christ
Jewish writers, proofs of God's existence, 70 ff.
Johnson, Samuel, 257
Jonson, Ben, 13*n*, 18, 110
Josephus, 71, 188, 206
"Judas, Sir," 135
Judicial astrology, defined, 192; attacks on, 192 ff.
Julian Calendar, 197, 210, 212
Julian the Apostate, 57, 94, 96
Julian Period, 212, 213

Kempner, Nadja, 165*n*
Kyd, Thomas, 41, 94

Lactantius, 106, 249*n*
Lanquet, Thomas, 200
Laudonnière, René de, 20, 21

Law, T. G., 33
Lee, Sir Sidney, 40
Leicester, Robert Dudley, Earl of, 28, 29, 30, 31, 33, 34, 259
Lessius, Leonard, 257
Letter to a Deist (Stillingfleet), 96
Levett, John, 163
Lie, The (Ralegh), 128, 138; answers to, 56
Literary and Critical Remarks on . . . Divines and Philosophers . . ., 190*n*; excerpts, 191 f.
Livelie, Edward, 204*n*
Loarte, Gaspar, 65
Locke, John, 256
Look to It: for I'll Stab Ye (Rowlands), text, 89
Love's Labour's Lost (Shakespeare), basis of theories about existence of a "School of Night," 262-70 *passim*
Lower, William, 46
Lucian, 92, 94, 96
Lucretius, 69, 86, 92
Lunary years, 202, 210
Lying, 158
Lyly, John, 85

Machiavelli, Niccolo, 92; a technique of, 149; indebtedness of Ralegh's political philosophy to, 150, 161-71; writings known to Elizabethans, 162; three general patterns of uses to which Ralegh put writings of, 166
Machiavellianism, 84, 88, 100; synonym for atheism, 162, 272; existence before it was tagged with a name, 163
McKerrow, R. B., 226, 227
Magic, defense of natural, 174, 175-81; threefold classification, 175; definition, 176; partition into two categories, 176 ff.; what the term embraces: ideas of King James and

Index

Magic (*Continued*)
  of Ralegh, 178; legitimate uses of scientific study, 179
Man, nature of, 124; freedom, 124, 130; self-knowledge, 125
Manifestation (Parsons), 32
Marlowe, Christopher, 5, 17, 26, 36, 92, 94, 95, 148; association of Ralegh and, 40 ff., 130, 264, 269; Baines' note on, 40*n*, 41, 42, 72, 201; reference to Aristotle in play, 237
Marston, John, 143
Martyr, Peter, *see* Peter Martyr of Anghiera
Massacre at Paris (Marlowe), 237
Mathematics, attitude of Ralegh, 181; of Elizabethans, 181*n*
Maxims of State, The (Ralegh), 12, 137, 164, 165; earliest title: later editions, 167
Measurement of time, 175, 197-218; *see entries under* Chronology
"Men before Adam," 175, 197-218; *see also* Chronology
Milles, Thomas, 103, 163
Milton, John, 5; prefatory note for *The Cabinet-Council*, 164
Miracles, 174, 175; of Christ and of Moses, 70 f., 72, 74, 87, 182 f., 183 f.; definitions and argument, 181-85
Mirandola, Pico della, 176, 182
Missionary zeal of colonizers, 20 ff.
Mohun, alias, *see* Cornelius, John
Monarchs, commentary on, 111, 151
Montaigne, M. E. de, 219, 200, 220, 229, 232; on authority of Aristotle, 239
Mooney, John, *see* Cornelius, John
Moral basis of worldly aims and success, 150-71 *passim*
More, Sir George, 51, 78, 82
More, Sir William, 51

Mornay, Philip de, 80, 83, 95*n*, 100, 108, 125*n*, 128, 141, 182, 200; ... *Trueness of the Christian Religion*, 63, 72 ff., 82*n*, 128*n*; argument for use of reason in support of religion, 72-78; three major topics treated, 75 ff.
Morton, Thomas, 103, 145
Moses, 76, 100, 112, 203; miracles, 70 f., 72, 87, 183 f.; time computation, 204; authority of laws of, 235

Nashe, Thomas, 64, 67, 85, 87, 90, 93, 94, 95*n*, 132, 199*n*, 201, 213, 265; references to Sextus Empiricus, 226 f., 228; dedications to Sir George Carey and family, 268
Nations, origin: after the deluge, 187, 189; *see also* Resettlement of the earth
Natural astrology, 176, 192-96; *see entries under* Astrology
Natural History (Pliny the Elder), 94
Naturalists linked with atheists, 90 f.
Natural philosophy, belief in and treatment of, 172-79 *passim*, 193, 196, 198, 202 ff., 235; natural magic the perfection of, 177, 181
Nature, relation to God, 101; Christ's superfine knowledge, 182; attitude toward study of, 183; wisdom of divinity and, distinguished, 184
Naunton, Sir Robert, 9*n*
Navigator's Supply, The (Barlow), 52
Necromancy, 178
Newton, Sir Isaac, 197
New World, *see* Colonization in New World
Noah's Ark, *see* Deluge
Northumberland, Earl of, *see* Percy, Henry
Nosce Teipsum (Davies), 144

Index

Oath-breaking, 157
Of Simulation and Dissimulation (Bacon), 159
"Of the Fundamental Laws of Human Belief" (Stewart), 260
Of the Vanity . . . of Arts and Sciences (Agrippa), 228, 234
"Of the Voyage for Guiana" ("by or for" Ralegh), 22 f.
Of Wisdom (Charron), 200, 232n
Oldys, William, 24, 25
Orbe Novo, De (Peter Martyr), 20, 45
Origen, 119, 176
Origines sacrae (Stillingfleet), 189
Osborne, Francis, 135, 259
Outlines of Pyrrhonism comp. by Sextus Empiricus, 221-29 *passim*, 233
Oxford, Earl of, 19
Oxford (college), dominated by Aristotelianism, 140 f.
Oxinden, Henry, 17
Oxyges, flood of, 185, 189

Paracelsus, 92, 173n
Paradoxes and Problems (Donne), 93
Parsons, Robert ("Andreas Philopater," pseud.), 27, 80, 85, 95n, 108, 141, 183; charges against Ralegh in his *Responsio*, 15, 25-40 *passim*; statements re teachings of "School of Atheism," 25, 26, 99, 132; criticisms of, 31 f.; widespread publication of his work, 39; "Books of Resolution" as treatise against atheism, 63 ff.; bibliographical history, 65 ff.; topics treated: arguments, 68 ff.; method parallels Mornay's, 74
Passionate Man's Pilgrimage, The (Ralegh), 138
"Passionate Shepherd to his Love, The" (Marlowe), 42
Patrick, Mary Mills, 273

Paul, St., 71, 133, 177
Percy, Henry, Earl of Northumberland, 44, 53, 54, 59, 105, 263, 264, 265, 267; long-standing friendship with Ralegh, 269
Perkins, William, 84, 194n
Pernius, John, pseud., *see* Creswell, Joseph
Persian monarchs' reigns, 204n, 205 f.
Peter Martyr of Anghiera, 20
Pharaoh's magicians, 183
Phelippes, Thomas, 35, 36
Philip II, 27, 28, 34
"Philopater, Andreas," pseud., *see* Parsons, Robert
Philosophical principles, *see* Principles
Philosophy, natural, *see* Natural philosophy
Philotas (Daniel), 270
Pilgrimage (Purchas), 45
Plato, 69, 70, 92, 118, 122, 126, 200; on publishing scientific discoveries, 179; one-time preeminence over Aristotle: Protestant leanings toward, 239
Platonism of Ralegh, 120n, 128
Pliny the Elder, 91, 94, 200; translation of his *History* justified, 182n; on Moses, 184n
Plotinus, 70
Poems of Ralegh, 11, 18, 56, 128, 138, 162n
Political writings: Ralegh's indebtedness to Machiavelli, 161-71
Polybius, 13
Pomponazzi, Pietro, 127n
Popham, Chief Justice, 58, 94
Porphyry, 71, 72, 77, 95, 96, 250
Praz, Mario, 163, 165
Predestination, 113
Prerogative of Parliaments, The (Ralegh), 166, 167
Prescience, 113
Prestall, John, 34n

Pretending religion, 167
Prince, The (Machiavelli), 162, 163, 166
Prince, The; or, Maxims of State, original title of *Maxims of State* (q.v.)
Principal Navigations, The (Hakluyt), 45, 52
Principles, rejection of, as eternally valid, 231-36 *passim*, 272
Printing, 179
Proclus the Platonist, 108
Proctor, John, 41
Ptolemy, 194, 206n
Puckering, Sir John, Lord Keeper, 34, 41n
Purchas His Pilgrimage, 45
Puritan influence, 35
Pyrrhonic system, 87, 90, 132; skepticism, 220 ff., 273; principal tenets and characteristics, 222; works in which known to Elizabethans, 228
Pyrrho of Elis, 221, 223

Quintus Fabius, 168

Ralegh, Lady (Elizabeth Throckmorton), 18; story of Ralegh's marriage to, 3; his letter to, a minor classic, 138
Ralegh, Carew, 47, 49n, 50, 101, 139, 143n
Ralegh, Philip, 37n
Ralegh, Sir Walter, early career, 3, 9, 17; and beliefs, 4; story of his marriage, 3n, 149n; personality: characteristics, 4, 11, 54, 271; why he and associates called atheists, 4; the Guiana enterprise, 3, 22, 251 (*see also The Discovery of Guiana*); intellectual pursuits and development, 4, 18; changes in opinions about, in his own and later centuries, 5, 254-62, 271; reasons for softening of public attitude: transformed to symbol of English patriotism, 5; restudy of his life prompted by three qualifications united in him, 6; review of his alleged religious skepticism indispensable to discussion of his philosophical skepticism, 6; diversity of interests and employments, 8; character, 9 f.; speech from the scaffold: impression made: effects: publication, 10, 134 f., 136, 149, 150, 159, 224; materials which make it possible to get at opinions of, 11; aids to, and complications attending, understanding of his words, 11; difficulty in tracing development of his thought, 14; inclination to digression and personal comment, 14, 270; how comments of friends and enemies as source of information must be used, 15; charged with sponsoring a "school of atheism," 15, 25-40 *passim*, 99, 132, 264; the Cerne Abbas investigation, 15, 43, 44, 46-52, 98n, 101, 132, 134, 139n, 262, 271; effort to restore Elizabethan proportions of thought of, 16; records that form basis of information about, 17-60; fragmentary knowledge of his early life, opinions, and beliefs, 17; a scholar at Oxford, 18, 47, 139; the 1580's the years of designs for colonization, 20 ff.; intermingling of conquest and piety, 20; works dedicated to, as part of colonization campaign, 20-25 *passim*; the Virginia venture, 21, 23n, 24, 34, 43, 44, 45, 189; Parsons' charges against, 25-40 *passim*; attacks upon, in Jesuit replies to the Queen's proclamation, 28 ff., 149; reasons for Catholic antagonism, 34, 35, 39; connection with Puritans, 35; attitude toward the Jesuits, 36 ff., 52; duties as Lord Lieutenant

of Cornwall, 37; debate with Ironside on nature of God and the soul, 37, 47, 48, 49, 72, 75, 80, 97, 139-47 *passim*, 237, 238; a powerful favorite of Queen, 39; career as symbol of anti-Spanish feeling, 39, 40, 255; placed in company of other individuals suspected of atheism, 40 ff.; association with Marlowe, 40-42; with Harriot, 43-46; at Sir George Trenchard's supper party, 47; no formal charges against, or action taken, at Cerne Abbas, 51; illustrations showing drift of popular opinion about, 52-60; damaging criticisms of, by Sir Robert Cecil and Henry Howard, 53; target of verse libels and lampoons, 54 ff.; held largely responsible for downfall of Essex: reached a new low in popular esteem, 54; attempted suicide, 56, 149; effect upon public opinion, of his trial for treason, 54, 57, 59; details of the trial, 57 ff.; words used by his judges in the trials of 1603 and 1618, 57, 58, 158*n*, 254; scholarly pursuits in the Tower, culminated in his *History*, 58; meanings of atheism as semantic context in which charges of atheism against, may be interpreted, 61-97; on controversial usage in words, 62; ideas about reason, 96, 102, 230, 235, 239, 242, 273; conclusions about conduct of debate on atheism, valuable for understanding of his position, 96 f.; and in reconciling contradictory evidence of what he said and what said about him, 97; abundant records of his views provided in writings, 98; opinions on God and the soul, 99-147; excerpts from his *History* on the being of God, 99-104; views on the creation: linked with God's providence, 104-8; why belief in providence had special importance for, 109-15; denial of the authority of Aristotle, 106, 219, 236-41 *passim*, 272; interest in the causes of man's conduct, 111; scathing review of conduct of monarchs, 111, 151; contributions to literature on the soul, in *A Treatise of the Soul*, and in Chap. II of the *History*, 115-32; praise of human understanding, 121; argument for immortality, 122; on how man resembles God, 123; traditional quality of thought, 125 ff.; both Platonic and Aristotelian traditions represented, 128; causes of "modernizing" the beliefs of, 129 ff.; ideas on the Scriptures and salvation, 132-39, 198; questions of his faith in the specific terms of church doctrine and creed, 134; MS with fullest account of execution, 135; Stukeley considered betrayer of, 135; writings and recorded utterances permeated by religious point of view, 137 ff.; letter to wife became a minor classic, 138; formal advice to son, 138, 154 ff.; grief at his death, 138; best-known stanza, or "epitaph," 139; clue to the significance of his impatience with Ironside's definitions, 145; love of, and cleverness in, debate, 146; rebellion against Aristotle and school logic the key to much of his thought, 147; "inward atheism" or Machiavellianism, 148 ff.; some of the most disputed actions in life of, 149; providential interpretation of history underlying all his discourses on morality, 150; moral basis of the "architecture of fortune": practical politics, or the rights and wrongs of gaining wealth and position, 150-171; argument for obedience to

Ralegh, Sir Walter (*Continued*) God's commandments, 152; doctrine of degree invoked, 153; pages of his Preface that could stand alone as an essay: major themes of moralizing touched upon, 154 ff.; strictures on ambition, 156; on oathbreaking, 157; on lying, 159; relative unimportance in the history of political thought, but significant as a purveyor of that thought, 161; political ethics and their indebtedness to Machiavelli, 161 ff.; summary of uses of Machiavelli's writings: three general patterns, 166 ff.; last word on abuses of power politics: best-known paragraph of his *History, text,* 170; change in, between early and later years, 171; patron of, and relations with, men of science, 172, 174; experiments in chemistry and medicine, 172, 173; opinions on definition and limitations: of natural magic and of demonology, 174, 175-81; of miracles, 174, 181-85; of the deluge, Noah's Ark, and the resettlement of the earth, 175, 185-92; of astrology, 175, 192-96; of chronology, 175, 197-218; would have no "men before Adam," 175, 218; on the legitimate uses of scientific study, 179; admiration for pure science and for mathematics, 181; flair for identifying self with subject through own wealth of experience, 189; his knowledge of science and literalness of interpretation, questioned, 190 ff.; steered course between authority of Holy Writ and damnation of the black art, 196; conscientious efforts to get at the truth, 214 ff.; survey of his beliefs shows that charges of atheism cannot be made to stick, 218; obedient to religious code yet anxious to enlarge limits of free intellectual inquiry, 218; wrongly labeled a religious skeptic, 219; philosophic skepticism, 220-53, 272; acceptance or rejection of authority, 230-53 *passim;* the best statement of his skeptical philosophy is in passage attacking Aristotle's denial of the Creation in time, *text,* 230 f.; rejection of the "principles" as eternally valid, 231-36 *passim;* several major issues by which place among contemporaries defined, 243; historical method and some credulities considered, 244-53; mixture of hardheaded practicality and easy gullibility, 250; speech in Parliament re the Brownists, 252*n;* why gossip softened into legend, conflicts into conflicting evidence, 255; Tercentenary Commemoration, 255*n;* widely dispersed comments on the man, his *History,* and the quality and independence of his thinking, 256-62; traditions about atheism of, 257 ff.; and misconduct, 258; and independence in philosophy, 259; commentary upon, as a freethinker, 260; theories about his association with a "School of Night," 262-71; conclusions about beliefs and reputation of, 271-75; causes to which reputation as atheist, traceable, 271; seen as an influential worker in a transitional period, 272; importance in history of ideas, 273; *see also entries for subjects and persons mentioned in above group, e.g.,* Chronology; Parsons, Robert

—— literary work: three major works published in lifetime, 11; miscellaneous prose in the collected *Works,*

11; poems, 11, 18, 56, 128, 138, 162n; posthumous fame made printing of his "Remains" a desirable venture, 11; posthumous works credited to, 12, 22; problems of authenticity and originality, 12 ff., 116n; translations, 12; borrowed material, 12; letters, 138; political writings, 161-71; *see also under following titles: Cabinet-Council, Causes of the Magnificency . . . of Cities; Discourse of War; Discourse Touching a Marriage . . . ; Discovery of Guiana; History of the World; Instructions to His Son . . . ; The Lie; Maxims of State; "Of the Voyage for Guiana"; Passionate Man's Pilgrimage; Prerogative of Parliaments; Remains; Report . . . about the Isles of Azores, A (the Revenge)* ; *Seat of Government; Skeptic; Treatise of the Soul; Tubus historicus . . . ; Works*
Ralegh, Walter, the son, 18, 149n, 155n; formal advice to, 138, 154 ff.; death in Guiana, 138
Ralegh His Ghost (Lessius, tr. by A. B.), 257
Ramus, 237
Rationalism, term, 6
Rational soul, 117, 121
Reason, in support of religion, a major thesis of writers, 72; Ralegh's ideas, 96, 235, 239, 273; limitation of, applied to knowledge of God, 102; experience exalted over, 230, 242
Regnal years, calculations, 204, 205, 207, 211
Remains, posthumous (Ralegh), 11; Ralegh's speech from scaffold published in, 224
Reply to a Libel ("W.C."), 32

Report . . . about the Isles of Azores, A (Ralegh), 14; *see also Revenge*
Resettlement of the earth and origins of the nations, 187, 189, 196, 198, 203, 209; philosophy and method by which Ralegh endeavored to make credible, 208; *see also* Deluge
Resolution, *see Books of Resolution*
Responsio (Parsons), 25 f., 32; editions and translations, 39
Revenge (Ralegh), 11, 23; *see also Report . . . about the Isles of Azores*
Riches and honor, *see* Worldly aims and success
Rowlands, Samuel, 88, 226 f., 228
Royden, Matthew, 263
Ruffinus, 119

Sanchez, Francesco, 274
Sandys, Sir Edwin, 64
Sansovino, Francesco, 165, 166, 168
Sarmiento, Pedro, 39n, 146, 247
Scaliger, Joseph, 212, 246, 247
Scarlett, Francis, 50
Schoolmen, 220, 238, 239
"School of Atheism," Ralegh charged with sponsoring, 15, 25-40 *passim*; Parsons' statement re its teachings, 25, 26, 99, 132; identification with "School of Night," 264
"School of Night," 7, 15; theories about existence of, and Ralegh's association with, 5, 254, 262-71; supposed allusion in *Love's Labour's Lost,* 262 ff.; nucleus of, 263; identification with "School of Atheism": coterie opposed to, 264; problems of text, 265 ff.; members and their personal relations, 267 ff.; doctrines credited to, vs. opinions of Ralegh, 270; value of studies of, 270 f.

Science, Ralegh as patron: his own experiments, 172 ff.; distinction between the use and abuse of, 177; legitimate uses: wisdom of publishing discoveries, 179; admiration for "pure," 181; Ralegh's knowledge of, questioned, 190
Scriptures, Jewish, 70; Ralegh's acceptance of authority of, 130, 132 ff., 175, 186, 198, 202 ff.; chronology, 197
Scudamour, Lord, 99
Seat of Government (Ralegh), 224
Second Part of the Book of Christian Exercise, The . . . (anon.) 66, 67
Sects, evils in spread of, 89
Selden, John, 259
Seneca, 170
Senses, outward and inward, 121; and sensation, 223 ff.
Sensitive soul, 116, 121
Sethus Calvisius, 246
Sextus Empiricus, 132n; book on Pyrrhonism, 221-29 *passim*, 233, 273
Shadow of Night, The (Chapman), 263, 266
Shakespeare, 5, 55, 255; whether allusions in *Love's Labour's Lost* are intended for an actual coterie, termed "School of Night," 262-70 *passim*
Shirley, John, 8, 13, 15, 16, 199n, 258
"Sir Walter Ralegh His Lamentation," 255n
Sir Walter Ralegh's Skeptic; or, Speculations, title of first edition of *The Skeptic* (q.v.), 224
Sidney, Sir Philip, 19, 63, 85, 226, 245, 265
Similitude, term, 123
Skeptic, The (Sextus Empiricus, tr. by Ralegh), 12, 42, 164, 216, 224; Pyrrhonism the source of, 220, 224,

227; adaptations of thought and method in, 224 ff.; title, date, and other works in first edition: reprintings, 224; conclusions about, 229 f.; linked to speculations on religion, 131
Skepticism, term, 6; dominant popular meanings, 219; long important in Greek and Roman thought, 220; philosophic, 220-53 *passim*; Pyrrhonic, 220-30; Academic, 221 f., 230, 235; a weapon for attack upon dogmatism, 220, 235; key to Ralegh's and to its utility, 272
Soul, Mornay's theories, 77; Ralegh's contributions to the literature on, 115-32; Aristotle's definition, 116, 140; tripartite powers, 116 ff., 121; relation to body, 117, 122; debate between Ironside and the Raleghs on God and, 139 ff.; *see also* Ironside, Ralph
Southampton, Earl of, 264
Spain, attitude of Ralegh, 39, 255; of Jesuits, 39
Spaniards in the New World, 189
Spenser, Edmund, 4, 55, 255
Spirit and soul, 124
Stanhope, George, 67
Stanley, Thomas, 227
Stapleton, Thomas, 28, 29, 34, 39
Stars, conjunction of, 186; influence, 192 ff. (*see also* Astrology)
Statecraft, principles of, 161 ff.
Steel Glass, The (Gascoigne), 18
Sterrell, William (alias *Saintmain*), 35
Stewart, Dugald, 260
Still, John, 59
Stillingfleet, Edward, 96, 190, 209n, 256
Storton, Lady, 36
Stuart, Arabella, 30
Stukeley, Sir Lewis, 135, 255
Summer's Last Will and Testament (Nashe), 226, 227

Index

Tannenbaum, Samuel A., 40
Tercentenary Commemoration, Ralegh, 255*n*
Terminology, skepticism, 6; Elizabethan meanings of atheism and its derivatives, 6 f., 61 ff., 148; terms into which later generations have divided "atheism," 96; image and similitude, 123; soul and spirit, 124
Terrors of Night, The (Nashe), 268
Thomas Aquinas, St., 126, 183*n*, 239
Thorndike, Lynn, 275
Throckmorton, Elizabeth, Ralegh's treatment of, and marriage to, 3*n*; *see* Ralegh, Lady
Thucydides, 261
Time, measurement of, 175, 197-218; *see entries under* Chronology
Torniellus, 246, 247
Tounson, Robert, 134
Tourneur, Cyril, 87, 88, 92
Treasury of Ancient and Modern Times, The (Milles), 103
Treatise of the Nature of God (Morton), 145
Treatise of the Soul, A (Ralegh), statements of belief, and refutations of heresies, with excerpts, 115-32 *passim;* its only printing, 115; comparisons between Chap. II of the *History* and, 116, 123 ff.; question of authenticity, 116*n*, 125*n*
Treatise of Unbelief (Jackson), 79, 82*n*, 84
Treatise on the Deluge, A (Catcott), 190
Trenchard, Mrs., 38*n*
Trenchard, Sir George, 36, 37, 49; Ralegh-Ironside debate at supper party of: guests, 47 f.
Tropes, defined: purpose, 222
Tropics, heat of, 242
Tubus historicus . . . (Ralegh), 214*n*
Twyne, Thomas, 92*n*

Udall, John, 35
Understanding, human, 121 f.
Unmasking of the Politic Atheist, The (Hull), 85
Ussher, James, Abp., 207, 213

Vanini, Lucilio, 274
Varro, Marcus, 69
Vaughan, William, 65, 90
Vegetative soul, 116, 121
Verstegen, Richard, 28, 33, 39
Virginia colonization ventures, 21, 23*n*, 24, 34, 43, 189; Harriot's *Report* on, 44, 45
Vives, Ludovicus, 186, 188*n*, 200, 239

Walpole, Henry, 28
Walsingham, Sir Francis, 28, 33
War, deception in, 158, 159*n*, 168
Ward, Seth, 105
Warner, Walter, 59
Warning for Worldlings, A (Corderoy), 79, 83, 127
Watson, William, 32, 65, 95
Watts, William, 241
"W.C." replies to Parsons, 32
What You Will (Marston), 143
Whear, Diggory, 256
Whittle, vicar, 47
Whyte, Rowland, 52
Williams, John, 37, 49
Wilson, Sir Thomas, 9*n*
Winter, Thomas, 102
Witchcraft and conjuring, 176, 178
Women, souls, 118
Wonderful Workmanship of the World, The (Daneau, tr. by Twyne), 91, 92*n*
Wood, Anthony à, 12, 18, 45, 132, 154*n*; statement about Harriot, 104 f.
Woolton, John, 125*n*

292 Index

Work Concerning the Trueness of the Christian Religion, A (Mornay), 63, 72 ff., 82n, 128n

Works, collected, of Ralegh, 11, 115, 167, 224

Worldly aims and success, 114, 148-71; moral basis, 150; futility, 152; application to specific problems, 155 ff.; principles and ethics of statecraft, in political writings of Ralegh: influence of Machiavelli, 161-71

Yates, Frances A., 265, 268

Year, measurements, 202, 210; regnal years, 204, 205, 207, 211

Zanchius, Hieronymus, 123n, 126n

Zeitlin, Jacob, 240n

Zoroaster, 175